Managerial Discretion in Government Decision Making

Beyond the Street Level

MANAGERIAL DISCRETION IN GOVERNMENT DECISION MAKING

BEYOND THE STREET LEVEL

Jacqueline Vaughn, PhD

Professor, Department of Political Science
Northern Arizona University
Flagstaff, Arizona

Eric E. Otenyo, PhD

Assistant Professor, Department of Political Science
Northern Arizona University
Flagstaff, Arizona

JONES AND BARTLETT PUBLISHERS
Sudbury, Massachusetts
BOSTON   TORONTO   LONDON   SINGAPORE

World Headquarters

Jones and Bartlett Publishers	Jones and Bartlett Publishers Canada	Jones and Bartlett Publishers International
40 Tall Pine Drive	6339 Ormindale Way	Barb House, Barb Mews
Sudbury, MA 01776	Mississauga, Ontario L5V 1J2	London W6 7PA
978-443-5000	CANADA	UK
info@jbpub.com		
www.jbpub.com		

Jones and Bartlett's books and products are available through most bookstores and online booksellers. To contact Jones and Bartlett Publishers directly, call 800-832-0034, fax 978-443-8000, or visit our website, www.jbpub.com.

Substantial discounts on bulk quantities of Jones and Bartlett's publications are available to corporations, professional associations, and other qualified organizations. For details and specific discount information, contact the special sales department at Jones and Bartlett via the above contact information or send an email to specialsales@jbpub.com.

Production Credits
Publisher: Michael Brown
Executive Editor: David Cella
Editorial Assistant: Lisa Gordon
Production Assistant: Jennifer M. Ryan
Associate Marketing Manager: Laura Kavigian
Manufacturing Buyer: Amy Bacus
Composition: NK Graphics/Group 360
Cover Design: Kate Ternullo
Cover Printing: Malloy, Inc.
Text Printing: Malloy, Inc.
Cover Image: © Corbis

Library of Congress Cataloging-in-Publication Data
Vaughn, Jacqueline.
　　Managerial discretion in government decision making : beyond the street level / Jacqueline Vaughn, Eric Otenyo.
　　　　p. cm.
　　Includes bibliographical references.
　　ISBN-13: 978-0-7637-4656-8 (alk. paper)
　　ISBN-10: 0-7637-4656-8
　　1. Public administration—United States.　2. Public administration—Decision making.　3. Administrative discretion—United States.　4. Administrative agencies—United States—Management.　5. United States—Politics and government.　I. Otenyo, Eric Edwin. II. Title.
　　JK421.S95 2006
　　352.3'3—dc22　　2006025678
　　6048

Printed in the United States of America
10　09　08　07　06　　10　9　8　7　6　5　4　3　2　1

To my dearest friend and retail therapist, Heidi Land Wilson
—J.V.

To the memory of my father, Julius H. Otenyo
—E.O.

CONTENTS

Introduction

Mayvis Coyle, an 82-year-old woman, received a $114 jaywalking ticket from a Los Angeles Police Department (LAPD) motorcycle officer on February 15, 2006. Coyle said that she began shuffling across the street with her cane in one hand and groceries in another when the traffic light was green, but was unable to reach the other side before it turned red, and that is why she received the citation. Coyle recounted that the officer repeatedly shouted at her, "You're obstructing the flow of traffic!" She added, "I don't like being talked to like I'm a 6-year-old. This is the first ticket I ever got in my life for trying to cross the street." Coyle, who is a retired hairdresser and rancher, lives by herself in a mobile home park during the winter and her hometown in Colorado during the summer. She does not have a telephone, so the owner of the mobile home park takes messages for her.

The media immediately picked up her story, with headlines reading: "Guilty of 'Crossing While Elderly,'" "Stroll the Street of Death," and "Old Woman Fined for Walking Slowly." Internationally, newspapers in India, Germany, and the United Kingdom portrayed the police department as uncaring and irresponsible. The *Glasgow Daily Record* wrote "Stick Your Fine." Television news crews rushed to interview Coyle, and one daytime talk show host was reportedly interested in having her on the show. Angry letters flooded the LAPD, and many others were sent to the San Fernando Police Department, a smaller city agency in the region but not the one that issued the ticket. The San Fernando police quickly sent out a press release noting that they were victims of mistaken identity.

Others got involved in the incident once it was widely reported in the press. The American Association of Retired Persons published a commentary about the incident on its Web site, as did other senior citizen organizations. Reporters and city officials timed the lights at the same intersection where Coyle had tried to cross to see how long it would take them, without a cane. A member of the city council directed transportation officials to investigate, and shortly thereafter, the timing of the walk signal was lengthened to allow pedestrians more time to cross.

"I didn't want all this publicity," Coyle said. "But I'm not objecting to being used if it gets the lights changed and gets respect for the elderly. I think people can see I'm being sincere. I'm speaking for all those seniors who can't get across the street"

(*San Jose Mercury News* 2006). Coyle says that she believes the officer should have gotten off his motorcycle when he saw that she was struggling and helped her cross the street. She decided to fight the citation in court, and received several donations to pay her fine if she lost her case, which was reviewed by the Los Angeles City Attorney's Office. A Superior Court Commissioner ruled that Coyle was guilty of the crime in a June 20, 2006 letter, but he suspended the fine.

The police department's explanation of the incident was different from that reported by Coyle and the media. One officer told reporters that the violation had nothing to do with the time it took to cross the street. CNN used a video clip on its broadcast in which Sergeant Mike Zabowski of the LAPD said, "The ticket is strictly for stepping off the curb illegally against the traffic control and pedestrian control saying not to." The department said the officer saw Coyle begin to cross the street after the "Don't Walk" sign began flashing, signaling it was about to change. "While many people may look at that and say the LAPD should have a greater heart and should care more that this was an 82-year-old woman, our desire is that this 82-year-old woman, and all citizens of L.A., conduct themselves in a manner that is safe," the deputy chief of operations noted. An elderly woman was struck and killed by a car in the same area just eight days earlier.

Was this a case of, as one *Los Angeles Times* writer called it, "a jaywalking ticket from an overeager LAPD crime buster for not making it across in time"? Or did the police officer respond appropriately in determining whether or not a citation should be issued, adhering to the city's ordinances that had been voted on and approved by representative, elected officials?[1]

Another California incident illustrates the issues that can arise when a public official makes a decision of a different sort. Stanley "Tookie" Williams, a co-founder of the Crips, a notorious Los Angeles street gang, was convicted of brutally murdering four people during two armed robberies between February and March 1979. In one incident, he and his accomplices entered a convenience store and shot the victim in the back of the head, execution-style. Two weeks later, he also murdered three members of an Asian family while robbing their motel business, referring to the victims as "Buddha-heads." Based on the testimony of his accomplices and a ballistic analysis of the shotgun used in the crimes, a jury sentenced him to death,

---

[1]The accounts of the Coyle incident varied considerably in the media, and there were inconsistencies from one source to another. See, "Woman, 82, Ticketed for Crossing Too Slow," *Los Angeles Daily News,* April 11, 2006 (http:www.dailynews.com; accessed on April 13, 2006); Amanda Covarrubias and Cynthia H. Cho, "She Has the World at Her Not-So-Fleet-Feet," *Los Angeles Times,* April 14, 2006 (http://www.latimes.com/news; accessed May 10, 2006); Steve Lopez, "Guilty of 'Crossing While Elderly,'" *Los Angeles Times,* April 15, 2006 (http://www.latimes.com/news; accessed May 10, 2006); Transcript, *Cable News Network,* April 11, 2006 (http://transcripts.cnn.com; accessed May 10, 2006); "Judge Waives Fine Against Elderly Woman Given Jaywalking Ticket," *San Jose Mercury News,* July 8, 2006 (http://www.mercurynews.com; accessed July 14, 2006).

despite Williams' claims that he was innocent. Upon appeal, his case was reviewed and denied several times during a 24-year period, although the Ninth Circuit Court of Appeals, in an unprecedented step, urged the governor of California to seriously consider Williams' clemency petition.

During his incarceration on death row, Williams wrote children's books that advocated nonviolence and provided alternatives to gangster lifestyles. In 2004, he also helped broker a peace agreement that ended one of the deadliest gang wars in the United States. The change in Williams' life—especially his role as an advocate against gangs and violence—earned him much admiration and fueled a small-scale movement to have his death sentence reduced to life imprisonment or release from death row.

With his appeals exhausted, Williams' only chance to have his sentence commuted was through Executive Clemency from the governor. California's Constitution gives the governor the power to reduce and commute sentences as well as to pardon prisoners. As one attorney wrote, "The long appellate process had morphed a murderer into a peacemaker." Williams was nominated on several occasions for the prestigious Nobel Peace Prize (Linder 2005). The governor, Arnold Schwarzenegger, had the discretion to save Williams' life or to uphold the court's death sentence. Several celebrities, including actor Jamie Foxx and civil rights leader Jesse Jackson, argued that Williams' work and actions merited clemency based on his redemption as a former gang member. His supporters also included Archbishop Desmond Tutu and rapper Snoop Dogg, who had once been a member of the Crips himself.

In 14 states, the governor has sole authority to grant clemency petitions, and in 8 more, the governor must have a recommendation of clemency from a board or advisory group. In 10 other states, the governor receives a non-binding recommendation from a board or advisory group, and in three, a board or advisory group determines clemency. To date, three broad grants of clemency have been granted to death row inmates:

- 1986: New Mexico Governor Tony Anaya to all inmates ($N = 5$)
- 1991: Ohio Governor Richard Celeste to eight inmates
- 2003: Illinois Governor George Ryan to all inmates ($N = 167$)

Nationally, between 1976 and 2006, 229 death row inmates were granted clemency for humanitarian reasons, according to the Death Penalty Information Center. For the most part, clemency was awarded only where there were serious doubts about the defendant's guilt or the governor's conclusions regarding the processes leading to the death sentence. Since 1967, more than 1,000 persons had been on California's death row, but none had been granted clemency under the five governors who served during that time (Death Penalty Information Center 2006).

Governor Schwarzenegger denied Williams' request for clemency and Stanley Williams was executed at the San Quentin State Prison by lethal injection on

December 13, 2005. He was the second inmate to be executed in California in 2005 and the twelfth since the death penalty was reinstated in the 1970s. In response to Williams' clemency request, Schwarzenegger wrote:

> Clemency decisions are always difficult, and this one is no exception. After reviewing and weighing the showing Williams has made in support of his clemency request, there is nothing that compels me to nullify the jury's decision of guilt and sentence and the many court decisions during the last 24 years upholding the jury's decision with a grant of clemency (Schwarzenegger 2005).

This case is representative of the kind of political choices that members of the executive branch must face in their daily decision-making tasks. A previous governor had also faced the stark reality of the problem of discretion in public administration and management in general. The process leading to Williams' execution mirrored that of another death row inmate, Caryl Chessman, in 1960. Chessman also had written popular books while in prison but was executed despite appeals to then-California Governor Pat Brown that the sentence be commuted to life in prison. Brown later commented that "his refusal to ignore politics and commute Chessman's sentence to life imprisonment was his greatest personal failure" (Schwarzenegger 2005).

The Concept of Administrative Discretion

Although both of these examples took place in California, their significance is national in scope because they underscore an important element in organizational behavior: administrative discretion. There are different variations in the manner in which discretion is defined and conceptualized.

A starting point is that discretion is the freedom to make a choice among possible courses of action or inaction (West 1985). For one scholar, a public officer has discretion whenever the effective limits on his power leave him free to make a choice (Davis 1969). Another describes discretion as "the idea that administrative officials should be free to employ their expertise and training in the pursuit of the policy responsibilities delegated to them" (Bryner 1986). Yet another definition is that discretionary decisions are those that involve the choice to carefully weigh all pros and cons, in contrast to other decisions that are constrained by rules and regulations (Handler 1986). Lastly, discretion is rarely either absolute or absent (Jowell 1975). It can range anywhere between high and low.

Discretion, therefore, embraces ideas about judgment, discernment, liberty, and license. It is about judging among competing values, choosing a best possible solution, and being free to extend the rights and duties of office. Discretion is often part of the way decisions are made to conform to professional, community, legal, and moral norms.

From a purely administrative point of view, the police officer who made the decision to issue the ticket to the 82-year-old woman used his discretion as what scholars term a *street-level bureaucrat*. This term was used extensively in the 1980s to describe what happens at the point where public policy translates into practice in human service–related venues such as schools, courts, and public assistance programs. Researchers examined various agencies and concluded that policy implementation comes down to the individuals who work directly with clients and the public—for example, teachers, public safety officers, case workers, and other employees who literally work on the front lines in communities. These individuals face enormous pressure in trying to do their jobs because they work with limited resources, sometimes with clients in an adversarial setting, and may have target goals and objectives or quotas that are difficult to meet. These circumstances force them to make decisions—that is, to exercise their discretion in ways that upper-level bureaucrats may not understand in order to get their jobs done.

Governor Schwarzenegger's decision not to commute Tookie Williams' sentence from death to life imprisonment, while broadly based on law, was also discretionary in scope. The governor, however, does not make decisions at the street level, but rather acts as an administrative manager or executive of the state.

While recognizing the importance of discretion at the street level, the central theme of this book is that discretion is also important at other levels of government that involve the management of public organizations. Understanding administrative discretion becomes an essential part of studying how presidents, governors, county and city managers, and other chief executives in public organizations function and make decisions. This discussion is especially timely because, in the years surrounding the new millennium, these managers have become both increasingly active and increasingly visible. Prior years were not any different; in fact, the contrary is true. Arguably, what is different is that there has been a remarkable intensity in the use of discretion.

The Historical Foundation of Administrative Discretion

The historical foundation of administrative discretion is somewhat difficult to pinpoint, although it stems from the progressive reforms of the late nineteenth and early twentieth centuries, and the development of the civil service system. Prior to that time, appointments to serve in the federal government were based on who—not what—one knew and to which political party someone belonged. The *spoils system* (also known as *patronage*) is usually associated with President Andrew Jackson, who, after his election in 1828, promptly filled the administration with his friends and supporters. Most fit the essential requirement of "fitness of character" that had typified previous presidential appointees, and although there was more representation from the Western regions of the country, almost all were men from elite families and education. The spoils system continued under President Abraham Lincoln and throughout the post–Civil War period until the early 1880s.

Patronage politics allowed elected officials to choose government employees with little or no interference. At the time, federal jobs (especially the coveted title of postmaster) were handed out as a way of maintaining electoral coalitions and building loyalty. A person with a federal job was considered to be someone who would agree to support the government as a sign of appreciation. But patronage also meant that employment in the federal government was in a constant state of turmoil as elected individuals came and went, bringing in and taking out their friends and family members. The practice was even more pervasive at the state and local levels of government. The period is characterized as the zenith of administrative discretion in hiring for public service.

Reform of the spoils system came in 1883 with passage of the Pendleton Act. The statute was a product of reforms in Great Britain that was imported to the United States and finalized in exhaustive Senate debates. Its premise was that the federal government should hire individuals with experience in the tasks assigned, rather than just give jobs out or promote persons on the basis of associational loyalty. The foundation of the Pendleton Act is the use of competitive examinations, designed to ensure that the person best suited for the position is hired. In Britain, applicants took essay examinations, but these were considered impractical for the United States. One slight modification was made with respect to the tenure of public service employees. In much of Europe, government service was considered to be for life, which was unacceptable to American reformers. Civil service employees were assured of relative job security under the new law, meaning they could not be fired for not becoming active in politics. But the civil service was also designed to be politically neutral, eliminating termination because of one's political beliefs. To guard against reprisals, the Pendleton Act demanded that in the initial selection process, employees be considered in a non-partisan atmosphere. Other provisions included a probationary period of six months, which did allow some discretion in firing those who were truly unqualified, and a requirement that drunkards would be ineligible for government positions.

The ideas behind the Pendleton Act were lofty, but they did not eliminate the use of discretion in hiring by the president. Congress was not able to force the president to hire employees based only on merit because the system of separation of powers did not allow one branch to have that much control over another. Safeguards were put into effect in an attempt to minimize patronage, such as the requirement that not all of the members of the new Civil Service Commission be from the same political party. But the law also allowed the president to remove members of the commission without any restrictions on his ability to do so, limiting, at least to some degree, its overall independence (Van Riper 1958).

Some presidents have openly flaunted the rationale behind the Pendleton Act, although not directly endorsing a return to patronage. Under President Woodrow Wilson, for instance, several positions within the Department of State were politically connected to the department's secretary, William Jennings Bryant, who had run as a candidate for president, enthusiastically supporting patronage as part of the appointment process. Administrative discretion also stayed alive and well at the state and local levels of government, where the concept of a merit system was not introduced for more than two decades in most jurisdictions.

Factors Affecting Managerial Discretion

Two unrelated influences have exerted considerable pressure on executives at all levels of government to be more visible. The first unintended consequence of the continued reification of management practices that emphasized the empowerment of managers, especially in response to the need to achieve greater effectiveness and efficiency in the provision of public services, was the expansion of managerial and executive discretion. Technological progress has given greater visibility to executive and managerial practices, and new information communication technologies have expanded visibility of executive action to unprecedented levels. Computer-based systems, including the Internet, have empowered members of the public to probe managerial and executive activities and helped expose discretionary actions, including successful, effective, and efficient strategies, and perhaps, most profoundly, questionable decisions. The new management strategies, often labeled "reinvention of government" or "new public management," have supported the transplantation of private sector techniques to solve public policy problems.

Even before the private sector could claim absolute superiority, important private sector managers and chief executives were in the news facing charges of corruption and mismanagement. The stories of managerial abuses within Texas-based Enron and other giant corporations appear to be merely the tip of the iceberg in the larger problems of scrutinizing the role of discretion in managerial decision-making. From all indications, managerial discretion in the private sector seems to be better studied than in the public realm. Unfortunately, debates on managerial decisions in the public sector are front-page news items only when abuse is detected.

In the public realm, discretionary decisions are often confrontational. This is because of the democratic nature of the environment in which public decisions are made. From a systems perspective, public discontent is almost certain whenever the feedback process identifies discontent in the policy output or outcome. Then, managerial decisions become the focus of attention in public discourse.

Another influence affecting managerial discretion and visibility is the September 11, 2001 terrorist attacks on the United States, which created an environment where security concerns became the central focus of most administrative government units. Inevitably, managers had to reshape agencies to closely monitor activities that were considered essential to securing the nation and keeping the workplace safe. Leadership and, more specifically, discretionary decision-making were required to enable each unit to tailor broad national changes to each agency. In December 2005, the post–September 11 experiment with government reorganization was used with the Federal Emergency Management Agency (FEMA), as officials faced enhanced public scrutiny following the devastation of hurricanes Rita and Katrina along the Gulf Coast. These two events, and the criticism of government that followed, focused new attention on an important dimension of a previously existent but largely ignored area of public administration.

Germane to the central issue of managerial and executive discretion is that whenever discretionary decisions raise the possibility that the balance of power in government institutions is tilting in favor of the executive branch, a corresponding amount of public distrust and scrutiny of the work of public officials becomes inevitable. Perhaps, without our knowing it, the steady growth of discretionary decision-making has not been challenged enough. The general reaction is for legislative bodies to reexamine powers granted to the executives. While most managers (elected and appointed) function within the confines of primary laws, cases in which limits to law or vagueness allow for less scrutinized uses of discretion.

Discretion in decision making is expected and desirable so long as it is used fairly and appropriately. Discretion, it is argued, enables managers to handle situations that require leadership. For the most part, managerial discretion is couched within a political dynamic. The overwhelming problem for public managers is to strike a balance and arrive at decisions that do not lead to litigation and waste public resources. In other words, discretion is fine so long as it is not abused. What remains unclear is what constitutes abuse.

Managers in the public sector may feel that they need to gain personal control over institutions because of political competition. Working in tandem with allies, managers often make choices that affect both the public and bureaucracy. Most frequently, managerial competence can help avoid disastrous choices. Because public managers make final decisions within their jurisdictions, nearly every level of decision making has some element of discretion.

However, there are areas in which the enabling statutes as well as organizational structures and practice allow discretion. Conventional wisdom holds that for managers in public organizations, the most obvious areas where the use of discretion is expected are appointment and hiring powers, the freedom to reorganize bureaus, pardon powers, leeway in proposing budgets, and quite frequently, the ability to spend discretionary funds. Perhaps it is worth emphasizing appointment and hiring powers in the context of enhancing public management. One manager put it well when he wrote, "Public managers should have no less discretionary latitude in personnel matters than their private sector counterparts. Successful managers in private industry are measured on their ability to hire, train, develop, promote, and manage high quality people. No less should be expected of public managers" (Leidlein 1993, 392).

Each manager in the public sector attempts to leave an imprint on an agency. How this is done is a function of several factors, including political capital, resources, skill, and institutional support. Whenever called upon to make discretionary decisions, the most obvious way is to use a political calculus. Chief executives should be politically perceptive, but they must also pay attention to broad management issues. They can discharge managerial duties directly or indirectly. They must still be managers of their deputies who handle the routine managerial functions.

The Study of Managerial Discretion

Even though discretion is vitally important at top managerial levels, surprisingly, the theory of administrative discretion is better developed in studies of street-level bureaucrats. For decades, scholars have grappled with ideas on policy implementers making decisions based on realities on the ground. The preeminent scholar in the field, Martin Lipsky, identified groups that qualify as street-level positions. His examples of street-level bureaucrats include teachers, police officers, and law enforcement personnel, including court staff, public lawyers, social workers, and health workers. Knowing who populates these groups helps sharpen our focus (Lipsky 1980).

However, because the demand for street-level services tends to be quite high, different administrations have tried to enhance efficiency by using online service delivery systems. By eliminating person-to-person contacts, administrative systems are, in effect, controlling discretion. Most government units with "one-stop-shop" portals check discretion through automated and programmed decision-making approaches. Online programs check discretion because they provide only certain options and eliminate the ability for clients to have special circumstances, or more colloquially, "to bend the rules." The use of computer services is often a function of availability or access and possession of requisite skills. Technically, access and ability to use computers rations the services. This was predicted by Lipsky, who wrote before the onset of large-scale e-government programs as defined in the federal E-Government Act of 2002.

The downside of online service delivery systems is that there will always be situations in which more flexibility is required. Perhaps this is the heart of Lipsky's theory. He believed that setting procedures that promote predictability relieves employees from having to be responsive to client demands. If there is an explicit procedure for a given situation, the employee must defer to that, even when it is at the expense of the client. Therefore, even with new technologies, administrators must still confront some level of discretionary decision-making. For those in executive-level positions, there is very little contact with members of the public but executives are empowered to make decisions with wide ramifications.

Few major studies attempt to describe the dynamics of discretionary decision-making in the American political system. With the exception of Huber and Shipan's discussion of the legislative context of discretion in selected developed countries, not much has been written to identify key concerns in discretionary decision-making at the managerial level (Huber and Shipan 2002).

The problem is that there is little reflection upon managerial discretion and broad leadership of executive roles within the public sector (Milakovich and Gordon 2004, 243). In addition, "the questions of administrative discretion, of allowable judicial deference to managerial expertise and professionalism, are unsettled in many important respects" (Bertelli and Lynn 2003, 265). At least two authors attempt to provide a conceptual framework for understanding managerial discretion in the public sector (Migue and Belanger 1973; Watson 1981).

Another study bridges, albeit briefly, the gap between street-level and managerial discretion analyses (Carrington 1999). Carrington's single paragraph statement on socialization and discretion explains, in large measure, the connection between the vast body of discretion at the street level and that of the managerial cadres. Perhaps the missing link is the socialization process. Managers in the public sector can affect the socialization process through their own examples as well as attitudinal training initiatives. Although Carrington's work is based on his study of police and law enforcement agencies in New York City, it has wide applications throughout the public bureaucracy.

For example, professional associations have been known to socialize managers to strive for more productivity, efficiency, effectiveness, ethical behavior and economy. The key to making managerial choices that meet those standards is therefore to embrace those values in making decisions. Public managers who ignore or condone acts of injustice or inappropriate behavior without regard for civil and statutory rights send similar signals to street-level organizational membership. When an organization's management allows practices that bend the rules, leading to abuses of street-level discretion, the ultimate solution is to hold management accountable.

Socialization, whether conducted through orientation sessions for new employees, or acquired on the job through organizational citizenship, is key to understanding discretion at both levels of organizational hierarchies. Carrington therefore argues for greater professionalism as a strategy for limiting abuses to power and discretion. He adds that it is prudent to "use the socialization process to introduce values that will enhance an employee's discretionary decision-making" (Carrington 1999, 9).

Managerial Discretion in the Private Sector

There are, however, numerous studies on managerial discretion in private sector organizations. Most are methodologically advanced and range from statistical analyses of the impact of managerial discretion to calculations on leverage in a firm (Morellee 2004). It is generally understood that managerial risk-taking guides discretionary action and could have far-reaching impacts on industry stocks (Chen 2003). However, risk taking does not occur outside the confines of managerial agency, company disclosure, and authority structures (Singh 2003). In the realm of business studies, models abound on the costs of managerial discretion. It is widely held that optimal managerial discretion affects incentive structures in any given firm (Liu 2004; Alderson and Betker 2003; Chambers et al. 2001).

There are also numerous doctoral dissertations that examine various aspects of managerial discretion worldwide. Vilmos Misangyi (2002) provides an excellent reflection on theories of managerial discretion in the private sector. His research deals with the power of chief executive officers (CEOs) in making decisions and taking actions on behalf of the firms they lead. Misangyi and others contend that the key motivation in discretionary actions has much to do with obtaining profits. Therefore, issues of strategy are important variables in choices made. Firm ownership structures, the number of outside directors, and industry competitiveness appear to be key factors affecting limits on decision making in private firms. While Misangyi contends that the profit maximization paradigm dominates business models, he refutes that managers with discretion are not necessarily constrained to the pursuit of profitability (Misangyi 2002).

This is not surprising and is relevant to an understanding of discretionary decision-making in general. In the public sector, the current drive to implement customer-friendly management styles would benefit from reinforcing arguments for maximization of justice, fairness, equity, and other normative values outside the realm of profits. As in the public sector, managerial discretion can be high or low and affect the firm in several ways depending on other intervening variables (Alderson and Betker 2003). The effects of increased managerial discretion on performance are well documented in another study on private firms (Cho 1999). Clearly, managerial discretion is a key variable in goal attainment at the firm level.

Historically, the advocacy of "business-like" public administration can be traced to the post-Progressive Era reforms, especially the classical orthodoxy of Frederick

Taylor (1923). An efficiency expert, Taylor sought to determine the "one best way" of making businesses more productive, using what he called scientific management techniques. For instance, through time and motion studies, he conducted various experiments to see if even common tasks, such as shoveling dirt, could be broken down into a series of steps that could be replicated by individual employees, and which method would produce the biggest pile of dirt in a set time.

Other perspectives (White 1926; Willoughby 1927) looked at organizational structure as a basis for increasing productivity, contending that placing authority in a strong chief executive to make decisions would enhance organizational effectiveness. A chief executive, they noted, should have hierarchical authority, a unified command in decision making, and a role within a strict division of labor. This type of organizational matrix focused authority on a single individual, but that individual would have the ability to delegate authority as needed. A similar approach was taken by Chester Barnard (1948), whose book, entitled *The Function of the Chief Executive,* serves as the model for the development of many corporate structures.

The discipline of public administration was not dormant over the next four decades, but the focus on efficiency gave way to other concerns, including civil rights, discrimination and affirmative action, budgetary planning, organizational behavior, civil service reform, and retrenchment as revenues for public sector agencies declined. By 1980, scholars began to take another look at what many considered to be a blurring of the distinctions between the public and private sectors. Graham Allison's comparison of public and private management found that there were some functions that were similar, such as establishing objectives and priorities, or devising operational plans. He also noted that the responsibility for management of the internal components of an organization (staffing, personnel management, performance evaluation) were the same, as was the management of external constituencies, such as the media. But Allison also found differences, such as the shorter time horizons of public sector managers (including their tenure in the organization), a lack of agreed-upon performance measures in public organizations compared to businesses, the lack of a governmental "bottom line," and the greater public scrutiny that public managers face (Allison 1980).

By the early 1990s, another business-like model would gain attention from decision-makers, including support from President Bill Clinton. David Osborne and Ted Gaebler's book entitled *Reinventing Government* used the phrase popularized by 1992 presidential candidate Ross Perot to *run government like a business* to describe the way business principles and techniques could be applied to public organizations. By using the same kind of market incentives and economic models used by successful corporations, they argued, government could be made more efficient and better able to serve the public. Even the nomenclature is changed in their model. Managers become *policy entrepreneurs;* those being served are *customers* or *clients;* excessive bureaucracy and rules are replaced by an organizational *mission;* and tasks are conceived of and implemented by *teams* rather than from a top-down hierarchy. Like businesses, public organizations have stakeholders (the community), emphasize competition, engage in profit making, and focus on outcomes (Osborne and Gaebler 1992). This so called New Public Management approach became a justification for reform as part of an emerging change in values and expectations about the role of government.

Mounting social problems and decreasing revenues have created a "do less with more" attitude in the public sector, along with an increasing sensitivity to meeting what are perceived to be public preferences. There is, therefore, the expectation that public sector managers will not only make organizations more effective, but also that they will have the necessary discretion to make decisions that will meet those preferences. While placing an emphasis on creativity in serving customers, as is the case with business, new public managers allow for greater discretion among lower echelon officers (Peters 2001, 19). These newly empowered managers are expected to demonstrate their entrepreneurial competence in solving public problems regardless of the goals of the political system as a whole.

By the turn of the twenty-first century, still another model emerged that melded the reinvention of government and new public management into the New Public Service. As happened previously, the New Public Management's nomenclature and structure changed. For example, *customers* are changed to *citizens* and, rather than being market driven, government accountability is driven by the law, community values, political norms, professional standards, and the interests of citizens. The New Public Management viewed discretion as a key tool that gave wide latitude to managers to meet entrepreneurial goals, while the New Public Service accepted discretion as necessary but constrained (Denhardt and Denhardt 2003).

The complexity of this model is staggering. Public administrators are called upon to be responsive to all the competing norms, values, and preferences of our complex governance system. Accountability is not, and cannot be made, simple. It is a mistake, in our estimation, to oversimplify the nature of democratic accountability by focusing on only a narrow set of performance measures or by attempting to mimic market forces, or, worse, by simply hiding behind notions of neutral expertise. To do so calls into question the nature of democracy as well as the role of citizenship and a public service dedicated to serving citizens in the public interest (Denhardt and Denhardt 2003, 137).

About This Book

Our book is one of the few concerned with discretion from the perspective of public managers. It investigates the extent to which public service managers exercise discretion and describes decision points at which managerial discretion occurs. The book relies on several cases to illustrate how different managers use discretion at all levels of government.

Analytically, the book is divided into five chapters. Chapter 1 introduces the nature of the issue and discusses discretion beyond the street-level discourse. The starting point is the recognition that managers face choices in which they have to make discretionary decisions. Luther Gulick and other early pioneers of the field of public administration expressed this sentiment several decades ago (Carrington 1999, 4). Chapter 2 focuses on discretion in local government, especially the work of mayors, city managers, and school administrators. This chapter is also illustrated with examples of how other high-level municipal officials use discretion. Chapter 3 describes and analyzes the context of discretion at the state level, focusing on how governors use discretion in different decision situations. As presented in this introduction, state-level discretion sometimes involves life and death decisions that are unlike those made at any other level of government. Chapter 4 reflects upon discretion in organizations under the executive office of the president as well as the president's use of executive orders. After all, the president is the foremost public service manager. Through the use of executive orders, the interplay between discretion and the enabling constitutional–legal structures is examined. Chapter 5 attempts to respond to the question, "Just how much discretion should managers have?" It has been said repeatedly that managers must have some discretion but they must use it wisely. This concluding chapter revisits the key philosophical arguments in discourses on confining, structuring, and checking discretion.

As in all scholarly discourse, it is important to clarify the terminology used in this book. The text refers to managers, administrators, and executives as titles somewhat interchangeably. Our purpose is to focus the discussion of discretion on the public sector only, although some principles and ideas may be applicable to the private sector as well.

But unlike business and industry where the titles Chief Executive Officer or Comptroller are more precise, public service entails a remarkable spectrum of nomenclature, some of which represent efforts to embrace gender or diversity.

Unfortunately, there is no clear line of demarcation among the various titles that allows for distinction among positions in the public sector. For that reason, we have tried to describe the actions of those who have positions involving the supervision of other employees, and whose decisions affect policy outcomes. That may not cover the entire universe of local, state, and federal bureaus, departments, and agencies, but it is a starting point in a literature that is still in its infancy. We apologize in advance to anyone we may have left out.

CHAPTER 1

Beyond Street-Level Discourse

Illinois Governor James Thompson issued an executive order on November 12, 1980 declaring a hiring freeze that stopped state officials from hiring any employee, filling any vacancy, creating any new position, or taking any similar action. The order affected 60,000 state positions, and on average, about 5,000 of those jobs opened up each year because of resignations, retirements, reorganizations, or deaths.

One of the key provisions of this executive order was that no exceptions were permitted without the governor's express permission. The hiring freeze was violated regularly, however, when Thompson also created the Governor's Office of Personnel (GOP), which operated as a screening agency to limit state employment and beneficial employment-related decisions to those who were supported by the state's Republican Party. In determining whether to ask the governor for permission to take action on a personnel matter, the GOP looked at several factors, including whether the individual voted in Republican primaries in past elections, had made contributions to the party or Republican candidates, had joined or promised to work for the party, and was supported by local or state party officials.

This *de facto* system of political patronage allowed the governor to populate his administration with employees who agreed with his Republican agenda and ideology. It was also, five persons alleged, a violation of the First Amendment. They filed suit against the state in a key 1990 case that made its way to the U.S. Supreme Court, *Rutan v. Republican Party of Illinois*. Cynthia Rutan, a rehabilitation counselor who had worked for the state since 1974, claimed that she had repeatedly been denied promotions to supervisory positions because she had not worked for or supported the Republican Party. Franklin Taylor, a road equipment operator who worked for the Illinois Department of Transportation, said that he had been denied a promotion because local Republican leaders did not support him. James Moore alleged he was not hired as a state prison guard because he did not have party support. Two other plaintiffs, Ricky Standefer and Dan O'Brien, joined the suit, arguing that they had not been recalled to work after they had been laid off, even though fellow employees were brought back. Standefer argued that the retaliation was because he had voted in a Democratic primary election, and O'Brien said that he later obtained a lower paying position only after he received the support of the chairman of the local Republican Party.

In contesting the suit, the state of Illinois contended that there was a significant state interest in supporting the patronage system to ensure it has effective and efficient employees. The state also noted that politically loyal employees were needed as a way of making sure policies were properly implemented. The GOP, they said, did not constitute an impediment to the First Amendment protections of association and speech. The state had made no effort to attempt to coerce employees to change political parties, attorneys argued, and there was no punitive action taken. In addition, there is no entitlement to promotion, transfer, or rehire, and no "right" to a valuable government benefit inherent in state employment.

The District Court dismissed the employees' suit, and the United States Court of Appeals for the Second Circuit agreed, noting that patronage practices violate the First Amendment only when they are the substantial equivalent of a dismissal, or when an employment decision would lead a reasonable person to resign. On appeal to the U.S. Supreme Court, the key issue was whether the First Amendment's proscription of patronage dismissals extends to promotion, transfer, recall, or hiring decisions involving public employment positions for which party affiliation is not an appropriate requirement. Based on precedent decisions, the Court ruled in a 5–4 decision that conditioning public employment on the provision of support for the favored political party unquestionably inhibits protected belief and association. "The First Amendment," the Court said in its majority opinion, "prevents the government, except in the most compelling circumstances, from wielding its power to interfere with its employees' freedom to believe and associate, or to not believe and not associate."

In contrast, the minority opinion was that political leaders at all levels of government "increasingly complain of the helplessness of elected government, unprotected by 'party discipline,' before the demands of small and cohesive interest groups," predicting that the Court's ruling "may well have disastrous consequences for our political system." The dissenters also noted that the government's role as employer was different than its capacity as a regulator of private conduct: private citizens cannot be prevented from wearing long hair, but police officers can.

Thompson's original order had attempted to formalize a system that had previously been very informal, using his authority as governor to institutionalize a Republican administration. Was this an overextension of gubernatorial discretion or an appropriate way to approach public policymaking?

Managerial and Administrative Discretion

Public managers and administrators are individuals who supervise the activities of public employees. Analytically, there are at least two types of managers: the appointed and elected. Starting with the premise that managers are leaders, the conceptual focus can be refined to recognize the distinct roles of the highest level members of public organizations. From a leadership perspective, it is possible to identify three levels of managerial tasks: executive, managerial, and supervisory (Gortner, Mahler, and Nicholson 1997, 334). Even within the managerial cadre there are different levels of responsible leaders, such as middle managers.

This book focuses on public managers at the apex of their organizational structures. Elected executives and public managers include the president, governors, and mayors. Legislators in weak-mayor systems may perform managerial functions but, for the most part, we like to emphasize their roles as legislators. In the context of discretionary powers, perhaps the significant point concerning the roles of political executives is that they matter and, perhaps, the range of their discretionary actions shapes what government actually delivers (O'Toole 2000; Cartier 2005, 630). Appointed managers include bureau chiefs, agency directors, city and county managers, department heads, and supervisors in civil service positions. In general, the highest ranked federal managers, including department secretaries and directors, are political appointees, while most of the civil service managers are careerist appointees.

Organization theory specialists recognize political chiefs as having tremendous responsibilities for making policy. In fact, policy implementation studies consider discretionary experimentation as part of a valuable leadership strategy (Nakamura and Smallwood 1980, 112–33). Discretionary experimentation with policy is one of the characteristics that can distinguish between successful and less successful leaders. The issue is how organizational leaders use their discretionary abilities to effect change. While policy making is part of executive and managerial responsibility, it is not the only task for bureau chiefs; executives also have a considerable degree of discretion in policy making, especially transformational leaders. More important is the political leader's ability to frame policy problems. How issues are framed often determines the levels and types of discretionary actions that occur during policy implementation (Hammond and Knott 2000, 59).

Appointment powers are another key element in executive leadership and management. The political system makes assumptions that appointed and elected managers have legitimate concerns in pursuing their policy goals and proposals. The window for discretionary decision-making is sometimes enlarged because elected managers have a fairly brief tenure (Aberbach and Rockman 1988, 610).

Appointment concerns are at the core of policy implementation in all public bureaus, for various good reasons. Classical works, especially Machiavelli, recognized the need for a prince to surround himself with a competent cadre of public officials. In a sense, the quality of political appointments is a key factor in determining rates of programmatic failures or success. Leaders who appoint individuals with a desire to transform society are most likely to be intensely experimental.

There is an expectation that when administrations change, newly appointed managers choose new directions for their agencies. Change provides greater opportunities for exercising discretion than is often acknowledged. "For their part, senior career executives must discover whether changes at the top of their agencies and bureaus imply changes in policy directions and alterations in opportunities for exercising discretion" (Aberbach and Rockman 1976, 456). For the most part, the new changes are structured by the ideological norms established in each administration. The key criterion for managerial Senior Executive Service (SES) appointments in the U.S. system since the administration of President Richard Nixon is "loyalty." Some observers believe that loyalists are likely to be manipulated and make decisions based on established party norms and ideology (Aberbach and Rockman 1995, 841–2; Gerhardt 2000, 133). How one measures intangibles such as loyalty is problematic, but it usually implies that a manager follows priorities and policies established by higher levels within the hierarchy, often without question.

How managers reduce and resolve conflicts with career bureaucrats and how the legislature checks and controls discretion is considered basic to understanding executive power and leadership. Managers are expected to play roles that include serving as a leader, entrepreneur, resource allocator, disturbance handler, and as monitor of the implementation of public policy. Because these are enormous and often overtly political roles, the public expects greater accountability from managers whenever they make discretionary decisions. Ignoring the realities of discretionary power in public management undermines any attempts at understanding decision making.

The challenge, therefore, is to understand practices and processes informing the exercise, control, and confinement of managerial power and discretion. Most literature recognizes that managerial power exists in public organizations. Norton Long's essay, "Power and Administration" (1949), established that "the life-blood of administration is power. Its attainment, maintenance, increase, dissipation, and loss are subjects the practitioner and student can ill afford to neglect." While examples of the abuse of power abound, just how much of this power is discretionary is not a very well developed field of inquiry. The question of discretionary power within public management begs increased attention in the field of public administration.

Perspectives on Discretion in Decision Making

Decision making continues to be at the core of public administration and management. From the outset, it is useful to point out that discretion is a part of the broad continuum of decision-making processes that involve the act of making choices. It is a determination of a question and a judgment or opinion in a case in which there has been some form of deliberation. It is well known that most policy makers are dependent on a number of advisors who help them think through the choices they make. Although there are numerous frameworks for discussing decision making, much work needs to be done in dissecting the nature of exercising discretion at policy levels. Exercising executive and managerial discretion requires a close look at a variety of conscious and judgmental choices.

Much like legal discretion, managerial and executive discretion have far reaching consequences, and it becomes useful to investigate how discretion is conceived. One of the reasons why public trust in government has plummeted has to do with cynicism about discretionary decision-making. In part, choices made by a majority of public managers and exe cutives fall within the realm of discretion.

Cynicism is exacerbated when policy choices appear to treat segments of society dissimilarly. There are times when executive and managerial actions, particularly policy alterations, provide a recipe for malfeasance and nonfeasance in the form of selective allocation of resources and prejudice. This is particularly true when official policies do not clearly establish criteria for decision making (Ball, Krane, and Lauth 1985, 103). Public managers need to be constantly reminded that guidance on factors to be considered before discretionary decision-making is made helps to minimize unjustifiable inconsistencies among individual decision-makers.

Much of the scholarly work on managerial and executive discretion in public organizations has not been sufficiently embedded in self-conscious decision-making theories. While this is not to say that the work on the technicalities of decision making ignores discretion, there is a need to elevate the empiricism and examine the ethics of decision choices. Empiricism helps in understanding institutional constraints, especially the limits of legal provisions. After all, the past actions of executives and managers, especially those who have used too much discretion, often led to negative outcomes. Such actions require constant probing and evaluation. Experience can dictate how an individual public manager and executive make discretionary decisions (Manley-Casimir 1977, 84).

When it comes to decision making by discretion, some studies make a strong case for caution. In addition, it is useful for decision makers to include key administrative values such as representation, economy, efficiency, effectiveness, fairness, and transparency. While all of these values are important, this discussion only mentions a few. For example, public managers, in the discharge of their duties, may employ discretion to promote representation as a value (Rourke 1984; Mosher 1982). But if they act in a policy framework established outside the law, that is, using discretionary power, chances are that the promotion of representativeness might lead to competition among societal groups (Lowi 1969).

David Dillman explains the importance of discretion in enhancing efficiency and effectiveness more profoundly than previous authors. He contends that discretion is often necessary to ensure that things are done (2002, 178). The reasons for articulating administrative values are numerous. For example, not embracing transparency is likely to lead to corruption, which in turn leads to further distrust in the administrative process. Discretion is more than being cautious. There has to be some consideration of the consequences of decisions taken, especially evaluating decisions based on whether they are right and just. As John Burke points out, these are important values in achieving an ethically sound decision (1996).

Decision making in areas where "high discretion" is necessary requires similar principles, especially careful prioritization of values to be promoted. High discretion may in most cases refer to what the literature terms "strong discretion," a situation in which managers are not bound by previously established standards (Dworkin 1979; Toews 1981, 3). Thus, in certain emergency circumstances, almost all decisions are discretionary. Executives and managers dealing with emergencies and disasters must necessarily consider the risks associated with each of the choices they make.

Among the most important decisions to be made in disaster management are the prevention of loss of life, recovery of life and property, security, public safety, relief, and reconstruction, just to name a few. On the one hand, it might seem obvious that officials would take every measure possible to reduce the loss of human life and property when resources are at their disposal to do so. But their discretion to act may be limited or constrained by statutes, regulations, or even political considerations that sometimes seem inappropriate under the circumstances.

For instance, during the California Fire Siege of 2003, local and state resources were stretched thin as multiple fires burned almost simultaneously in Los Angeles, Riverside, San Diego, San Bernardino, and Ventura counties. The three fires that burned in San Diego County between October 25 and 27, 2003 resulted in the loss of 16 lives and 3,241 structures, with suppression costs surpassing $43 million. After the blazes were extinguished, numerous reports were prepared that assessed state and local officials' actions, with particular criticism aimed at airspace management during the fires.

Federal, state, and local governments each have policies on aircraft "cutoff" and "shutdown" times that determine when airplanes and helicopters may be dispatched, and these times are often inconsistent with one another. California's policy states that aircraft may not be dispatched to arrive at an incident any later than 30 minutes before the official time of sunset in the jurisdiction. The federal policy is consistent with the state policy, except that it references only air tankers and does not specifically address helicopter use. Cutoff policies, under federal regulations, relate to restrictions on the dispatching of air tankers in low ambient light conditions. The aircraft cannot be dispatched to arrive at a fire earlier than 30 minutes after the official sunrise, or later than 30 minutes before official sunset, unless an approved aerial supervisor is on the scene. Shutdown refers to the time when all low-level aviation and single-engine aircraft operations cease for the night, normally 30 minutes after sunset. Federal policy does not permit nighttime aviation fire suppression operations, nor does the State.

San Diego's Cedar Fire was reported at 5:37 PM on October 25, three minutes after the aircraft cutoff time. As a result, no aircraft were dispatched to the fire at that time but were ordered for immediate use the next morning. The county sheriff's office contacted fire officials and offered the use of their helicopter but the offer was declined due to their interpretation of the cutoff policy. California also has a "No Divert" policy that allows an incident commander at a fire to prohibit aircraft resources from being used if there is recognition of critical problems that might require those airplanes to be sent elsewhere. However, the policy does not distinguish between airborne aircraft and those held on the ground. In San Diego, aircraft were held on the ground for use in structure protection needs anticipated on another fire in the region. However, weather and visibility conditions prohibited safe operation on the other fire, so aircraft sat idle on the ground. Military aircraft were also available for use, including heavy-lift helicopters used for water drop operations, but the federal Economy Act of 1932 limits the utilization of military assets prior to the complete use of all civilian resources. Those craft did not become available for use in combating the fire until considerably later.

Critics, including a San Diego–area member of Congress who lost his home in the fires, argued that unnecessary adherence to federal and state policies had slowed the response to the widespread blazes. Congressman Duncan Hunter, a Republican who is head of the House Armed Services Committee, had arranged with Federal officials to send in air tankers from Colorado to help fight the fires. Two other unused air tankers sat on the ground at a nearby military base. He accused the governor, forest, and fire protection officials of delaying needed help. County officials and others argued that the sunset rule and the decision not to allow local helicopter pilots to attack the fire when it was relatively small may have been responsible for expanding the fire, making it the largest in California's history.

The seriousness of each value plays the biggest part in the politics of executive decision-making. In those extraordinary circumstances, it may not just be about promotion and attainment of certain values. There are also rules to be followed and roles to be played. Public managers acting outside the parameters of rules and roles then risk public condemnation, especially if the policy outcomes are not favorable to large sectors of the population. Yet, from a conceptual point of view, the discretionary part of decision making may not necessarily be governed by rules or existing policies (Handler 1992, 3; Pinkele 1986). Besides, managers acting on their own discretion may choose to ignore established rules or do nothing at all, which are termed *inaction decisions* (Davis 1969, 4).

From a rational decision-making perspective, what is particularly noticeable about discretionary decision-making is that it is a complex process. Each public manager and executive has to make choices that have policy ramifications. By looking at specific examples, we can discern a great deal about the way discretion works at the top levels of public organizations. Conceptually, providing greater insight into discretionary decision-making might lead to improved public management. Most importantly, research on the intent of managerial action needs to focus on logically verifiable political choices rather than pitching arguments in positivist arguments.

Discussions and study of the political environment assist in understanding the exercise of managerial discretion. It is political reasoning that underlies selective policy choices. So long as we are a democracy, public policy will continue to be dependent on how specific policy issues shape discretionary actions.

Managerial and executive actions that have the potential for injustice undermine democratic governance. Theoretically, discretion is permissible to the extent that public officials use it in a non-abusive and responsible way. As much as discretion is important, when it is at odds with political accountability, there is a real danger that democratic governance, especially the rule of law, may be in jeopardy (Bryner 1986, 2; Dillman 2002, 166). Without factoring in the role of politics, it is difficult to build a coherent theory of executive and managerial discretion.

In tandem with the concept of the administration–politics dichotomy is the twin idea of forfeiture and delegation. Public administration is generally understood to be the execution of public policy. Public policies emanate from legislative directives worded in less than precise ways. The legislature, being an imperfect body, does not enact perfect laws, hence, some gray areas are left for administrators to interpret and implement. The concept of forfeiture and delegation is a powerful one for understanding the use of discretion in managerial decision-making.

Even though legislative bodies delegate responsibility to managers and other administrators, they also reserve the power to oversee administrative decisions. Legislative bodies may question the potential for abuse of discretion and often establish rules to contend with this possibility. Formal legislative ethics committees, for instance, institutionalize reviews of legislative behavior, and oversight functions allow legislators to examine the implementation of public policy. At the federal level, reviews undertaken by the Government Accountability Office (GAO) provide more intense scrutiny of specific policies. Congress also sometimes subrogates its delegated power through judicial review, which is often justified when the legislature detects an abuse of managerial and administrative power.

Legislative bodies are not the only ones that contend with the potential problem of abuse of discretion. Courts, too, have become arenas for resolving problems associated with the abuse of discretionary power. While administrators and managers must be cognizant of the provisions of various aspects of federal and state administrative procedure acts, certain decisions at the managerial level are best analyzed within a constitutional framework.

Decisions made by managers that might lead to constitutional questions are seldom reversed in favor of procedures. At the local level, council ordinances and charters might override procedural guidelines embraced in administrative regulations. Managers, therefore, exercise discretion within a legal–constitutional framework, with the central question being the extent to which the primary law guarantees executive power to managers. Stated differently, the focus is to understand the dynamics of separation of powers between top management in a public agency and the lower-level offices.

Discretion, in this context, is about the delegation of responsibilities among the various layers of government. This leads to the important concept of federalism, which plays a large part in the apportionment of discretionary power among the various levels of government in the United States.

Federalism and Its Place in Understanding Managerial Discretion

Federalism and intergovernmental relations structure executive and managerial discretion in formulating and managing public policies. Federalism is seldom lost in the search for analytical tools for studying discretion in decision making. It is possible to hypothesize that the outcome of a given policy is a function of the amount of discretion permitted each layer of government within the federal system. By tracing the actions and the roles of the different layers of government, we can determine the authority structures and base environments through which managers and executives manage public policies. Even though creative federalism has allowed for both competition and cooperation in the delivery of various public services, the core foundation principles of American intergovernmental relations left much ambivalence on the parameters for policy making within the various jurisdictions. The subsequent dynamism and changes in the federal idea across different administrations suggests that politics informs the discretionary conduct permitted policymakers at different levels.

One way of understanding executive and managerial discretion is by examining how federalism affects political decision-making. A federal system is one in which authority is divided between at least two levels of government, such as the national government and various state governments in the U.S. Federations are usually distinguished by territory, so that a state government's authority extends only to the geographical area over which it has jurisdiction. "Coming together" federations are those where independent states join by ceding or pooling sovereign powers in certain domains for the sake of goods otherwise unattainable, such as national defense (Stepan 1999).

Historically, the federalist model was established in the United States after the Articles of Confederation failed to provide sufficient authority for the new government in 1781. The powers granted to the national government were too weak to provide for defense, interstate commerce, and law enforcement. The subsequent Constitutional Convention of 1787 was designed to revise the Articles, but it also touched off a national debate on how much power should be given to the states and how much should be given to the national government, which is the classic split of a federalist system. The Anti-Federalists believed that centralization of authority in the national government allowed leaders too much discretion, and would put the states at risk of having their authority usurped by a body too far from local interests. The Federalists, led by James Madison, Alexander Hamilton, and John Jay, wrote a series of essays that explored possible models for dividing power so that neither the centralized government nor the states would have total control.

The issue is discussed in the *Federalist 10* and *41* and other historical documents (Mason 1972; Drake and Nelson 1999; Sutton 2002, 38). Importantly, at the general level, dispersion of powers was considered a rational strategy against corruption in the various units (Beer 1993, 233). Yet at a much broader level, the problem of national security and rights remained an issue in the delicate balancing act of apportioning discretion among the various units of government. For instance, in *Federalist 41*, the writer notes that the powers conferred to the American Union government prudently chained the discretion of its own government. By prioritizing national security and maintenance of harmony with the states, the federal constitution set bounds on the use of power for its own safety. Security against foreign danger was no doubt as important to the founders as it is against international terrorist groups such as al-Qaida. In the area of security, most scholars would argue, it made rational sense to provide absolute discretion to the federal government when authorizing the power to raise troops and equip fleets. While this section is not intended to be a discussion of the enumerated powers of the federal government, it is worthwhile to discern the principles that inform federal discretionary powers.

There are other numerous responsibilities and tasks for which only the federal government has absolute discretion. For example, in financial matters, the Constitution only permits the federal government the authority to mint monies. The Federal Reserve Act of 1913 established Federal Reserve Bank to furnish elastic currency and manage the banking system in the country. Although the Federal

Reserve Bank has considerable discretion in carrying out its responsibilities, it is still accountable to Congress. Legislation checks discretion by requiring that the Reserve Bank reports annually to Congress. In addition, the GAO and the Federal Reserve Board's Office of Inspector General can audit the Federal Reserve Bank's activities. Because Congress appropriates all monies spent by all public agencies, a unit's misuse of discretionary power can be stopped technically by being written out of law and by denial of funds.

Beyond specific administrative critical operational tasks, the Constitution also conferred to the federal government powers to restrain states from certain injurious acts. There were also certain miscellaneous objects of general utility that were considered more efficaciously the province of the federal government (Madison 1961). For the most part, acts of the federal government that exceed the enumerated powers of that government under the Constitution violate cardinal principles.

The framers knew that states had certain advantages in managing unique situations. They recognized the unique characters of individuals, families, neighborhoods, local governments, and private associations. The framers, therefore, restrained the federal government from undertaking activities that limited the policymaking discretion of the states where there was constitutional authority for local action. Moreover, the intent of the constitution was to grant the states the "maximum administrative discretion possible" where federal oversight of state administration was neither necessary nor desirable. The broad objective was to avoid federal regulation of state activities, especially in a manner that would interfere with functions essential to the states' separate responsibilities and independence.

Modern managerial activities and functions of the federal government have been partly codified in operational statutes such as the Federal Activities Inventory Reform Act of 1998. Presidents have articulated their individual executive understandings of principles of federalism in their policy statements and authoritative pronouncements.

Nixon's New Federalism, for instance, increased the influence and executive discretion of elected officials in state and local governments. In fact, Nixon encouraged the implementation of administrative reforms that supported an expedited and simplified application of the block grants provided by the national government. President Jimmy Carter approached federalism much differently, perhaps unenthusiastically (O'Toole, Jr., 2005, 139). Perhaps federalism and intergovernmental relations received a more sustained enthusiasm and attention from the return of the Republican Party with Ronald Reagan's almost religious articulation of devolutionary policy formulation and implementation strategies. From a comparative perspective, the changes to intergovernmental relations were not profound under George H.W. Bush. Regardless of the forms of intergovernmental relationship, the core principles continue to be an arena of scholarly attention especially in terms of discretionary authority dispersed to various jurisdictions. Yet importantly, policy makers have continued to make value judgments regarding the kinds of policies that are permissible at each entity of the federal system. President Bill Clinton used his powers to promulgate an Executive Order in August 1999 that used unambiguous language to explain his view of federalism.

In formulating and implementing policies that have federalism implications, agencies shall be guided by the following fundamental federalism principles:

(a) Federalism is rooted in the belief that issues that are not national in scope or significance are most appropriately addressed by the level of government closest to the people.

(b) The people of the States created the national government and delegated to it enumerated governmental powers. All other sovereign powers save those expressly prohibited the States by the Constitution, are reserved to the States or to the people.

(c) The constitutional relationship among sovereign governments, State and national, is inherent in the very structure of the Constitution and is formalized in and protected by the Tenth Amendment to the Constitution.

(d) The people of the States are free, subject only to restrictions in the Constitution itself or in constitutionally authorized Acts of Congress, to define the moral, political, and legal character of their lives.

(e) The Framers recognized that the States possess unique authorities, qualities, and abilities to meet the needs of the people and should function as laboratories of democracy (Executive Order 13132 of August 4, 1999, Section 2).

Limitations on State and Local Discretion

Every policy that the national government delegates to the state and local units reflects a series of choices that involve managerial discretion. Decision choices include responding to the question: Which governmental level should handle or solve an aspect of public policy? Discretion concerns arise when a local jurisdiction fails to deliver services adequately, for instance. Questions of just how much should local jurisdictions be doing abound. While the constitution established the broad framework to structure regional and local actions, some problems are far too big to be delegated to local and state bureaucracies. Moreover, the idea of Intergovernmental Bodies (IGB) implies there are problems that are beyond the control of local governments (Agranoff 1990). Changes in federalism have added new players to the scene. For example, standardized testing implies that local school districts have lost a degree of discretion in how they run and assess education programs. This is because the federal government mandated local governments to embrace the concept of standardized tests to determine deficiencies in education systems across the nation.

Although state and local governments deal with the street-level implementation of national policies, the federal government retains a large measure of discretionary power over what state and local jurisdictions can do. It does this in numerous ways; federal influence begins at the level of identifying and adopting the public agenda. Federal actions create excuses for making proposals that affect state and local units (Derthick 2000, 175–195). Officials who fail to meet federal standards may be criticized by their supervisors, who often aspire to national recognition.

The federal government exercises influence, in large part, by stimulating demands from groups within the state and by placing "extra" resources and influence at their disposal. Many tactics involve using federal funding as carrots and sticks. This forces state agencies to act as clients, or more appropriately, as allies of federal agencies. Federal government officials know this and often seek to create allies at the state level by establishing agencies specifically for managing federal funds. This provides the federal government with the ability to achieve compliance and integrate its values and priorities within local and state government systems.

These strategies reduce or confine discretionary activities at the local level. Autonomy at the lower levels of government is therefore guaranteed only to the extent that it furthers federal goals. Federal patron agencies and their state counterparts might be expected to have shared values and goals without the federal agency taking steps to assure this, even if they only share programmatic functions. To meet federal requirements, state agencies are given only enough autonomy to ensure federal objectives are met.

Other strategies that limit the discretion of local and state governments are more visible. The federal government shapes discretionary activities of state and local governments through myriad programs. For example, grant-in-aid programs are a form of contract in which compliance is made unavoidable. Beyond that, a variety of other legal and fiscal techniques are employed by the national government to encourage acceptance of its regulatory standards. The four most prevalent strategies for confining discretionary actions at state levels are direct orders, crosscutting requirements, crossover sanctions and partial preemption.

Direct orders include the Equal Employment Opportunity Act (EEO) of 1972, which bars job discrimination at all levels of government; the Marine Protection Research and Sanctuaries Act of 1977; the Fair Labor Standards Act, and the Food Stamp Act (1977, amended in 2004). Direct orders are legally permissible.

For instance, in the case of the Food Stamp program, the act defines who is eligible for benefits and how one becomes eligible. Through a standard Eligibility Verification System (EVS), state Departments of Economic Security coordinate regional food security needs for families in their respective state jurisdictions. The federal government, through the Department of Agriculture, also provides guidelines, codified in the Code of Federal Regulations (CFR), for retailers outlining the type of merchandise they may sell and the amount of business to anticipate from the program. The CFR also includes rules under which states administer the program. Generally, each state's Plan of Operation includes a State–Federal Agreement, Budget Projection, and a Program Activity Statement. In the case of food stamps, states seemingly have little discretionary authority because of overriding federal standards.

Crosscutting requirements are widely recognized and generally applicable requirements imposed on grants across the board to further various national social and economic policies. For instance, Title VI of the Civil Rights Act of 1964 stipulates that no person should be excluded from receiving federal services on the basis of race or ethnicity. In other words, programs receiving federal financial assistance are required to enforce the anti-discrimination law. Over the years, crosscutting requirements have been enacted to protect persons with disabilities, the elderly, and women in the implementation of education policies. These rules apply horizontally to all or most federal agencies and their assisted programs.

Crossover sanctions rely upon the federal power of the purse. They impose federal fiscal sanctions in one program area or activity to influence state and local policy in another. The distinguishing feature is that failure to comply means reduction of funds or termination of funding. For instance, federal requirements that billboards be removed from highways were a carrot and stick approach with crossover implications. The sanctions, like the crosscutting requirements, are tied directly to the grant-in-aid system. Federal power in these cases is derived from the constitutional authority to protect the general welfare.

Finally, partial preemption structures discretion when the federal government exercises its authority to preempt certain state and local activities under the Constitution's supremacy clause and commerce power. Preemption in this case is only partial. Federal laws establish basic policies, but administrative responsibility may be delegated to the states or localities if they meet certain nationally-determined conditions or standards.

The Water Quality Act of 1965 was an early example of this strategy. The general structure of federal preemptive action is for states to enforce federal regulations and water pollution standards. What this means is that if the state does not issue regulations acceptable to the federal government, then the federal agency or department takes over. If the state does not adopt and enforce the required regulations then the federal level of government assumes jurisdiction. The same structure has been used in implementing other environmental laws, such as the 1990 Clean Air Act.

From State and Local Discretion to Unfunded Federal Mandates

The federal government's role in preempting state and local discretion was legitimized in the 1970s through three mechanisms: block grants-in-aid, categorical grants, and general revenue sharing (GRS). The federal block grant programs were designed to promote federal priorities by providing funding for general purposes, such as community development or housing. The broad language in the block grant applications enabled nearly any entity to use its discretion in how the funds were to be spent, becoming a key element in the sharing of government powers (Milakovich and Gordon 2007, 134; Grodzins 2000, 56).

Categorical grants were similar in intent, but they required the recipient government to share a portion of the cost of the program by agreeing to match a certain portion of the expenses with their own funds. This type of grant moderated discretion, and it also caused some municipal governments to apply for funds whether the project was needed or not, simply because the proportional match was so low.

In contrast, general revenue sharing (GRS) was an experiment in administrative discretion that totally decentralized federal aid, with some unexpected results.

In 1971, President Richard Nixon's State of the Union message called for a "New Federalism" that was part of his "New American Revolution" message. The 1972 State and Local Fiscal Assistance Act allocated funds for distribution to state and local government on the basis of a formula that included population, tax effort, and personal income. There was no application process; municipalities simply received a check each year, and were required to report (very generally) where the money was spent. The GRS program was designed to be a temporary one, with the financial grants ending in 1976. Nixon predicted that there would be a "burst of creative energy" at the local level as officials had total discretion in deciding the best use of the funds (Wallin 1996).

Congress warmed to the idea as officials considered the grants a type of windfall that allowed them to prioritize projects based on their knowledge of local conditions and needs. President Gerald Ford called the program "a resounding success, as it supports and embodies his belief in the concept of Federalism—that unique aspect of the American system which permits and promotes creativity and freedom of action simultaneously at three levels of government." Ford sent Congress the State and Fiscal Assistance Act Amendments of 1975 to authorize extension of GRS with gradual increases in the level of funding, and increased public participation in determining the use of revenues (Ford 2006). Congress obliged, extending the program in 1976 and 1980, and reauthorizing funding for only local governments in 1983. GRS was terminated in 1986.

Studies of the implementation of GRS showed little creativity in how funds were used, however. The majority of cities used the funds as normal municipal revenue, maintaining existing services rather than initiating new ones, even though that option was available to them. Because the program was initially authorized to last only five years, local governments realized that the lifetime of the funding was probably short, so many used GRS for capital expenditures, building new facilities (especially city and county government buildings). This choice was both political and fiduciary. Officials realized that if new public sector jobs were created (such as police officers or planners), it was quite likely that those positions would have to be eliminated once the money ran out. Similarly, any new programs that were funded through GRS would be cut, forcing the programs to be terminated, or—worse yet— would need to be supported by pre-GRS tax revenues. As a result, funding was often used for public works projects, such as building bridges or repairing sewer systems (Caputo and Cole 1977; Larkey 1979; Marando 1990; McKenna et al. 1990; Wallin 1998).

On the other hand, federal or state attempts at imposing laws and regulations on other governments in the form of unfunded mandates adds to the complexity of use the of managerial discretion at the lower units of government. The legitimating of mandates began in the 1970s and continued into the twenty-first century. The era of cooperative federalism promoted coercive federal roles epitomized by mandates, sometimes considered a tool of coercion applied by the federal government against protesting state and local officials. This increased role reflects the growing interdependence of national, state, and local political systems that redefine the workings of the federal system. Federal mandates have become a major instrument of national policy and are seen as a logical and appropriate tool to promote greater national uniformity. In terms of discretionary discourse, they present another avenue through which state and local actions are confined and structured.

Unfunded mandates prescribed and legislated by upper governmental authority can become an economic burden on states and municipalities that are charged with implementing them. Usually these mandates are enforced through the threat of withholding funding from states and local governments if they fail to comply (Posner 1998). There have been instances when some states chose to disregard federal mandates and accepted the subsequent loss of federal revenue. In 1974, at the height of an energy crisis that had drivers waiting in line for hours to get fuel at gas stations, Congress instituted a 55-mph national speed limit. The move was designed to conserve fuel, and had a secondary goal of reducing highway fatalities by slowing drivers down. The U.S. Department of Energy had found that gas mileage drops sharply at speeds over 60 mph, and that for each 5 mph over 60, drivers pay the equivalent of an additional 20 cents per gallon of gas.

After a while, several states raised their 55 mph speed limit on freeways despite losing federal highway dollars. The penalty for noncompliance cost them less than to enforce the mandated speed limit. Congress lifted the 55 mph limit in 1995, but states still have discretion to set their own speed limits, even on federal highways. Along with highway funding, there are forms of other statutory compliance such as the requirement that to qualify for federal monies, agencies have to achieve a degree of training competence. The same applies to employment and fair labor standards federal requirements. The reality is that the federal government has effectively used mandates to control the lower levels of government or confine institutional program and policy abilities.

A more recent federal initiative is the No Child Left Behind Act (NCLB) of 2002, which reauthorized the Elementary and Secondary Education Act and established national testing standards. Studies show that the act has led to increased state government expenditures on education.

Several states, including Illinois, Connecticut, and Utah, began to oppose the NCLB policies. Connecticut filed suit in federal court against Congress in 2005, charging that requiring testing under the NCLB was a violation of the Unfunded Mandates Reform Act of 1995 (UMRA). The statute was enacted to address concerns about federal statutes and regulations that require nonfederal parties to implement federal legislative programs without receiving enabling federal funds. UMRA requires that a report be made as to how the federal government should relate to the other layers of government. UMRA generates information about the nature of federal mandates "but does not preclude the implementation of such mandates" (GAO 2005).

A first-year retrospective evaluation of UMRA found that the legislation did increase the quality and quantity of information about federal mandates (1998). This information is vital for ensuring sound intergovernmental relations. UMRA created an environment for Congress to estimate ways of minimizing costs to the state and local governments. During its first year, UMRA succeeded because Congress knew that the changes in federal policy would affect the budgets of the federal and state governments. But it did not eliminate the constraints faced by lower levels of government with reference to meeting broad programmatic goals (GAO 2005). For example, in the post–September 11, 2001 era, many federal programs addressing Homeland Security, Avian Flu preparedness, border control, and immigration issues have created an imbalance in fiscal responsibility between the federal, state, local, and tribal governments.

When States Take Over a Federal Responsibility: Immigration

In 2006, the debates on illegal immigration compounded law enforcement problems, especially because the broad policy framework is the purview of the federal government. Fiscal stress overwhelmed states that have had to provide services to undocumented immigrants. For the most part, unfunded mandates are a good way for a federal government to gain uniformity in polices among the various states. The alternative is a group of fifty states that create their own standards and provide services in their own unique ways. The current immigration crisis is a good example of how chaotic public organization can be if each state is to determine its own policies in dealing with issues such as immigration.

It is not enough to state that federalism is a framework for managing managerial discretion. While federalism allocates responsibilities to different levels of government, it also presents significant obstacles to the operations of state and local governments. Although the federal government has ensured some degree of quality control and standardization, from the perspective of managerial discretion, the challenge is just how much power should be vested in centralized federal structures?

According to the U.S. Citizenship and Immigration Services (USCIS), there were approximately 7 million unauthorized immigrants living in the United States in 2000. Although immigrants are from all over the world, those entering from Mexico have dominated the immigration discourse, in part because at least 4.8 million undocumented immigrants are Mexican. Moreover, the border between Mexico and the United States is considered, for the most part, to be fairly porous. Between 1990 and 2000, Arizona experienced a surge of immigration from less than 100,000 to an estimated 283,000 illegal immigrants (USCIS 2003, 7). Even more staggering were the numbers of those attempting to illegally cross into the United States annually. In 2004, nearly half of the 1.1 million illegal immigrants apprehended by Border Patrol agents crossed the border in Arizona (Meeks 2005). The large numbers of illegal crossings into Arizona have created massive political problems in the state and, more profoundly, intergovernmental relations with the federal government. Illegal crossings have resulted in numerous deaths in the desert and have received enormous media attention both locally, nationally, and internationally.

Policymakers in the United States and Mexico have met periodically to discuss solutions to the problems that stem from illegal immigration. Former Mexico President Vicente Fox was very vocal on the subject and urged President Bush to provide amnesty to undocumented Mexican workers. Since his election, Fox's agenda was to get legal status for those living illegally in the United States (Papademetriou 2003). On the other hand, President Bush's heightened concern with border security issues has been grounded within the larger post–September 11, 2001 anti-terrorism policy framework. It is not that the state of Arizona is oblivious to the security parameters or labor market logic of immigration into the United States. Arizona, as a border state, has paid close attention to the debate on immigration from a purely local and pragmatic position.

The primary concern has been the impact of immigration on state and local resources, especially health, schools, and other social service systems. Because children of illegal immigrants must be accommodated in state schools and be taught

English, the opponents of illegal immigration have raised issues concerning the state's continued ability to provide education and health services for those children (Gonzalez 2005). Although voters in Arizona passed Proposition 203 in 2000 banning bilingual education for children with limited English proficiency, the challenge of teaching children in two languages is a major problem in the state. With regard to health care, hundreds of illegal immigrants are injured on their way into Arizona. Others, especially uninsured women with children, have to deal with an unfamiliar, complex, expensive health care system they can hardly navigate or afford. There have been numerous studies that document the inability of undocumented immigrant workers to pay high medical costs (Banks 2005). In addition, the Arizona prison system is no longer capable of supporting thousands of illegal immigrants, especially those involved in violence and in other illegal activities including drug trafficking (Carroll and Villa 2005).

Among the problems associated with illegal crossings is the loss of life. For instance, according to the federal Department of Homeland Security (DHS), Arizona's border claimed the lives of 141 immigrants in 2004, 63 from exposure (U.S. Department of Homeland Security, 2004). Immigrant rights groups believe the number is significantly higher, however. Border crossing deaths represent the human dimension of illegal immigration.

The state and local government response to illegal immigration varies. For example, the Arizona Border Control (ABC) Initiative received widespread support from key constituencies in the state. ABC started in March 2004 as a collective effort by several agencies to thwart illegal border crossings, terrorist activity, and drug smuggling along the border. The DHS supported the initiative, which was successful in apprehending at least 400,000 illegal immigrants along the Arizona border in less than a year's time in 2004. Prior to that initiative, the increase in Arizona's border crossings was attributed to tougher restrictions on other popular routes like San Diego, California where a wall restricted some movement. In El Paso, Texas, greater scrutiny and surveillance had restricted easy access across the borders.

The second reaction to illegal immigration is the Minuteman Civil Defense Corps, volunteers whose objective is to forestall migrant smuggling. The Minuteman Project, originally organized in California, took up patrol along Arizona's border towns as a result of citizen frustration with federal and state bureaucracies (Hall and O'Driscoll 2005). One news item quoted a retired school administrator expressing his dissatisfaction. "I'm concerned about what's not being done by the government—hasn't been done for ages, apparently" ("Minutemen Back on Patrol" 2006).

The Minuteman Project in Arizona includes hundreds of volunteers from all over the Southwest who literally walk along the border and report sightings of illegal immigrants. The Minutemen claimed success for drawing national attention to the issue, and the problem became a central campaign issue in state politics.

Don Goldwater, nephew of the late Senator Barry Goldwater and a Republican candidate for governor in 2006, called for erecting a wall along the border with Mexico and threatened that he would put illegal immigrants in a tent city on the border and use their labor to build the wall ("Minutemen Back on Patrol" 2006). Arizona's legislature proposed and passed a bill to make illegal immigration a felony and also to cut funding for services provided to illegal immigrants, but Arizona Governor Janet Napolitano vetoed the bill (Diaz 2005).

In August 2005, Governor Bill Richardson of New Mexico declared a state of emergency, followed by Governor Napolitano. The governors claimed that the federal government was slow at forestalling illegal immigration into their neighboring states. The declaration of a state of emergency meant tapping into federal monies meant for disaster funding (Carroll and Gonzalez 2005).

The immigration debate further rose to national limelight when President George W. Bush announced in May 2006 that he would send National Guard troops to patrol the international border with Mexico. The president's decision was not considered a military offensive but rather a pragmatic attempt to control what many considered a national problem. President Bush viewed his executive approach as an additional measure to the proposed immigration reforms under discussion in Congress. He also made symbolic visits to the border states of Arizona, New Mexico, and Texas, where he gave speeches on the need for comprehensive immigration reform, including "guest worker" provisions and strengthening border security.

Although President Bush's decision to deploy troops was criticized by Mexican politicians, Border Patrol officials welcomed the decision because it augmented the services they provided. From an international politics perspective, any form of militarization can be interpreted as a less than friendly gesture, particularly because Mexico and the United States enjoy warm relations and are trade partners. Yet in terms of administrative exigencies, the border with Mexico has been traditionally seen as a weak spot in post–September 11 security management. This is besides the point that states neighboring Mexico were finding it hard to cope with providing basic services to undocumented aliens crossing into the country.

The USCIS is a unique federal administrative agency charged with important constitutional mandates (Ludd 1986, 16). In 1952, the agency was granted absolute power to define procedures that govern immigration policy. From historical evidence, it appears that because the United States is self-identified as a land of immigrants, the practical applications of the relevant law require the balancing of competing values. Clearly, by 2006, the mosaic of U.S. immigration policy was under stress, mostly from government actions or inaction. With the numbers of undocumented immigrants rising, political leadership, especially from elected executives, was essential. Immigration policy, therefore, provides opportunities to examine competing values that are at the core of subsequent administrative and managerial discretionary actions (Ludd 1986, 20). Immigration policy leadership is an area where hard choices are expected and must be made.

Explaining Managerial Discretion

While the arguments for tighter restrictions on the amount of discretionary power held by administrators abound, managerial discretion is frequently examined only in terms of constitutional standards. For ordinary administrators, flexibility is acceptable so as to implement programs in a manner acceptable to the large and diverse society (Shumavon and Hibbeln 1986). Yet we know that when discretionary power is too broad, justice may suffer from arbitrariness or when it is too narrow there might be inequalities in provision of public services.

Scholars believe that the elimination of unnecessary discretionary power and better control of necessary discretionary power are keys to successful administrative decision-making. Some warn that, without discretion, effective operation of government is impossible. In the early public administration literature, Ernst Freund contended that discretion permitted an adjustment to varying circumstances and avoidance of the undesirable standardization of restraints, particularly of government (1917). For most keen observers of both managerial and administrative powers, absolute discretion is considered an irrational practice in a democracy. A number of powerful theoretical propositions reinforce arguments for limited or measured managerial discretion.

The first consideration is that legislative bodies lack knowledge about the problems being addressed in statutory provisions, ordinances, and laws. Congress, for example, does not have the resources or the inclination to deal with complex, detailed regulations and is thus obliged to depend on experts to make policy decisions (Bryner, 1986; West 1985). As John Kotter explains, successful managers gain power by building reputations as experts. He notes that, "believing in the manager's expertise, others will often defer to the manager on those matters" (Kotter 1993, 14). While professional managers seek to protect their reputations and track records, elected managers, including mayors and presidents, seek reelection and a favorable place in history. Most seek to build enduring legacies and avoid making decisions that will undermine their achievements in history. Because of these limitations, Congress must delegate power and authority to management in public bureaucracies in the form of discretionary decision-making.

A second argument is that legislative bodies often have little time to follow through with the minute details of policies enacted in law. There is less time for majority building in individual cases in legislative bodies, and members must settle for consensus on general, rather than specific, statutory goals (West 1986; Leys 1943). "It is not possible for a legislature to draft statutes that have the capacity to speak authoritatively to all of the circumstances likely to arise in the administration of a program throughout its future history" (Morgan and Rhor 1982).

Third, managers are seen as more likely than legislative bodies to be able to monitor social and economic activity and develop flexible and rapid responses to changing conditions. Even when a specific law or ordinance has been passed, managers must make decisions concerning the setting of priorities, the balancing of conflicting goals, and the regulation of complex and poorly understood problems (Bryner 1986).

Fourth, because of the expansion of government over the years, legislative bodies provide managers with broad authority and discretion to execute policy as best they can based on what is "on the ground" (MacIntyre 1986). However, generally, the length of legislation shapes discretionary action. In other words, longer statutes are most likely to tell agencies what to do, and shorter ones give them more leeway. When statutes get longer, they consist of more and more specific policy instructions (Huber and Shipan 2002, 73–75).

There are those who read ulterior motives in the legislative delegation of authority to public managers. It could be that delegation to managers is an attractive way for politicians to deflect difficult policy choices. They can take credit when a policy works and blame the public managers when it fails (Bryner 1986). This line of thinking implies that legislative bodies delegate for narrow selfish interests that protect them from the wrath of their constituents in the subsystem politics. To rely on managerial discretion, there must also be a reliance on the moral character of public managers and their commitment to the protection and promotion of the public good (Kiel 1986).

Some policies are pursued under broad statutory statements of general purpose that offer little more guidance than to serve the public interest, while other statutes give specific detailed instruction to administrative agencies. In many instances, public agencies are given little guidance in their enabling statutes concerning how they should shape their regulatory agenda, set priorities, allocate scarce resources, and distribute the costs and benefits involved in the rules and regulations they issue (Bryner 1986).

Public agency managers must be accountable to the legislatures and the people they serve. Two values, accountability and responsiveness, are often in conflict, placing managers at the center of political activity as they attempt to balance competing pressures. Having noted the ambiguities in lawmaking, it is necessary to consider the basic arguments raised in favor of managerial discretion.

Support for Managerial Discretion

The very nature of legislative lawmaking, with its inherent constraints upon drafting specific direction for agency action, compels theoreticians and practitioners alike to accept the inevitability of managerial discretion (Ludd 1986). Proponents say that delegation is a convenience, primarily to relieve the legislature of a mass of detail, and to gain greater flexibility (West 1986). Supporters of managerial discretion view it as appropriate and even essential in assuring that expert work is guided to achieve political ends. They believe that while scientific expertise and technical calculations should determine policy formulation, the balance between political and scientific interpretations must be handled at the management level.

Woodrow Wilson was a proponent for managerial discretion, noting that the executive branch needed it to pursue its tasks in an efficient and effective manner and within agencies so that expertise and professionalism could be harnessed in the pursuit of public purposes. Wilson's theory of the separation of administration from politics exemplified this line of thinking.

Others who believed in the practice of administration by experts supported discretion for the same reason as Wilson. For example, contemporary writing states that discretion may provide opportunities for getting agencies to work effectively and efficiently (Dillman 2002, 178). However, the separation dichotomy appears to have run its course and discretion has taken on a separate meaning. At the presidential level, it was further actualized in the form of executive orders, discussed in greater detail in Chapter 4.

Managerial discretion may be viewed as a practical response to the inability to separate aspects of politics from administration. Managers may sometimes use discretion to overcome the many technical and political obstacles to development and implementation. Discretion at the managerial level also may enhance the government's capacity for responsiveness. Public managers with sufficient discretion may energize agencies for change and new policy direction. In the rulemaking process, defenders of managerial discretion observe that only agencies are capable of drafting rules appropriate to a specific situation. Such adaptations are best suited for guaranteeing individual justice and constitutional protections because each rule must be tailored to the specific considerations of the particular constituents of the proposed rule, or to the specific facts surrounding an administrative action (Ludd 1986). Discretion, when used wisely in rulemaking, may contribute to just and fair decision-making. Public managers must oversee this process. In fact, even the Constitution allows for discretion in the "necessary and proper" clause of Article 1, Section 8, which gives Congress the ability to delegate authority. For the most part, therefore, sub-delegation to managers is not unconstitutional so long as it is done pursuant to general guidelines (West 1986).

Opposition to Managerial Discretion

Those who oppose discretion prefer laws and regulations that are much more specific, directed, and confining upon public managers so that the possibilities for abuse do not present themselves. Allowing discretion also might lead to unintended consequences and perhaps the subjective interpretation of public policies. Opponents of managerial discretion argue that it threatens the idea of political accountability because partisan officials make important policy choices, and suggest that excessive managerial discretion endangers the idea of the rule of law.

They recommend several things, including that governmental actions be clear, specific, and applied in a non-discretionary manner to avoid inconsistencies and arbitrariness in policy formulation (Bryner 1986; Donnison 1982, 90; Titmuss 1987, 233). Beyond arbitrariness, there are numerous areas of concern, including creation of opportunities for malfeasance and nonfeasance in delivery of public services. Furthermore, there is a real possibility that too much discretion will produce policy actions that may not be broadly representative (Toews 1981, 3–4).

Managerial discretion also calls into question the structure of the separation of powers, checks, and balances, and other elements of constitutional democracy that rely on formal institutions and processes. It threatens the development of clear public choices, inhibits public debate and education concerning public policies, and contributes to perceptions of the "capture" of agencies by the interests that fall under their jurisdiction. A newer version of opposition to discretionary decision-making has emerged from the ideologically powerful, public-choice oriented school. In rhetorical terms, executives and managers who have embraced this school of thought have traditionally sought to reduce the role of bureaucrats in the polity. More profoundly, their concern is to narrow the scope of bureaucratic discretion and "latitude for independent advocacy" (Campbell 1993, 388).

The strongest voices against discretion charge that it often threatens constitutionalism. While supporters of delegation might argue that elected political executives such as mayors and governors need discretion as people's representatives, too much discretion challenges the essence of the doctrine of separation of powers and democratic practice in general.

Bonnie Honig presents this dynamic more forcefully by stating that critics of government expansion and use of discretion have the tendency to appeal to courts to resist the reach of executive power, which increases during emergencies, as events such as terrorist attacks in 2001 and hurricanes in 2005 have shown. This means that the only way to understand the full role of discretion is by paying attention to legal concerns raised in numerous court proceedings. Honig argues that courts have deferred many security- and emergency-related issues to the executive branch (2003).

The Courts and Managerial Discretion

The question of the constitutional basis for managerial discretion warrants further examination. According to Gary Bryner, the only concern of the courts in the matter of managerial discretion is to ascertain whether the will of legislative bodies has been obeyed (1986). This leads to the exploration of judicial processes, since reviews of agency decisions can be sought in the courts, although there are significant limits on the scope and nature of the review process. A difficult question may lead to U.S. Supreme Court action.

Those who take an activist approach to judicial review state that it can provide administrative agencies with the necessary direction to accomplish their statutory mandates. It may assist in designing the standards Congress and state legislatures may have failed to provide in the original legislation creating the specific administrative and managerial function. Advocates of judicial review declare that it can supply the ever present need for governmental accountability because it can be the instrument through which equilibrium is established in the government. Supporters of judicial review also contend that the final arbiter of governmental action or inaction must be the one branch of our government that is insulated from direct political manipulation: the federal judiciary. According to this position, the possibility of the courts expanding the limits for a broader scope of review into discretionary decision-making is highly unlikely (Ludd, 1986).

For other observers of the courts, the fear is that the system has been inconsistent on the question of delegation, both with regard to legality and the allowable limits of discretion. This contention is supported by some court decision rulings that delegation was appropriate provided that clearly-articulated legislative directives delimited it. The court's traditional doctrine was that legislative delegation is unconstitutional unless accompanied by meaningful standards, but legislative bodies have often been unable or unwilling to provide meaningful guidance for administrative discretion. Thus, courts should require administrators to provide this type of guidance within a reasonable time. The courts' oversight of administration has been enlarged along both substantive and procedural dimensions, largely through judicial precedent, but also through the result of statutory provisions (West 1986).

Statutory and Other Types of Constraints on Discretion

Statutes represent still another constraint on the use of discretion, as do administrative rules, and other types of quasi-legislative procedures. Congress and state and local legislative bodies can monitor and control agency decisions by enacting laws and by exercising the power of legislative veto. Statutory limitations on decision making are common, but they have been supplanted in recent years through the process of administrative rulemaking.

Under Franklin D. Roosevelt's New Deal, there was a flood of new legislation that greatly enhanced the centralization of federal power. New public policies were developed that affected nearly every sector of American life, from assistance to the poor and elderly, agricultural subsidies, and banking and securities laws to others affecting natural resources, utilities and power, and wildlife. With so many statutes came the realization that there was no way to keep track of the many regulations that would be needed to implement the new policies. That void was filled with the creation of the *Federal Register,* which publishes all documents and notices related to regulatory activities. The *Code of Federal Regulations* (CFR) serves as the compilation of actions taken to implement statutes. Since it began publication in 1938, the CFR has expanded to 50 subject areas, called titles, that cover every element of federal activity. Title 7, for instance, covers regulations related to agriculture, while Title 23 deals with highways, and Title 35 covers the Panama Canal.

To set limits on managerial discretion, Congress enacted the Administrative Procedure Act of 1946 (APA). The statute divides all administrative procedures into three categories: rulemaking, which is when agencies act like legislatures; adjudication, which is when agencies act like courts; and everything else. The last category is perhaps the most important, since it is the area where discretion is often most apparent (Shapiro 1986). The APA, as the name implies, outlines what agencies must do when they implement laws, identifying specific procedures that must be followed to insure conformity. For instance, the APA requires an agency to state the express purposes of what it is trying to do and its purpose in creating new regulations. Strict deadlines are included for notifying the public about a proposed regulation in the *Federal Register,* and for other types of participation. One of the few criteria that agencies must meet is that the substance of rules cannot constitute an "arbitrary or capricious abuse of discretion." But the APA does not provide any additional guidance on what that might mean (Kerwin 2003, 54–55).

Advocates for rulemaking feel it is superior to adjudicative procedure in many ways. All who may be interested are systematically notified. Tentative rules are published and written comments are received before final rules are adopted. Rulemaking allows all interested parties to participate, and frees managers and other senior administrators to consult with anyone in a position to help. Prospective rules are preferable to retroactive lawmaking because it allows legislative committees to provide supervision. Those opposed to rulemaking state that it is a quasi–legislative process that is unconstitutional, because the language requires that policy be made by elected representatives and that rulemaking violates the Constitution's specification of powers.

The idea that managers must have discretion when performing tasks challenges the theory of separation of powers in government. Yet, discretion is a must to render credibility to the search for effectiveness and efficiency in the provision of services. If and when discretion is necessary, there must be ways of controlling and structuring it. The ideas presented in this chapter inform the practice of discretion in American government and the key arguments for understanding discretion, and how it is important in the administrative and managerial discourse in the country's democratic environment. Chapter 2 focuses on managerial issues at the local level, applying theory to practice in the municipal setting.

CHAPTER 2

Managerial Discretion in Local Government

In 1954, the Mount Soledad War Memorial Association built a cross in a San Diego city park to honor veterans of the Korean War. The city agreed to let the memorial be built, and for 35 years, the cross received little attention. But in 1989, Phillip Paulson, a Vietnam veteran who was also an atheist, filed suit claiming that the cross was a religious symbol that violated the Constitution's provisions that government not favor one religion over another. City officials decided to respond by trying to sell the land to the memorial association, an action that was fully within the scope of their discretion. On two separate occasions, they even obtained sufficient voter approval to authorize the sale. But the courts ruled that the attempt to sell the park was also unconstitutional, because the city was unfairly favoring buyers who wanted to keep the cross where it was. The city appealed the case all the way to the U.S. Supreme Court, which refused to consider it, and in 2004, city voters rejected a third attempt to sell the park's land.

The city then turned to two local members of Congress, who slipped a provision into another piece of legislation that designated the memorial a national monument, allowing the federal government to accept a donation of the land from the City of San Diego, and also directing the National Park Service to help maintain it. But in 2005, the city council rejected a proposal to donate the land to the federal government. Supporters of the cross memorial launched a ballot measure that asked voters to override the city council vote, and a month later, the members of the council rescinded their earlier decision. In June 2005, nearly three-quarters of the voters approved the measure, directing the city once again to donate the land. In October 2005, a judge ruled against the city, saying both the ballot proposition and the proposed transfer of land to the federal government were unconstitutional. While the city appealed the ruling again, the judge told officials in May 2006 that they had 90 days to remove the cross or face a fine of $5,000 per day. In the meantime, the city attorney wrote a letter to President George W. Bush asking him to intervene.

Seventeen years after Paulson filed his suit, supporters cheered when President Bush held a ceremony in the Oval Office transferring the 29-foot cross and war memorial to the federal government. The August 14, 2006 action was not the end, however; Paulson's attorney had already filed papers in federal court to void the transfer of the monument and to have the court declare the action unconstitutional.

Aside from the issue of the separation of church and state, San Diego officials faced a number of problems in deciding what course of action to take. On the one hand, city officials were using their discretion to take an action they believed to be both appropriate and legitimate. As representatives of their constituents, they were responsible for following public sentiment which had been expressed by voters in the ballot proposition. But on the other hand, by politicizing the issue of the cross and the park, officials were accused of fanning the flames, at the expense of the veterans' memorial, to gain re-election. As one law professor noted, "What politician wants to be the mayor that tears down the cross on Mount Soledad?" By sticking with the voting majority, city officials also faced the reality that they were not only paying their own legal costs, but if they lost the appeal against Paulson, which the city attorney said was probable, they would have to pay his legal bills as well (Strumpf 2006). In this instance, managerial use of discretion resulted in an expensive legal and political lesson.

Local Government Management

The sheer fact that there are more governments at the local level than at the state and national level means there is greater diversity in the types of discretionary managerial decisions that are made. The U.S. Department of Labor's Bureau of Labor Statistics notes that there are about 87,500 local governments in the United States, including about 19,400 municipal governments, 16,500 townships, 13,500 school districts, and 35,100 limited purpose special districts for services such as fire, water, and wastewater systems. In Illinois alone, there are an estimated 6,900 local government units. As of 2004, there were about 5.5 million persons employed by local governments, excluding education and hospitals. Professional and related occupations account for 21 percent of employees, and management, business, and financial occupations constitute another 11 percent of the workforce. First-line supervisors and managers have a median annual earning rate of $20.24 per hour, with a city manager receiving just under $90,000 in compensation, a fire chief about $70,000, a purchasing director making $59,000 and a chief librarian making $56,000. In contrast, the median annual income for local elected officials is under $8,000 per year (U.S. Department of Labor 2006).

With low salaries relative to those working in the private sector, local governments have tremendous difficulties recruiting and retaining managers, especially when they are subject to the limitations on discretion outlined in Chapter 1. The federal system confines their maneuverability, and makes decision making an exceptionally arduous task in comparison to managers at the national and state levels. For the most part, managers' roles and power are prescribed by state legislatures. Some observers believe that state governments have, in effect, usurped local discretion, hindering cities and other local governments from addressing their own problems (Andrisani, Hakim, and Savas 2002).

Because city managers are an example of managerial positions, it helps to place in perspective their general formal roles. In most council-manager cities, the formal duties of the city manager include supervising all or most parts of city government; overseeing the enforcement of all laws and ordinances; hiring, disciplining, and removing employees according to applicable policies and law; preparing an annual budget and guiding its implementation after adoption; advising council members on the city's finances; making and controlling purchases; and keeping the public informed on government operations (Stillman 1974, 131).

The relationship between the city manager and the governing body is often described as a partnership, with the city council as senior partner. This suggests vulnerability on the part of the city manager and administrative staff. The general theory and practice is that the city manager implements policies established by the city council. There is also diversity and variations in discretionary power among various levels of government. For example, the potential exists for city managers in the council-manager form of government to exercise greater discretion in certain policy areas. This is because in the mayor-council system, policy guidelines embrace a strong sense of community and the public good.

There is sometimes a concern that the council-manager model relies far more on the manager's administrative prerogatives. The general assumption is that a city manager is a professional often selected from a national pool who has less familiarity with localized concerns (Loveridge 1971, 46; Nalbandian 1991, 31). It follows that in the strong manager-council arrangement, no one individual may be held accountable for policy failure. Typically, the mayor in the council-manager city is seen as weak, and most mayors perform ceremonial roles, are a link to the public, promote and represent the city, and preside over council meetings. The mayor is characterized as having a leadership, rather than a managerial, role (Svara 2002, 45).

In small rural townships, the managerial capacity for discretionary decision-making is often hampered because typically, as tasks and issues became more complex, elected officials rely on outside consultants to advise them (Bender and Zolty 1986, 119–120). This strategy provides elected officials with a temporary neutral buffer for making decisions. Another strategy is to make use of citizen advisory committees, which increase community involvement in decision making and decrease the amount of direct pressure and discretion available to senior managers in rural communities. Citizen advisory committees are important in making decisions in areas such as planning and zoning, public safety operations, and economic development.

A loose typology of discretionary decision points can be constructed based upon five broad responsibilities in the local manager's docket. These areas of managerial oversight are:

1. Appointment and staffing powers
2. Legislative processes
3. Policy implementation
4. Contracting
5. Finance.

These five areas are not mutually exclusive but reinforce each other, providing an insight into the role of managerial discretion in local government.

Appointment and Staffing Powers

Appointments are considered a key responsibility of the executive at all levels of government, with the federal system serving as the model for local and state officials. The need for the national government to provide some mechanism for appointments of public officials was present at the nation's constitution-making convention (Gerhardt 2000, 17–19). At that time, the task was to evaluate grants of authority to the executive branch and simultaneously provide for limits to those powers. Delegates grappled with the key question of which offices merited or did not merit constitutional protection. Much like the president and governor, the mayor and city manager have legally sanctioned appointment powers, sometimes sharing the responsibility for appointments with various commissions, city boards, and committees. Appointments to certain commissions could be a sensitive and charged issue. For example, in areas with rich tourism interests, an appointment to a Tourism Commission elicits much public debate. A Tourism Commission establishes, maintains, and coordinates relationships with agencies and organizations that promote tourism. The Commission also develops plans to enhance a city's tourism infrastructure and, through an allocations subcommittee, advises the mayor and council on the appropriate use of city lodging tax funds. Similar responsibilities are held by appointees to city boards including Procurement Appeals Boards and various committees whose members serve at the mayor's discretion. These include a large variety of administrative bodies performing a host of tasks. For example, most mid-to-large cities have created commissions on People with Disabilities, Ethics, Transportation, Equal Opportunity, License Review, and Parks and Recreation.

There are other similarities in appointment processes as well. In weak mayor systems such as Los Angeles, the city charter has required the council to confirm members of commissions appointed by the mayor since 2000, much like senatorial confirmation of presidential appointees. The role of political logic in appointments is unmistakable. Even though managers might not choose to characterize their duties as inherently political, the reality on the ground requires that they deal with political issues. Appointments and staffing decisions also leave room for decisions based on factors besides merit, as one recent court case illustrates.

Springfield is the home of the Massachusetts Career Development Institute (MCDI), a city-run school that serves welfare mothers, the homeless, immigrants, and displaced workers who are trying to learn a new trade. In July 2005, one of MCDI's directors was sentenced to a year in prison for handing out "no-show jobs" at the facility to friends and family members, including his son-in-law. The director had worked at the facility since the early 1970s; at his sentencing hearing, he was characterized as an Italian immigrant with a history of service to his church and to the community. The school's former executive director, who had also been the chairman of the city's Police Commission, was convicted of handing out city jobs in exchange for sex. Both defendants had been placed in positions of authority that allowed them considerable discretion in hiring decisions.

Although most city administrators prefer to be viewed as politically neutral, tasks such as naming a new police chief are often politicized (Nalbandian 1991, 80–81). The selection of a police chief was, until the early 1950s, a relatively routine matter. Most appointments were made from the ranks of current police officers, often based purely on seniority. But a number of events changed hiring patterns and led to substantive reforms that made the appointment process much more visible. On December 25, 1951, about 50 Los Angeles Police Department (LAPD) officers beat 7 young men in their custody, including 5 Mexican Americans, in what came to be known as "Bloody Christmas." Activist groups called for an investigation into charges of police brutality, seeking greater civilian control over police actions. The newly-appointed police chief, however, had already announced that he was launching an effort to make the department more professional, and more importantly, autonomous. External investigations into the brutality complaints were stifled, and the LAPD gained a reputation of being above the law and hostile to minority communities (Escobar 2003).

Similar events continued to take place in Los Angeles (and in other cities with a large minority population) during the 1960s and 1970s, increasing the visibility of police chiefs and their handling of incidents involving minorities. The 1965 Watts Riot, which led to 34 deaths, 1,000 injured persons, and an estimated $200 million in property damage, began after a white LAPD officer stopped a black motorist he believed to be intoxicated. A second white officer arrived on the scene, and was alleged to have hit with his baton several of the crowd members who had gathered. News of the assault quickly spread throughout the city and, combined with already escalating racial tensions, anger disrupted against the all-white LAPD and white shopkeepers in the neighborhood. For five days, more than 35,000 people rioted in the Watts neighborhood, and over 16,000 National Guard officers and city and county police were brought in to stop the rioting. The Watts Riot changed the political landscape of both California and Los Angeles, eventually leading to minority representation in many urban police departments.

In the 1980 Miami Rebellion, Arthur McDuffie, a black insurance executive, was badly beaten by four white police officers. McDuffie was riding a motorcycle, ran a red light, and led police on a high speed chase. He was driving on a suspended license and had numerous traffic violations on his record, and allegedly ran from officers before being subdued. He died four days later from multiple skull fractures from a blunt object. All four officers were acquitted of manslaughter charges. Street violence began after a protest involving over 5,000 residents. After three days, 18 people had been killed, more than 400 were injured, 1,100 were arrested, and the city estimated damage at more than $100 million.

The 1990s witnessed a rash of police brutality incidents. Perhaps the most infamous beating was that of Rodney King, who was beaten by LAPD officers after a traffic stop for speeding in 1991. King, a black man, was alleged to have emerged from his car in an aggressive manner that police said suggested he was high on drugs. Before King was handcuffed, officers hit and kicked him nearly 60 times, finally subduing him with a stun gun. The beating was captured on tape by a bystander, and the incident was replayed worldwide. King subsequently brought charges of brutality against four police officers, and the trial was moved out of the area to an all-white suburb. When the men were acquitted nearly a year later, protesters gathered in South Central Los Angeles, and rioting spread quickly there and in other cities throughout the United States. After three days of violence in which U.S. Army troops were brought in by President George H.W. Bush, more than 50 people had been killed, 400 were injured, and 17,000 were arrested. Damage estimates were more than $1 billion, placing additional pressure on the city's embattled police chief.

In 1994, a veteran New York City police officer choked Anthony Baez to death, but the defendant was acquitted of criminally negligent homicide despite at least eleven other brutality complaints. San Francisco police subdued burglary suspect Aaron Williams and repeatedly sprayed him with pepper spray in June 1995; he died after officers failed to monitor his breathing, which was affected by the spray.

Highly publicized incidents continued into the next decade as well. In Houston, Hiji Eugene Harrison was shot to death by a deputy during a routine traffic stop in 2005; the officer involved said that Harrison had tried to take his gun. In the aftermath of Hurricane Katrina, New Orleans police were videotaped beating an elderly black man who was on the street after curfew.

In all of these cases, the Chief of Police became a key political figure as well as a manager. Surveys have shown that the criteria for selecting the police chief have changed in an attempt to choose individuals who are capable of handling explosive or highly publicized situations. Two studies found that experience in managing police, and extensive training and education, were identified as the two most important criteria for selecting qualified potential police chiefs (Dantzker 1994; Dantzker 1996). What initially may have been a localized decision has become an important appointment with national implications, putting additional pressure on the persons making those appointments.

Legislative Processes

Depending on the enabling statutes, mayors play a big part in legislative processes and some have veto powers, which councils can override. Their level of discretion varies from one locality to another and in some cities, the mayor has considerable discretion. For instance, in smaller communities, a mayor can technically amend an ordinance. In larger cities including New York, mayoral participation in legislative processes is very similar to that of governors and even the president. For example, a mayor might propose legislation following a catastrophic occurrence or to fulfill a party agenda. New York Mayor Michael R. Bloomberg, for example, introduced legislation after the tragic events of September 11, 2001 to make skyscrapers safer. Bloomberg worked closely with the buildings department commissioner, Patricia L. Lancaster, taking his cues from the findings of a report on the World Trade Center Building Code Task Force. In a similar example, Mayor Anthony Williams introduced housing legislation in Washington DC to meet the growing challenges of homelessness in the nation's capital (Lazere 2001).

Other problems have triggered legislative leadership from mayors and city managers. The influx of illegal immigrants has forced mayors to increase their attention to the challenges they pose for city services, regardless of the size of the municipality. In 2003, Seattle Mayor Greg Nickels, for example, introduced a law prohibiting city employees and police from inquiring about a person's immigration status. In comparison, the Pennsylvania town of Hazelton passed the Illegal Immigration Relief Act in July 2006, one of the strictest ordinances in the country. The mayor said that growing numbers of immigrants had damaged the city's way of life, leading to problems with violent crime, crowded schools, increasing hospital costs, and demands for services. The ordinance, which the mayor had proposed a year earlier, makes landlords who rent to illegal immigrants subject to a $1,000 fine, and takes away business licenses from companies who employ illegal immigrants.

Similarly, New York Mayor Bloomberg used an Executive Order to reverse the city's practice of "don't ask, don't tell" that governed the interaction between city workers and immigrants in the city. The 2003 policy shift became controversial, forcing the mayor to review it. In an effort to limit the change's impact, he ordered that city workers could inquire about someone's status only in certain instances. The previous policy had prohibited city agencies from reporting a person's immigration status to federal authorities, an approach that was meant to protect undocumented but otherwise law-abiding immigrants seeking medical treatment, police assistance, or other city services. Bloomberg's order reversed that course, and allowed workers to report illegal immigrants. The mayor argued that he was making changes to comply with new federal laws and a court decision.

Policy Implementation

Jurisdiction

Although the city charter in a council-manager form of government defines the formal powers of the manager in terms similar to those conferring power to the mayor in a mayor-council charter, the two operate in quite different ways. The city manager's role as policy maker is detailed in city charters or enabling ordinances. The problem is usually how to acknowledge this role (Nalbandian 1991, 24–25). Most have to decide their role in policymaking but it often embraces innovation and advocacy (Loveridge 1971, 45–50). The latter hinges upon on a manager's competence and ability to bring expertise and experience to the council. Those qualities can significantly affect policy implementation. For instance, research shows that a vast majority of chief executives—including city managers—have the power to propose a budget. However, one may also find journalistic accounts of "iron fist" managers controlling budgets to a degree that minimizes the council's role. The traditional means of attaining a successful budgetary process is to work with the council in drafting the budget (Loveridge 1971, 49).

While control of budgets is an important area of political power, an increasingly more prevalent contentious issue is the battle for control of policy implementation. Jurisdictions often fight over policy direction in areas that pose direct challenges to urban governance. Although constitutional guidelines allocate broad responsibilities to local authorities, takeovers by higher levels are not unusual. For instance, when the Chicago Housing Authority was plagued with mismanagement, the federal government, through the Department of Housing and Urban Development (HUD), took over control of 40,000 housing units in the largest federal takeover of a housing project. Its board resigned after publicly acknowledging the authority was out of control (Terry 1995).

There is no question that mayors can leverage policy directives in their jurisdictions. Many observers link mayoral discretion to the structure of local government, especially to debunk the popular perspective that mayors are all too powerful and are domineering. Evidence suggests that facilitative mayors are less controlling than "high-leadership" mayors who get enmeshed in operational detail and are often at loggerheads with city managers. However, a mayor "has an impact on the level of council involvement in goal setting and policy making" (Svara 2002, 49).

Certainly, managerial mayors usually have a greater ability to oppose legislation and to execute the law in ways that fit their broader administrative styles. Arguably mayors with considerable legislative power—those who can be tie breakers in council meetings—may have tremendous potential to change the direction of local governance. However, it is also known that weak leaders—defined as mayors without much power to appoint key administrative officials such as police chief—do have some important leverage and can use their discretion to affect policy implementation. A prime example of how that discretion is used involves school governance.

Education Policy

Recent mayoral change initiatives in local government education policy change initiatives reflect a pattern of growing executive response to issues that are considered vital to a city's quality of life. Education, as policy scholar Deborah Stone contends, is one of the most important policy areas for strengthening the upward mobility of groups considered politically weak (Stone 2002, 386). Rightfully, education policy is an area generally considered to be under the direct purview of local legislatures. Formally, no big city mayor has policy oversight in how school districts are run and most do not wish to be embroiled in school politics. Yet, actions of leading large city mayors triggered public debate over use of executives' discretion in controlling education policy and agendas in city schools. Here is how one columnist presented the issue.

> "Mr. Giuliani, who has spent weeks embroiled in the politics of who would be the next Chancellor of the city schools, is but one of the mayors around the country who find themselves caught up in the local, often chaotic, business of education. In truth, big-city mayors generally have no formal power to do anything about public schools. But either because the problems are so grave, because the need to do something is so obvious, because the lines between what's a school problem and what's a city problem have become hopelessly blurred, or because they figure they are going to get blamed anyway, mayors increasingly are defining the problems of the public schools as their problems" (Applebome 1995).

Over the last 15 years, local government officials (especially mayors) have become increasingly active in taking over the administration of public schools when problems have become so acute they felt that a takeover was necessary. In most cases, the change in school management was a result of the Elementary and Secondary Education Act of 2001, better known as No Child Left Behind. This federal legislation requires schools to develop accountability provisions to make sure every child is learning, with individual schools being ranked according to their performance. Chicago Mayor Richard M. Daley took over operation of the city's schools in 1995 after the Illinois state legislature formally transferred responsibility to the mayor after his persistent calls for change in the way schools were run. Mayor Daley subsequently cut a deal with the teachers' unions to assure stable labor–management relations.

A similar takeover occurred in Cleveland, where the state legislature turned school operations over to the mayor. In Detroit, Mayor Dennis Archer was appointed as the Acting Chief Executive Officer of the city's schools in 1999. Through a series of legislative maneuvers, the mayor was given the power to appoint the majority of the members of the school board, effectively shifting power from the schools to his office. "Any mayor in the country will tell you that the number one issue facing cities isn't crime or jobs anymore, it's public education. Mayors have every reason to take on the responsibility" (Hathaway 1999).

School takeovers have not been without incident. Policy stakeholders, including teachers, school administrators, students, parents, unions, business interests, and elected officials, have taken opposing sides on the matter. Parents, for example, question the rationale of taking over entire districts because not all schools are on "watch lists" due to their substandard performance. Unions are concerned about the loss of jobs following takeovers. The duel of different policy interests and stakeholders can be seen vividly, for example, in the case of Los Angeles, with more than 730,000 students, and the nation's second largest school district.

Los Angeles Mayor Antonio Villaraigosa announced his takeover strategy in his first State of the City address in April 2006. Mayor Villaraigosa's proposal was modeled on mayoral takeovers in Chicago, Boston, and New York, where a council of mayors from cities within the district had broad education policy oversight. Villaragosa's plan did not envision disbanding the Los Angeles Board of Education, but the decision-making responsibility would be relegated to parents. Although Villaragosa, like other mayors, wanted accountability to shift to the mayor's office, the entire plan required state legislation (Boghossian 2006; Villaraigosa 2006).

Unions concerned that the takeover would lead to teacher and staff layoffs contested the takeover attempt. The United Teachers of Los Angeles saw the takeover as an issue of concern, especially the perception that "mayoral control" should not replace "mayoral participation" (Blume 2006). This perception viewed the mayor's plan as an attempt to "replace a failing school bureaucracy with his own." The takeover was also framed in racial and ideological terms as some commentators regarded the mayor's plan as a Hispanic ploy to control schools in the area, and an effort at forcing homeowners to pay for it through higher taxes. The takeover debate was often characterized as an attempt to find solutions for failing schools that include illegal immigrants as students, and whose test scores were generally poor.

On the other hand, the business community was more cautious. The Los Angeles Chamber of Commerce, for instance, issued public statements urging collaborative strategies. California governor Arnold Schwarzenegger embraced the mayor's school takeover plan, stating that "it is inexcusable" that more than 30 percent of students in the district dropped out of schools (Blood 2006). But the problems associated with the running of schools are not confined to performance and dropout rates. Another equally serious policy issue is violence in schools, which now has become a major problem facing local school boards.

Violence in the Schools

Journalists and education experts attribute school violence to troubled students who lack parental supervision and students who have few opportunities for recreation and jobs in their communities, easy access to weapons, and watch violent movies, video, and digital electronic games. Still others are involved with substance abuse and criminal activities.

Greater attention to school violence has coincided with incidents that have been both deadly and widely publicized, especially in the late 1990s. Both mayors and school district personnel have responded to incidents involving disruptive students, and the potential for violence against both teachers and students. In October 1997, a 17-year-old student at a school in Hattisburg, Mississippi brought a gun to school and later was found guilty of murdering two persons and committing aggravated assault on seven others. In March 1998, two pre-teen students at the Westside Middle School in Jonesboro, Arkansas killed five and wounded 10 others in a school shooting. A 15-year-old boy killed four and attempted murder on 26 others in May 1998 at a school in Springfield, Oregon.

The most widely publicized, and one of the most deadly incidents took place on April 20, 1999, when 12 students and a teacher were killed, and 23 others wounded, at Columbine High School in Littleton, Colorado. The two students who opened fire on their classmates and then killed themselves in the attack were members of an anti-culture clique who said they had been influenced by Hollywood violence. Prior to the killings, they documented their anger on home videos. Exactly a month later, a 15-year-old boy at Heritage High School in Conyers, Georgia injured six students in a shooting where he told the prosecutor he had admired the two boys who committed the Columbine shootings. Just days before the one-year anniversary of the Columbine incident, a *Wall Street Journal*/NBC News poll found that 70 percent of Americans believed such a shooting could occur at a school in their own community (Cable News Network 1999b).

The problem is not limited to teenagers, however, with more and more incidents being reported at the lower grade levels. California reported that from 1995 to 2001, the rates of vandalism and other offenses dropped among elementary school students, while crimes against persons, such as assault, nearly doubled. Minneapolis schools suspended over 500 kindergartners in a two-year period for fighting, indecent exposure, and a persistent lack of cooperation, among other offenses. In Greenville, South Carolina, schools suspended 132 first-graders, 75 kindergartners, and 2 preschoolers from 2001 to 2002. The percentage of elementary school teachers who say they have been attacked has risen, and principals and safety experts say they are seeing more violence and aggression than ever among their youngest students. They point to what they see as an alarming rise in assaults and threats to both classmates and teachers (Toppo 2003).

Although much of the work done in school administration is discretionary, most hardly think of it that way (Heilmann 2006). In the area of disciplinary decisions, the majority of school principals work under broad guidelines based on specific school district policies. There are also a combination of intervention and prevention programs developed by professional organizations, including surveillance, conflict resolution training, and education for perpetrators and victims. Many intervention and prevention programs integrate the school, family, and community in efforts to create a safe environment. These collaborative efforts to meet the health, education, and welfare needs of students are believed decrease acts of violence. For example, campuses that invite students to participate in quality after-school activities recognize at-risk students and deal with discipline issues in conjunction with parental support (Elliott, Williams, and Hamburg 1998, 382–384).

Administrators, teachers, families, and agency representatives spend a considerable amount of time identifying needs, developing a trial program, and evaluating preliminary results before adopting policies and implementing a school-wide or district violence prevention program. Not all these efforts stop school violence, and occasionally some students act impulsively and often, violently. Highly visible acts of school violence draw attention to urban and rural school districts. Although urban communities often lack adequate financial resources to maintain safe working and learning environments, the incidence of violence in rural areas also worries policy makers (Hyman and Snook 1999, 9).

At the federal level, the U.S. Department of Education has established committees and funded research to address the problem. Their reports encourage school managers to take action. Most of the federal programs emphasize discipline rather than prevention strategies (Hyman and Snook 1999, 20). Strict discipline policies, therefore, have been the preferred option in most school districts. They are the foundation of zero tolerance procedures implemented by school districts throughout the nation. Administrators often use their discretion to suspend and expel disruptive students. Minor infractions like "insubordination" and "disruptive behavior" may lead to expulsion, although these behaviors are not the criminal behaviors legislators intended zero tolerance policies to prevent (Skiba and Peterson 2000).

Several authors recount how and why more than 90 percent of school districts in America have adopted "zero-tolerance" policies for crimes and offenses usually related to weapons and assaults on school property (Morris and Wells, 2000). Most of these policies mandate predetermined consequences regardless of individual circumstances. Civil libertarians oppose these policies and contend they unfairly target minority and socially disadvantaged students. Harvard University's Civil Rights Project officials agree that the zero-tolerance policies and other tougher forms of school discipline are "part of the tsunami of intolerance" for bad behavior that also harshly punishes lesser offenses such as dress code violations, tardiness, and other minor misbehaviors. Taking away a school administrator's discretion "is a stupid, stupid, stupid, policy" according to one Temple University psychologist, commenting on a Philadelphia zero-tolerance policy that forces principals to report all violent incidents, even minor ones (Toppo 2003). Opponents also worry that eliminating discretion and flexibility in dealing with disciplinary problems is unfair and without merit. Advocates for zero-tolerance policies believe that such policies maintain order in learning situations. Many supporters, however, do believe discretion to exercise fairness is essential. The zero-tolerance policy thus invites debate on the use of discretion in school districts (Morris and Wells 2000).

The debate is likely to be organized around legislative intervention. States have reacted differently to the problem of violence in schools. Across the nation, evidence shows that legislation combines both punitive and protective measures. For instance, in Alabama, the 1995 law spells out some of the actions that must be followed if and when violence occurs. The law gives the state schools' superintendent the authority to intervene and assume direct management of any public school that is not in compliance with school safety and discipline requirements. All public schools in the state are also required to have written comprehensive school safety plans.

The Arizona Legislature enacted a law to ensure that schools were adequately prepared for all emergencies, including those emerging from incidences of violence. In April 2000, then-Governor Jane Hull signed into law Senate Bill 1559, which revised Arizona statutes and increased appropriations relating to school safety. The legislation requires all public schools to have emergency response plans. These plans are a joint effort involving both law enforcement, the Arizona Department of Emergency Management, and the Arizona Department of Education.

Since then, several hundred students have been arrested for making threats to other students or school personnel, or for "causing interference with or disruption of an educational institution." The law increased attention to student discipline at unprecedented levels. Administrators now contact authorities to press charges against students accused of verbal threats on the playground, including those uttering statements such as "I'm going to kill you." Also, incidents where a student pretends to use their finger as a gun and says, "Bang, you're dead," or has drawn a graphic picture of violence, draw the attention of law enforcement agencies. The law requires schools to become aware of situations such as these (Hilts-Scott 2001, 1).

Other legal strategies have emerged across the United States. For example, schools in Mississippi established a central data bank for reporting expulsions. The state's Department of Education requires that administrators note the date and reason for expulsion in an expelled student's permanent file. This file is sent to any school to which the student transferred (Mississippi 2001). In Texas, the state rewrote its education laws to require each district to adopt a code of student conduct and provide alternative education programs for disruptive students. The law allows teachers to remove these students from their classrooms. The expelled students cannot return without a review committee's recommendation and teachers' approval, and can also be sent to alternative education programs. Texas law also requires law enforcement officials to notify school districts when a student is arrested for any felony charges. This is also the case in Delaware, where school personnel must report crimes to law-enforcement officials, previously done at the discretion of school staff (Simonich 2004; USDOJ 2002).

Because some situations require immediate action by school administrators, leadership skills become important. The school leader's role is to maintain a safe environment for both students and staff. This role is often challenged by federal and state legislation, including local school and district policies. The problem is that school environments throughout the country are socially, economically, and geographically diverse. Congress has passed legislation in response to demands to regulate acceptable boundaries for student behavior and diminish school violence. Among these laws is the Gun-Free School Zones Act of 1990, which prohibits individuals from possessing firearms at a place they know is a school zone, and the Safe and Drug Free Schools and Communities Act of 1994. The later supports drug and violence prevention programs. These laws do not have specific language that captures the needs of all communities in the country, however. Another problem with the legislation lies in "goal incompatibility" (MacIntyre 1986, 72). Teachers and school administrators value the education of children, but they also want to provide a safe environment for children. The intent of the law is to punish, not educate, and neither goal is actualized. Teachers and administrators struggle to respond in a way that balances both goals: education and safety. School district managers are challenged to interpret these laws and create policies suited to the needs of their communities.

Another discretionary strategy is the adoption of school uniforms as a way of reducing the risk of violence and creating a more productive learning environment. Principals who choose this option have had their decisions backed up in court when they have been legally challenged. As of 2006, 21 states and the District of Columbia give local school districts the authority to require students to wear uniforms. In May 2000, the Philadelphia Board of Education became the first large board to require school uniforms for its 200,000 students in all grades in the city's 259 schools. About 80 percent of Chicago's public schools require uniforms, as do 60 percent of the schools in Miami, 30 percent in Boston, and 85 percent in Cleveland (Morris and Wells 2000).

Because administrators can be personally and professionally liable for their actions, school managers are less likely to deviate from the prescribed actions mandated by federal and state laws than they are to use discretion in the application of school and district policies. Politically active groups act as watchdogs to protect the legal rights of students. In the final analysis, school managers who are skilled in behavior management techniques and knowledgeable about policies are less likely to abuse their power (Shumavon and Hibbeln 1986, 7). They may choose from alternative disciplinary actions that keep troubled youth in school rather than on the street at risk of committing more violent acts.

Contracting

Historically, municipal government managers and officials have recognized that it was impossible for them to be all things to all people, and that sometimes, they would need to rely on others to provide services that citizens wanted or needed. In small communities, local government revenues did not allow managers to permanently hire the staff that they needed, especially for short-term projects or those requiring specialized equipment or expertise. During the 1980s and the Reagan Revolution, many municipalities experimented with, and then later adopted, programs that outsourced city services or staffing, referred to as privatization. Based on the belief that the public sector was too large to perform every necessary function effectively, the practice was designed initially to save money and to promote efficiency. At the same time, privatization created conflicts over the meshing of public and private services, the proper role of government, and the potential for the abuse of managerial discretion.

Contracting out has become increasing prevalent at the local government level, ranging from ambulance services and animal control to mental health services. The privatization movement presents challenges from several perspectives, including the provision of services by entities that are not accountable to the voters. Managers responsible for dealing with contracts have two primary responsibilities: making sure that the process follows appropriate policy guidelines, and taking action if contractors fail to perform as is expected or cause government to lose money. The abuse of discretion in awarding and monitoring contracts is not new, but it is gaining increasing scrutiny by both the public and the courts.

The list of legal actions involving abuses of discretion is long, involving cities of every size and in every part of the country. In one widely reported case, former Mayor Kenneth Saunders, Jr., of Asbury Park, New Jersey was sentenced to 33 months in prison in 2004 for plotting to offer bribes to a city council member in an effort to profit from waterfront redevelopment plans and contracts. Similarly, Mayor Paul Richards of Lynwood, California faced federal charges of steering a series of lucrative city contracts to a company he secretly owned. In a 2006 court case, Chicago's city clerk received a two-year prison sentence for taking bribes from an employee in his office who also doubled as the operator of a trucking company, and from a former city water department employee. Both incidents involved efforts to get companies into a city program that awarded hauling jobs to trucking firms.

One of the more intriguing cases took place in Chattanooga, Tennessee, where a county commissioner was sentenced to three years in prison in 2006 for extorting bribes in exchange for helping a fake computer company created by the Federal Bureau of Investigation (FBI) as part of the "Tennessee Waltz" corruption investigation. The official had faced a maximum of 40 years in prison and a $500,000 fine after an undercover agent pitched deals on behalf of the company to buy and sell used computers. Several other officials are awaiting trials in the same case.

In Paterson, New Jersey, Mayor Martin G. Barnes was convicted by a Federal District Court of participating in kickback deals, tax evasion, and mail fraud. The mayor was involved in dealings with United Gunite, a sewer and bridge construction and repair company that obtained contracts worth millions of dollars in several cities in the state. United Gunite had been the only bidder for sewer work in Paterson for several consecutive years, earning millions of dollars in contracts since 1994. Barnes, a Republican and the first African-American Mayor of the city, extorted money from contractors, received a monthly consulting fee from the city, and also filed false tax returns. According to widely publicized reports, his actions constituted one of the "most reprehensible types(s) of public conduct that you can find anywhere in the country" (Alaya and Martin 2002).

Some efforts have been made, however, to avoid even the appearance of impropriety among officials. Philadelphia's Mayor John F. Street signed an executive order banning city employees from accepting gifts, gratuities, or favors from people who do business with the city, and warned companies that those who offered gifts would be barred from receiving city contracts. Mayor Street's action reinforced provisions that were already included in the Philadelphia Home Rule Charter, City Ethics Code, and the State Ethics Act. One of his concerns was finding a way to restore confidence in city government at a time when perceived accountability in local government managers was low.

Creating New Departments

As part of the chief executive's tasks, mayors and managers can create new divisions and departments to tackle new social problems and issues. The new agencies might be small-scale units, temporary task forces, or committees that handle issues such as scholarships, after-school programs, partnerships between governments, or large-scale policy divisions. In general, it is easier to expand and augment existing governmental structures and units than to create new ones. When chief executives create new services and departments, the potential for conflict arises; most executives, therefore, prefer incremental changes to forming new agencies.

A case in point is Washington, DC Mayor Anthony Williams, who signed into law a bill enacted by the Council of the District of Columbia that combined the functional operations of the Department of Insurance and Securities Regulation (DISR) with those of the Department of Banking and Financial Institutions (DBFI). The new agency, renamed the Department of Insurance, Securities and Banking (DISB) was expected to take a comprehensive approach to regulating financial services, products and transactions, many of which had banking, insurance, and securities features. The goal was to have a single regulator for both traditional and non-traditional financial products. The Council sought to eliminate problems associated with coordinating enforcement efforts between agencies in the District of Columbia. Previously, operations were governed by a congressional statute—the Gramm-Leach-Bliley Act (1999)—that eliminated the separation between banking and insurance that had existed since the 1930s. The new agency would, over time, "change the nature of financial services businesses, as new products are introduced that are not exactly insurance, not quite banking, not entirely investments, but a blend of each" (Moore 2004).

A city's ability to create new institutions depends very much on its internal politics as well as whether a mayor is "entrepreneurial" (Kotter and Lawrence 1974, 105). Large cities, including New York, face the perennial problems of big government. For a city of 7 million, with a workforce of 350,000 government employees scattered in 48 different agencies, creating a new department is a huge political issue. Most city departments are already too large in themselves, making coordination difficult. For example, the New York Board of Education alone has more than 125,000 employees and a $10 billion budget in comparison with 40,000 in the police department.

This lack of coordination forced then-Mayor Rudolph Giuliani to sign Executive Order 43, which created a Technology Steering Committee comprised of the Office of Management and Budget, the Mayor's Office of Operations, and the Department of Information Technology and Telecommunications. Giuliani formed this coordinating unit to harmonize information exchange among various government agencies, especially budgetary and planning information-sharing processes. The new agency also served to manage IT issues including administration of the city's Technology Fund to improve electronic government structures, the creation of virtual agencies, and to support the city's data center.

Mayor Giuliani is widely considered an "entrepreneurial" leader. By measure of his accomplishments, for example, implementing the Compstat project in the police force, he was able to reduce crime rates in New York. Compstat analyzes statistics on crime rates in the city and deals with trends on a daily basis, basically serving as a strategy for performance measurement. He also was successful in introducing accountability procedures in city government, arguing that everyone must be accountable all the time (Giuliani 2002).

Finance

One of the most complex areas of municipal policymaking deals with revenues and expenditures. To some extent, local governments are constrained by state laws that require caps on spending limits, balanced budgets, or debt ceilings, although there are seldom audits of finance activities. But the imposition of taxes and decisions on how to spend revenues is almost always at the discretion of local managers.

It is a basic assumption in all systems of decentralized government that the political institutions created for the territorial subdivisions of the state, if they are to have any political credibility, must have some measure of independence in the level of revenue they raise and the choice of public goods on which to spend it. Area governments are assumed to need some power to decide at what rate taxes are assigned to them by the constitution or the national government, and some freedom to allocate their spending among the functions similarly devolved to them, according to their own sense of priority (Smith 1985, 99–100).

Local government managers have almost total discretion in determining what mix of revenue sources they will use, ranging from property taxes, sales taxes, and income taxes, to user fees, licenses, inspections, permits, and even gambling revenues. Tourist areas have commonly implemented surcharges on goods and services such as lodging, restaurants, rental cars, and alcohol. Property taxes have started rising in many cities, along with increases in user fees (libraries, parks, and recreation facilities) and charges for municipal services such as sewer and water fees (Krane 1998). In property-tax–dependent areas, increases in housing prices have been a bonus for governments, because the rates are typically based on the assessed value of the property. In 2006, some cities were actually beginning to experience a fiscal surplus, allowing officials to make spending decisions that might have been unheard of a decade ago. Homeowners, however, are sometimes critical of local governments that have started assessing their property every year, rather than every four years, as was a commonly accepted schedule. Managers are thus caught between the desire to maximize local revenues as home prices escalate, and the political reality of angry residents (especially those in the middle class, seniors, and young families), who find property taxes have gotten out of control or beyond their means to become homeowners.

At the same time, local government officials face shortfalls from state governments that are reducing the funding they have traditionally supplied. In some states, such as Michigan, property taxes are collected and sent directly to the state, which redistributes money from rich communities to needy ones, almost totally limiting local discretion on rates and revenues. California caps property tax increases at 2 percent per year, a system that pleases homeowners but has crippled local services and led to massive cuts in city staff and program hours. Pennsylvania, in contrast, has limited property tax increases by replacing funds with the income generated from slot machines (Scherer 2004).

While the level of discretionary spending pleases managers in those areas where revenues have risen, decreasing income from other sources has proved extremely frustrating. In Mesa, Arizona, for instance, voters rejected a May 2006 proposal for the city's first property tax since 1945, forcing city leaders to figure out how to make $14 million in immediate cuts. In addition to laying off current employees, the defeat meant a freeze on any new hiring and unfilled positions. Initial cuts targeted fire inspectors, a park ranger program, cultural arts grants, and funding for a local museum. High profile layoffs and program cuts seem designed to send a message to residents that life will not be going on as usual.

In Bismarck, North Dakota, voters were asked to approve a sales tax initiative in June 2006 that would raise an estimated $32 million for seven capital projects, improvements and enhancements of existing facilities, and property acquisition. Opponents said that because of rising home values, the existing property tax should be sufficient to fund city programs, while supporters said that without the increased sales tax, projects that have been on the back burner for 20 years would be postponed for another 10 to 20 years. Even though Bismarck officials tried to remind voters that the city's sales tax was lower than 22 other cities in North Dakota, opponents were not convinced. One resident who opposed the tax increase said he believed that there was not a widespread need for the projects that officials had selected for funding, noting that in a year or two, greater needs would surface, and a possible funding source would have been dedicated elsewhere. "The basic point is that people pay enough in taxes. Bismarck and its governmental entities get enough money for the things they truly need. If they are short in being able to provide everything we want, they have to set priorities" (Weixel 2006).

In both cases, citizens subsequently complained as services began to be cut, railing against the cities' managers for doing exactly what the ballot measures had told them to do. What might seem simple at first glance—reducing expenditures—was in fact a much more politically charged mandate that officials could not win no matter what direction they took. Fiscal discretion thus becomes a tool and a burden, as some observers note that the freedom to tax and the freedom to spend do not come without costs.

Managerial Discretion at the County Level

Although a great deal has been written about the operation of municipal government, less attention has been paid to counties, which also perform an important function in policymaking. Although they are considered political subdivisions of the states, which create them, county government is usually thought of in local terms. States have the ability to designate county boundaries, although some attempts have been made by residents to split counties as the population grows and demographic lines shift. In Wyoming, for instance, business owners sought to divide Fremont County in two, creating a new Wind River County. Fremont County is geographically huge (about the size of the state of Vermont) and some leaders argued that the existing county was shortchanging cities in the northern part, where it also gets most of its revenues from mineral revenues. In other states, split county initiatives have started when voters believed that the county was unresponsive to their needs because of distance or political divisions. Still, state legislatures control much of what counties can and cannot do.

In many cases, state governments initially performed relatively few functions, delegating to counties the responsibility for most services, such as building roads, constructing and operating jails, caring for the poor, and record keeping on property, births, deaths, and marriages. Many states now allow counties to provide additional services under their constitution, such as libraries, parks and recreation facilities, and city-like programs such as zoning and planning.

What differentiates counties from one another is often the way they organize and select their governing bodies and officers, typically known as commissioners or supervisors. State constitutions also usually require that some county officials be elected, such as a district attorney, assessor, judges, or elections officer. In other states, these positions are appointed by the governing board, somewhat diminishing the level of discretion they afford those individuals because they serve at the pleasure of the board. Appointed county officials vary considerably from one part of the country to another, depending upon the state. The chief administrative officer for a county, for instance, is almost always an appointee of the governing board, and may serve the same function as a city manager. Other appointees may be selected on the basis of a particular type of expertise, such as a medical examiner, public health officer, county counsel, finance director, or treasurer.

One of the unique aspects of American federalism is the fact that persons living in a city are also residents, and thus voters, in the county where the city is located. Counties also include unincorporated areas, so governing managers provide municipal-type services for residents in those areas as well. As is the case with city governments, managers have a considerable amount of discretion related to appointments, ordinances, policy implementation, contracts, and revenues. County boards may also have some quasi-judicial functions when they serve as tax assessment appeals board or land use regulators, even though members are not required to have any experience in such matters. The decision about whether a county ought to provide certain services may be constitutionally mandated, or residents might be required to form a special district (such as a fire district) if they decide they want those services but the county is unable to provide them.

Elected county officials tend to have considerable discretion in the activities in which they choose to become involved, although how much power they exercise is also a function of personality, the county government's structure, and sometimes, political forces. Sometimes county officials perform legislative-type duties, such as cases where they enact ordinances. Other county boards act in symbolic roles, giving awards to local youth, appearing at community functions, or presiding over parades and other events. These duties are not prescribed by law but are undertaken because of peer pressure, a sense of civic duty, or local customs and expectations that they participate.

Other typical county commission actions involving discretion involve the setting of tax rates and the application of certain types of fees. In North Carolina, county officials dealt with the issue of whether they had the authority to impose impact fees on land developers and home builders as a way of paying for new schools. Arguing that the state had delegated the financing of building schools to counties, and that property tax rates had already reached the breaking point, they noted that counties can charge impact fees that are reasonably related to the cost of building public schools in order to meet the demand created when additional residential construction is completed. Durham County, for instance, charges builders $2,000 for each new single-family home and $1,155 for each new apartment or condominium. The money is held in an escrow account and then used to support school capital improvements. In contrast, Shawnee County, Kansas officials decided to impose a new tax on stores that sell crack pipes, pipes, rolling papers, and other paraphernalia that is sold legally but often used for illegal drugs. The new tax, approved in 2006, is designed to pay for the county's drug rehabilitation programs.

Sometimes county discretion is taken too far, however. In 2006, in Ventura County, California, a federal district court declared an ordinance that set minimum budgets for the county's public safety agencies unconstitutional. The county's board of supervisors had adopted the ordinance in 1995, using a complex formula that resulted in annual funding increases of up to 10 percent for certain departments. In 2001, the board members voted to cap the annual increases at 4 percent, arguing that the increases had compromised their ability to fully fund other departments, violating their discretionary powers. A 2005 agreement that tied law enforcement budgets to the county's financial health, but gave those departments funding priority, was declared unconstitutional. The court ruled the ordinance was illegal because it stripped the board of its authority to set budgets for county departments. If it were allowed to stand, the justices said, other agencies could also claim a chunk of the county's budget by placing their own budget initiatives before voters (Saillant 2006).

In other cases, county boards may defer politically volatile or controversial decisions to the electorate, rather than using their discretion as representatives of the voters to make a decision. In Billings, Montana, for example, Yellowstone County commissioners voted to put two measures on the 2006 ballot that would limit sexually explicit materials and sexually-oriented businesses. Several members of the county commission declined to state their positions on the ballot measures, which would involve a zoning ordinance designed to reduce crime. Other commissioners said they were not sure whether they had the authority to regulate sexually-oriented businesses, which the commission's legal staff doubted would be constitutional under the First Amendment (Howard 2006).

Use of Discretion by the County Sheriff

Perhaps the most visible individual in county government is the sheriff, who may enjoy wide discretion depending on the level of support received from the political establishment and constituencies (ThePittsburghChannel.com 2006). From an administrative point of view, county sheriffs are policymakers because they shape public safety operations. They respond to law enforcement and crime prevention challenges much like street level police officers, but they also have the power to determine priorities within individual departments. From a technical point of view, however, sheriffs may not always have the same kind of discretion. As managers within the county government structure, they may have more limited control in budgetary issues than, for instance, a city manager in a large municipality. There are also situations where a county attorney probably has more discretion in determining how the office is run than the sheriff, who may share authority with city police. In some U.S. counties, sheriffs have no law enforcement powers at all. Their duties may be limited to providing courtroom services, managing jails or detention facilities, transportation to and from court, or building and event security.

As a manager, the sheriff also is involved in administrative tasks that range from fingerprinting services for employees in daycare facilities and schools to dog licenses to responses to requests for information from the media and the public. Some sheriff's offices develop public outreach and educational activities, such as drug prevention programs in schools, or neighborhood watch meetings in unincorporated areas of the county. In these types of activities, the level of discretion is low on a day-to-day basis.

But there are instances where the decisions made by the sheriff are highly discretionary as well as highly politicized. In 2005, the Allegheny, Pennsylvania County Sheriff's Office was overwhelmed with controversy. As one newspaper editorial explained in making its election day recommendations, "The incumbent presides over a corrupt office that includes a captain who was found guilty of perjury, employees who testified that commanders pressured them with implied threats over their jobs to give to the sheriff's political fundraisers, deputies who did landscaping on county time at the home of the chief deputy and a sheriff who pleads the Fifth Amendment to avoid self incrimination when called to testify by the counsel for one of his employees" (Voting Is Crucial 2005). The office was also part of a federal investigation, increasing the visibility of the sheriff, who subsequently resigned.

The new sheriff faced a county Jail Oversight Board in May 2006 after the media reported that pregnant inmates were being shackled to their beds before they gave birth at the hospital. The controversial practice had been going on for decades at the discretion of the sheriff's deputy in the birthing room in fear that the inmate might become violent or try to escape. The sheriff's policy was that male deputies were not allowed in a hospital room with inmates in labor, so they put restraints on them before leaving the room. "It's always been when a man is watching a woman," he said. The deputies fasten the shackles "and go smoke a cigarette." He said that although he wanted only female deputies to transport women in labor, a union contract prevented him from making the change (Sherman 2006). He had previously admitted that he remembered the practice from his time as a deputy more than 30 years ago, but did not know it was still happening routinely. Advocates for children of inmates said they have known about the shackling policy for years.

The issue in this case deals with whether the county sheriff could have used his discretion to end the practice, or whether there were legitimate reasons for continuing the policy. The county jail warden and a judge said that the shackling was necessary to make sure that the inmate is secure. "If you have someone who is a flight risk and the officer loosens restraints and the inmate escapes, the officer may lose his or her job. That's a concern." A judge agreed with the sheriff that some inmates in labor could present risks. "Some people are desperate and would attempt to flee under certain circumstances," she said, noting that those situations likely would be rare. The sheriff told the board members that a total ban on shackling could be excessive, however. His lawyers, he said, would consider changes to the department's policy manual that would allow deputies to defer to hospital staff to determine whether the inmate's restraints should be removed (Sherman 2006).

A second case of the use of discretion by a county sheriff also made news in 2006. For more than 30 years, the sheriff had charged inmates at the Homerville Jail in Clinch County, Georgia a fee of $18 per day for their room and board. Georgia law, however, does not give the sheriff the authority to charge such fees unless they are specifically authorized by statute, and no statute for per diem has ever been enacted. In 2004, the Southern Center for Human Rights and a law firm providing representation *pro bono* filed a federal class action lawsuit on behalf of pre-trial detainees after a former member of the Clinch County Commission alerted attorneys to her concern about the effect of the jail fees on poor black residents. The plaintiffs in the case were Mickel Jackson, who served time in the jail for three months, and Willie Williams, who was jailed for nine months. In some cases, the fees had mounted to over $3,000, which inmates had to pay regardless of whether they were convicted of a crime or had the ability to pay. Jackson was charged $1,471 and paid $713 in seven installment payments, over one-fifth of his annual income. Williams was released on bond to await trial, but only after he signed a promissory note agreeing to pay the jail $4,608 or face re-incarceration. The charges against Jackson were dismissed, but the sheriff refused to refund his money. Williams remained free on bond while he awaited trial. In April 2006, a U.S. District Court judge approved a settlement agreement in which the sheriff agreed to stop charging the fees. The action covered all pre-trial detainees from 2000 to 2004, estimated at about $27,000 (Southern Center for Human Rights 2006).

Discretion in the Maricopa County Sheriff's Office

Clearly, some discretion is needed by managers such as sheriffs in order to do their job without undue interference, or to maintain order. But in the highly publicized case of Maricopa County, Arizona sheriff Joe Arpaio, further scrutiny and discussion is appropriate. The state enumerates various powers and duties for sheriffs, including preserving the peace, operating the county jail, coordinating search and rescue operations, delivering process service notices, taking those accused of crimes before a judge, and assisting in court as needed. From a law enforcement perspective, Maricopa County is a geographically large area covering more than 9,200 square miles, with a population of more than 200,000. The sheriff is an elected official in the county, and Arpaio was first elected in 1992. He has always won re-election by a large margin, an indication of voters' support for his management style.

Prior to becoming sheriff, Arpaio served in the U.S. Army from 1950 to 1953 and joined the federal Drug Enforcement Administration in combating drug trafficking. He also served as a police officer in Washington, DC and Las Vegas. In 1996, when he ran for re-election, he had an 85 percent approval rating and enough support that no other candidates ran against him. He won again in 2000 and 2004. Although he has limited discretion in determining which criminals actually end up in jail, his authority to determine the operation of the jails is almost unlimited. It is this aspect of his management style that has earned him both notoriety and a series of lawsuits. He considers himself a "get tough" sheriff in the sense of the Old West, where the sheriff's power was absolute, with a small nod to the law, and seems to delight in the fact that he is often referred to as "America's toughest sheriff."

There are many examples that can be used to illustrate the controversial nature of his discretion as sheriff, many of which deal with the county budget. Shortly after taking office in 1993, Arpaio contended that jail overcrowding was exacerbated by a lack of county funding (his annual budget is about $400 million), so he started his Tent City to house over 2,000 prisoners in a canvas compound. He was convinced that prisoners should not live in conditions better than the general public, and that U.S. troops were living in tents, so inmates should, too. A pink neon "Vacancy" sign was hung over the entrance, and surplus military equipment was obtained under a Defense Department regulation that allows him to purchase them at little to no cost. To reduce jail expenses, he changed the jail menu and served bologna sandwiches, lowering the cost to 20 cents per meal, per inmate. Women began being housed in Tent City in 1996, and the site has become a magnet for visiting officials (Arpaio 2004; Arpaio 2006).

In another controversial move, chain gangs were established for both men and women, re-instituting a system that had been nearly eliminated as being too harsh and demeaning. He considers the chain gangs to be rehabilitation rather than punishment because inmates volunteer for them. In 1995, he realized that the all-white jail boxer shorts with MCSO stenciled on the back were being stolen and sold on the street as a novelty item. After losing $48,000 worth of the underwear, he had all inmate boxers dyed pink. Prisoners wear pink underwear because he believes it makes it more difficult for them to remain undetected should they escape. The new pink undershorts became so popular that a slightly altered version was sold for a $10 donation to fund the operations of the 3,200-member sheriff's posse. In just a few months, over $400,000 had been sold. Inmates wear black and white-striped uniforms as a security measure, making it more difficult for escapees to avoid detection. In jail, there is a ban on coffee, smoking, pornographic magazines, and movies, and television watching is restricted. Arpaio also initiated a program that provides housing and care for abused, neglected, and abandoned animals, along with those of persons who cannot take their pets to shelters for victims of domestic violence.

At face value, that might not sound like it would garner much attention. But the sheriff houses the animals in an old jail facility that is air conditioned, unlike Tent City, which uses only electric fans (Arpaio 2006).

As a county manager, the sheriff is responsible for maintaining a quality workforce through development and training. Arpaio has increased salaries for his deputies and provides incentive pay, improved equipment, and has elevated his office to a state-of-the-art facility. He relies on a carefully selected cadre of loyal employees to make him look good. Typical of his management style is the Professional Standards Bureau, headed by a deputy chief. This sector of law enforcement, also known as Internal Affairs, is critical to a law enforcement agency because it is these officers' responsibility to "police the police." Internal Affairs investigates two kinds of employee misconduct, those involving criminal activity (such as corruption, brutality, and infringements on civil rights), and those that violate internal procedures and policies. They may also investigate incidents where deadly force has been used or injuries occurred, providing checks and balances against violations of an inmate's constitutional rights. Internal Affairs is often perceived as the most effective means of providing oversight to the types of street-level discretion described in the introductory chapter of this book. But there are also instances where managerial discretion is tempered by accountability imposed by another branch of government: the court system.

Local Managerial Discretion and the Courts

Local government authority has long been a subject of legal debate as judges have had varying rulings on managerial discretion. In a 1868 case, *City of Clinton v. Cedar Rapids and Missouri Railroad Company,* Judge John Dillon argued against local government power, based on a case involving municipal investment practices. "Dillon's Rule," which was upheld by the U.S. Supreme Court in 1903 and 1923, allows state legislatures to determine the extent of authority and discretion exercised by local government officials. The ruling led to the Home Rule Movement, which called for limitations on how much state legislatures could interfere in municipal affairs. The movement's call for reform was followed by another court case in which Judge Thomas Cooley affirmed the right of local governments in Michigan to control their own actions, called "Cooley's Law." However, the overall trend has been for the courts to accept the idea that local government authority is granted, not inherent.

Recent court cases have reaffirmed local governments' discretionary authority. One legal scholar has demonstrated that the doctrine of "privilege" evident in mayoral discretion is no longer viable, using the example of a Massachusetts Supreme Judicial Court ruling in *McAuliffe v. Mayor of New Bedford* (1892). This ruling upheld the conviction of a preacher who had violated a municipal ordinance in presenting a public address on the Boston Common without securing a permit from the mayor (Van Alstyne 2004). In that case, the Boston Common was government-owned but the city ordinances lacked specific language to control the mayor's discretion in issuing permits.

In *City of Lakewood v. Plain Dealer Publishing Company* (1988), the U.S. Supreme Court allowed a challenge of the grant of unbridled discretion to public officials even if the challengers lacked the standing to raise such a claim. The court, ruling on mayoral discretion to issue permits, recognized that the "mere existence of the licensor's unfettered discretion, coupled with the power of prior restraint," can threaten First Amendment values even if such discretion and power are never actually abused. In this case, the mayor had the authority to grant permits to place news racks on public property. The city ordinance allowed the mayor to attach to the permit any "terms and conditions deemed necessary and reasonable." The language of the ordinance gave the mayor considerable discretion to the point that a permit could be denied simply by invoking "public interest concerns."

Similar arguments were presented in *Caren Cronk Thomas and Windy City Hemp Development Board v. Chicago Park District* (2002), which dealt with a Chicago Park District ordinance that required "a person to obtain a permit before conducting events involving more than fifty individuals in a municipal park." The plaintiffs' concern was a fear that the park district was vested with too much discretion and possibly failed to satisfy First Amendment requirements. The plaintiffs applied for a permit to hold a rally in a city park in March 1997 but the permit had been denied. The original plaintiff, Robert MacDonald, was an advocate of marijuana legalization who died during the course of litigation, and Caren Thomas and Windy City Hemp Development Board were substituted as plaintiffs. The district court enjoined the park district from enforcing certain provisions of its ordinance, but the Seventh Circuit reversed. While the court acknowledged the danger in giving officials broad discretion over which political rallies shall be permitted to be conducted on public property, "because they will be tempted to exercise that discretion in favor of political friends and against their political enemies," the case was dismissed (USDOJ 2002).

A similar case in New York City was filed in 1999 *Housing Works v. Howard Safir and Rudolph Giuliani*. The New York Civil Liberties Union (NYCLU), on behalf of Housing Works, filed a pre-trial brief against Mayor Rudolph Giuliani's administration. Their suit opposed an official city policy under which press conferences, rallies, and demonstrations that the mayor deemed to be of "extraordinary public interest" may take place on or near the steps of City Hall without limit on their size or duration. Other rallies and demonstrations are limited to 50 persons and to one hour.

The plaintiff sought a declaration that this policy violated the First Amendment, noting that other groups' meetings were permitted, but not a meeting to mark an AIDS Day observance in 1998. Instead, the city wanted the meeting to take place in the parking lot in front of City Hall. In addition, the New York Police Department used barricades to create the areas for the event. One week after denying Housing Works' request to hold a rally at City Hall, officials allowed other groups to hold rallies or events on or near the steps of City Hall. The court ruled that the current policy gave the mayor unfettered discretion to select the events that qualify for his exemption and limited protest activity at City Hall (NYCLU 2000). In these instances, accountability over a manager's use of discretion was decided in the judicial arena.

A Culture of Corruption?

The fact that several cities in the country continue to institute ethics training, whistle-blower reward and protection acts, reforms in contracting, and other measures to combat corruption, speaks volumes about the need to be consistent about integrity in managerial decision-making. Perhaps a few recent decisions by city officials demand a rethinking of the enabling organizational cultures that challenge conventional wisdom on good governance and integrity in the discharge of public services. Corruption is often thought to be the disease of politics and can be found in almost any public agency depending on how one defines it. Yet it is also well known that some public organizations are notorious for bribery, mismanagement, and waste. Although certainly not the most corrupt city in the United States, New Orleans came under considerable scrutiny following the devastation of Hurricane Katrina in 2005.

Nationally, both New Orleans and the State of Louisiana had acquired a reputation for corruption long before Katrina. The *New York Times* observed that perhaps no other state has "as eccentric and problematic a political culture as Louisiana" (Applebome and Alford 2005). The Public Corruption Convictions Report ranked the state third in the nation based on the number of federal corruption convictions of public officials per 100,000 during the period of 1993 to 2003, trailing Mississippi and North Dakota. One scholar proclaimed that Louisiana once had more professional politicians in jail than any other state (Key 1949).

The continued provision of federal money to the New Orleans Police Department's anticorruption efforts speaks volumes about the negative impact of corruption on the city's overall development (Flaherty 2005). The city's Metropolitan Crime Commission also received federal funding to maintain a hotline for reporting government corruption. Coupled with those efforts are initiatives from the FBI office in Baton Rouge, which prosecutes public corruption in the New Orleans area. Already, the New Orleans FBI office had two working teams in 2005, making New Orleans one of the five cities—including Chicago, Washington, DC, San Juan,

Puerto Rico, and Newark, New Jersey—where the agency has two or more public corruption squads.

New Orleans is not the only city that has been heavily scrutinized since Katrina, but by a simple count of media coverage of corruption and poor judgments within the policymaking body in the city, Detroit's leadership has continually battled a credibility gap. Perhaps the first concern has been that Detroit suffered an image problem as one of America's most dangerous cities. This image was perhaps dented further in 2002 when the city elected its youngest mayor, Kwame Kilpatrick, then 31 and variously referred to as the "Hip Hop Mayor." Kilpatrick had run against an older more experienced candidate, Gill Hill.

The issue was not so much the age factor but the Mayor's subsequent style of leadership and how it was reflected in the media. Specifically, Kilpatrick's misuse of public office raised questions about official integrity. Lingering perceptions that he violated the city's ethics ordinance were fueled by his own admission that he leased a new Lincoln Navigator for his wife through the police department's budget. The mayor, whose base has been African-American youth, also received press condemnation for hosting "wild parties" at the mayor's mansion. In addition, the mayor's uses of petty cash through city credit cards and miscellaneous expenses have often been characterized as inappropriate. There have also been reports of irregularities in the use of time cards (*Detropolis* 2004). Many of these irregularities were largely due, some believe, to a weak Board of Ethics.

In order to have a complete picture of corruption in large cities, perhaps one more example will suffice: Chicago. To comprehend corruption in Chicago, one needs to consider the logic and workings of machine politics. Much like New Orleans, the politics of machines is at the root of Chicago's long association with corruption. As one author states, "There is no city in America that has been as maligned as Chicago" (Taylor 2003). Republican mayor William Hale "Big Bill" Thompson, one of the influential mayors of the 1920s (1915–1923 and 1927–1931) was well known for running a corrupt administration. Mayor Thompson was widely believed to be on the payroll of famous Chicago gangsters including Al Capone. These allegations were reinforced by Thompson's failure to work with municipal reformers seeking to eradicate organized crime from the city. Instead, he turned against the reformers and reinforced the popular nationwide belief that Chicago's mayors are deeply entrenched into political feuds.

Under Mayor Richard J. Daley, City Hall became synonymous with "Chicago Machine" politics, where patronage dominated appointment and selection processes. Even though he was not convicted, many of Daley's associates were jailed for corruption. Daley, first elected as Mayor in 1958, was previously Chairman of the Cook County Democratic Central Committee. He was Chicago's longest serving mayor with 21 years in office, and was often dubbed "Mayor for Life"; he was mayor when he died in 1976. His son, Richard M. Daley, was elected mayor in 1989 and continues to wield considerable political power in city politics, and his administration also has been accused of corruption. A wide-ranging federal investigation is in progress to determine irregularities in contracts and hiring, leading to more than 30 convictions among his senior and cabinet-level administrators.

CHAPTER 3

Managerial Discretion at the State Level

On May 10, 2006, Kentucky Governor Ernie Fletcher was indicted by a grand jury on three misdemeanor counts alleging criminal conspiracy, first-degree official misconduct, and violation of the state's prohibition against political discrimination. These indictments came five days before the state's primary election, and were the result of an investigation into hiring practices by members of his administration. The allegations stated that the governor had "ordered, directed, and otherwise approved" the development and implementation of the Governor's Personnel Initiative, orchestrated by Fletcher to place political supporters in state merit jobs. Appointees were placed in each cabinet of government to check backgrounds of merit job applicants, including their political affiliation and campaign donation records. At least fifteen employees were hired, promoted, transferred, or dismissed under the "preselection" process (Loftus and Pitsch 2006).

Fletcher had served as a state legislator and as a member of Congress before becoming governor in 2003. Allegations against the governor began to develop in November 2004 when a Transportation Cabinet employee told the staff of the Executive Branch Ethics Commission that some merit hiring was based on politics, which led to an investigation by the Kentucky attorney general. A special grand jury indicted several state officials and the state Republican chairman in June and July 2005, and Fletcher said he would appoint a task force to improve the merit system. Less than three months later, the governor pardoned all those who had been indicted as well as issuing a blanket pardon to anyone else who might be indicted, although he did not include himself. In going before the grand jury, Fletcher invoked his Fifth Amendment right against self-incrimination, declining to testify in the face of what the attorney general called "overwhelming" evidence of wrongdoing. Several administration officials were subsequently fired by the governor, who accused them of using poor judgment or being overzealous in promoting administration goals.

The controversy escalated when the state's transportation secretary was indicted on new charges that he retaliated against a department employee who was a whistle blower in the investigation, alleging he vetoed a proposed bonus for her. More indictments were issued in the case against state officials and Republican Party leaders, and the members of the grand jury asked a judge to represent them if they were later sued. A three-judge Court of Appeals ruled that despite the governor's blanket amnesty, the grand jury could continue issuing indictments; the governor appealed the ruling to the Kentucky Supreme Court in December 2005. In February 2006, the governor appointed two lawyers to sit temporarily on the state Supreme Court, both of whom had been contributors to his political campaigns, and they were selected to hear Fletcher's appeal. They replaced two other justices, including the Supreme Court's chief justice, who had voluntarily disqualified themselves from the case because of close ties to the governor's office.

Under Kentucky law, the governor has the discretion of appointing justices to the Supreme Court, even when the case they will hear deals with charges against the governor who appoints them. The attorney general called the situation unprecedented, and asked the entire Supreme Court to disqualify the two new temporary justices, citing conflicts of interest. After Fletcher became the fourteenth person indicted by the grand jury, he told a reporter that he had no intention of pardoning himself. "My conscience is clear, and let me say to the people of Kentucky, we've worked very hard to make sure we've done everything to move this state forward. I'm very disappointed, but we'll continue to move forward. I'm not going to let this distract from moving this state forward." The Kentucky Supreme Court later ruled that the grand jury could not hand down indictments against people for whom the governor had issued a blanket pardon, stopping any further legal proceedings (Loftus and Pitsch 2006; Beardsley 2006).

By July 2006, the political fallout from the grand jury indictments had taken its toll on the Kentucky governor. A Republican Party-commissioned poll found that 69 percent of those responding said that they wanted someone other than Fletcher to be governor, saying that even his acquittal or the dismissal of legal charges would not change their views (Alessi 2006). Fletcher's fortune changed in August 2006 when a judge ruled that the governor could not be tried while in office, asking the parties to try to reach a settlement. Later that month, the judge signed an agreement dismissing the misdemeanor charges "with prejudice," a designation that prohibits the charges from being brought against him again. Fletcher did agree to acknowledge that the evidence "strongly indicates wrongdoing" by his administration, and that his actions were inappropriate. Another part of the agreement required the governor's four appointees to the Personnel Board to resign so that employees could receive a fair hearing. A day after the August 24 announcement of the settlement, Fletcher returned to the campaign trail seeking re-election as governor (Alford 2006).

The governor is the state-level equivalent of the city manager or county administrator at the local level. Depending upon the state, gubernatorial powers are enumerated in the constitution in either precise or exceptionally vague terminology, allowing substantial room for interpretation. With 50 different state constitutions, there are 50 different management styles, built partially on legal parameters and partially on each governor's personal style. In Kentucky, the amount of discretion the governor has in managing the state's personnel system is substantial, as seen in the case above. In other states, the constitution provides for shared powers among executive branch agencies so that too much power is not focused on one individual or political party. What is clear, however, is that within the last three decades, states have been given more responsibility and mandates by the federal government. The result has been that governors have more power and discretion than ever before.

Role of the Governor

The governor's role is to manage the executive branch of the state, and they are usually the most powerful personality in the state. They have the capability of shaping policies and the bureaucracy that implements them. Although executive roles are similar across the nation, there are wide variations in enabling constitutional frameworks, most of which specify what the governor is permitted to do. Limitations on executive power usually stem from case law and from accompanying legal commentaries, rather than sanctions found in the constitution. As a constitutional officer, powers are delegated by the people; a governor does not exist under common law or possess common law powers. However, when the state constitution grants the governor supreme executive authority, it implies the power necessary to secure the efficient and fair execution of the law, so long as that power is exercised within constitutional and statutory limitations. A governor receives power only through legislative enactment or by constitutional provision, and the governor cannot alter, expand, or diminish that power. The legislature of a state may not interfere with a state governor's exercise of gubernatorial powers that are granted by a state constitution (Ellis 2004, 4).

In the early years of the United States, state legislatures were more powerful than governors, although over time, they were able to expand their power and increase the prestige of the office. This resulted from the direct popular election of the governor, extended terms in office, the reintroduction of the gubernatorial veto, and the decline in the effectiveness of the legislature as the chief mechanism of state government.

The growth of autonomous or semi-autonomous state agencies and departments, however, mitigated any attempts by governors to control the state government, because oversight was usually vested in the state legislature. To facilitate the administration of the state, governors began to act more like managers, gradually advocating a strengthening of their power. In some states, this involved the consolidation of agencies, or the substitution of appointed department heads for independently elected individuals and fiscal reforms that granted governors power in the areas of budget preparation and implementation (Ellis 2004).

For the purpose of discussion, the governor's managerial role can be divided into seven categories, many of which are similar to those exercised by other executives within the public sector. In addition, governors have various responsibilities and duties that are more procedural or ceremonial.

Appointments

Governors have considerable discretion in making appointments to positions identified in the state constitution, part of their perceived need to build a team of managers to carry out policy. The number of appointments a governor can make varies from state to state; in Connecticut the governor appoints about 50 commissioners and deputies, 100 in Arizona, and about 50 in Kentucky. Appointments become more visible and discretion becomes more important during administrative transitions, when new governors want to have an immediate impact on developing a team to run the state (Roberts 2003).

Gubernatorial appointments can sometimes even affect the state legislature, as is the case in Hawaii. Governor Linda Lingle used her discretion in making an appointment to fill a seat in the legislature after a Democratic representative resigned in 2005. Her appointee joined the Democratic Party just three days after the previous member's resignation, making her eligible to fill the vacancy. In response, legislators passed a 2006 measure that would have given political parties the ability to decide who the governor should appoint to fill legislative vacancies. The bill also required that the political parties could choose only from those who are registered members of the party for at least six months prior to the appointment. The governor vetoed the bill, stating that "such a provision fails to recognize that this may unreasonably restrict the pool of potential candidates" (Kua 2006).

Some appointments are relatively benign, such as the governor's power to appoint members to the state Board of Barbering, while others wield considerable power. In many states, the governor controls the membership of the state's higher education board, which sets policies ranging from tuition levels and budgets to admissions and hiring. In Arizona, the governor appoints all of the members of the state Board of Regents, providing a substantive degree of influence over higher education in the state. One appointee, for instance, was a strong supporter of the governor who advanced her education agenda among the other members of the board. In Pennsylvania, the governor appoints six of the 32 members of the Board of Trustees of Pennsylvania State University, providing fewer opportunities for directing the board's agenda. In other states, the governor routinely appoints all or most of the members of commissions and boards with varying levels of jurisdiction and authority.

Governors use their discretion over appointments in both what they do and do not do. In Missouri, for instance, Governor Matt Blunt's 2006 choice of an influential Republican state legislator to the state's Ethics Commission drew heavy opposition. The commission has oversight for all campaign-related money in the state, including expenditures by candidates and lobbyists. The commission also handles all formal accusations of violations, imposing fines and referring some matters to prosecutors. One Democratic Party official referred to the appointee as "a political hack who will not aggressively enforce ethics laws." The appointment to the commission was also critical because the governor had delayed nominating replacements to the commission, which was unable to do much because the terms had expired for three of its six members, leaving it without a quorum to proceed. Among the issues languishing on its agenda were two formal complaints accusing Blunt of illegal campaign activities during the 2004 election (Mannies 2006).

Alaska Governor Frank Murkowski made news of a different sort for his appointments to the state judiciary. Applicants for judgeships are screened by the Alaska Judicial Council, a seven-member group made up of three attorneys, three public members, and the chief justice of the Alaska Supreme Court. The best qualified candidates, in the opinion of the council members, are forwarded to the governor, who picks one of the nominees. In 1968, Governor Walter Hickel appointed the first three female judges in the state; there are currently 63 judges in the state, and 52, or about 83 percent, are men. Over the last two decades, governors have appointed female judges about one-quarter of the time. But Governor Murkowski has appointed women just under five percent of the time; even though the Alaska Judicial Council has nominated at least one woman in 15 of the 21 appointments made by the governor. In one instance, three of the eight nominees were women, but the governor still appointed a man. Overall, he has appointed only one woman, who was named to a district court (Snifka 2006). The governor has, of course, the authority to choose who he wants to serve as judges, but the imbalance in gender on the bench has not gone unnoticed.

Former New York Governor George Pataki's discretion in making appointments was severely limited by the state legislature. Pataki, a Republican, made nearly a hundred nominations to state boards and commissions in 2006, but almost half were held up by the state senate for lack of confirmation. Observers said that some nominees were not confirmed as bargaining chips with the governor, who left office at the end of the year as part of an ongoing budget battle. Other delayed appointments were considered retribution for budget items the governor had vetoed, such as property tax rebates.

The governor's appointees were designed as one way the outgoing administration could leave a legacy behind for the new governor, if they were confirmed before the end of the year. Many of the positions paid salaries of $100,000 or more, and had substantive policy implications. Among the slots the Senate was holding up were appointments to the State University of New York Board of Trustees, the state's Public Service Commission, the Parole Board, and the Workers Compensation Board. Other nominees awaiting confirmation were for the Commission on Correction, the Thruway Authority Board, and the Racing and Wagering Board. Some of the positions were even for reappointment, making them less controversial.

Pataki's staff members attempted to pass off the delays as unintentional, but one key legislator said the action was appropriate given the way the governor had acted toward the state legislature (Karlin 2006). Although Pataki had the legal authority to make the appointments under the state's constitution, his ability to get those appointments confirmed, even after three terms as governor, was limited by partisan retaliation. In areas of authority such as appointments, legal power does not always equal political power.

Economic Development

Although many managerial tasks involving the day-to-day operations of the state are quite similar to those of any large organization, governors are also tasked with the responsibility for improving the state's economic climate. Because jobs are typically one of the key issues on the minds of voters, building workforce skills, spurring innovation through research and development, and aid new business development are essential items on a governor's agenda. This is also an area where a governor's personal style, initiative, and use of discretion can be essential as management tools.

After the recession of 2001, many economic analysts believed that individual states could take steps to develop regional clusters of innovation that would share markets, labor, new ideas, and products. These strategies implemented on a state/regional level rather than on the national level, put governors in a unique position to tailor initiatives to their own needs and resources. By boosting economic competitiveness, governors could create a business climate that sought to hold down wages, taxes, and infrastructure costs to improve their state's long-term economic prospects. Business clusters that have become the focus of gubernatorial initiatives are energy, with at least 20 states working to develop this industry; life sciences, with at least 16 states taking action to develop this cluster; the film industry, with at least 11 states providing tax incentives; and nanotechnology, with six governors focusing on efforts in higher education research, funding, and training (National Governors' Association 2006a).

Governors have considerable discretion in deciding which tools they can use to enhance economic development in their states. A 2006 survey by the National Governors' Association's Center for Best Practices identified the following actions that were taken by individual governors during the previous year.

- Exempting research and development activity from sales and use taxes (Idaho, Indiana)
- Establishing a fund to encourage research financed by a state budget surplus or tobacco settlement fund dollars (Connecticut, Washington)
- Partnering with universities to invest in research and development and innovation (Delaware, Georgia, Kentucky, Texas)
- Funding training opportunities to build workers' skills (Illinois, Michigan, New Mexico, North Carolina, Vermont)
- Creating state entrepreneurship centers (Illinois, Wisconsin)
- Increasing access to financial resources and venture capital (Arizona, Louisiana, Wisconsin)
- Offering incentives for targeted industries (Georgia, Maryland, North Carolina, Pennsylvania)
- Creating incentives for job creation (Georgia, Massachusetts, Missouri, New Hampshire, Oklahoma)
- Simplifying regulations and procedures (Arkansas, Virginia)
- Developing rural areas (Michigan)
- Providing tax incentives and loans (Georgia, Minnesota, Nebraska, New Mexico)
- Supporting tourism and producing promotional campaigns (Alaska, Idaho, Illinois, Nebraska, North Carolina, Ohio, Pennsylvania, South Carolina, Wisconsin)
- Attracting businesses through quality of life initiatives (Iowa, New York, Vermont)
- Marketing the state's businesses (Alaska, Florida, Georgia, Iowa, Maryland, New York, Wisconsin (National Governors' Association 2006a).

Although this list is lengthy, the programs themselves are similar in theme: promote the growth of the state's economy by finding new ways to solve old problems. In these instances, the governor's ability to be innovative is limited only by the inability to come up with a new name or acronym to describe what has often been tried before. In economic development, there is only one direction a governor can turn: growing the economy.

Emergency Management

Among the most fundamental responsibilities a governor has is responding to crises (Matheson 1986, 200). Crises include events such as disasters (natural and human-caused), health care emergencies, and public employee strikes or even employee walkouts. The governor has substantial discretion in determining a state's response, ranging from declaring a state of emergency in order to become eligible for federal aid, or ordering regulations to be waived or relaxed, or mobilizing resources to be sent to disaster sites. Emergency powers may also include mobilizing the state's National Guard units, requiring the evacuation of all or part of the population within an area involved in an emergency, commandeering the use of private property, authorizing emergency funding, and entering into mutual aid agreements with other states. Governors are responsible for petitioning the federal government for disaster aid, whether the crisis involves civil disobedience, terrorism, or natural disasters.

In August 2005, Louisiana Governor Kathleen Blanco was faced with one of the nation's costliest disasters when the state was hit with Hurricane Katrina, which ravaged the Gulf Coast. The U.S. National Hurricane Center had issued a statement on August 23 warning of the formation of a tropical storm.

For decades, experts had warned that New Orleans and nearby areas were vulnerable to storms and that protecting them would require a stronger storm management infrastructure, including the historic system of levees and canals that surround the city. Despite the warnings, successive administrations never pushed the issue to the national agenda. Even after the August storm was upgraded to a dangerous storm, the governor was slow at issuing a state of emergency for the state, waiting until several days later to do so. She waited several days to reach out to a multistate mutual aid compact for assistance.

What might seem like an easy decision is not always so easy. Governor Blanco, for instance, had to choose between relying on her own state's resources, which she could personally direct and manage, or calling upon the federal government for help. In choosing the later option, a governor gives up a considerable amount of power, political and otherwise. To some observers, Blanco appeared to be unable to decide at what point she would need to call upon other resources, which was perceived by some as evidence of her weak leadership that led to delays. Louisiana officials insisted they had begun to manage the situation nearly a week after the hurricane hit, but the battle for authority was already well underway.

The Bush administration sent the governor a proposed legal memorandum asking her to request a federal takeover of the evacuation of New Orleans as a way of gaining control over all local police and state National Guard units that were reporting directly to the governor. Louisiana rejected the White House request, complaining that the action would be comparable to a federal declaration of martial law. One source noted, "Quite frankly, if they'd been able to pull off taking it away from the locals, they then could have blamed everything on the locals." Blanco sought to keep the response at the state level, establishing a philanthropic fund for the state's victims and hiring a former Federal Emergency Management Agency (FEMA) director to advise her on relief efforts. The head of the federal Department of Homeland Security said one reason why federal assistance was not brought into the state more quickly was "because our constitutional system really places the primary authority in each state with the governor" (Roig-Franzia and Hsu 2005).

Federal officials claimed they had the authority to federalize National Guard units to quell civil disturbances under the Insurrection Act, attempting to unify the chains of command that were split among the three levels of government that were responding to the hurricane. After reports of looting, murder, and rape within the New Orleans Superdome, and armed criminals roaming the state, it appeared that neither New Orleans Mayor Ray Nagin nor Governor Blanco had the situation under control, after all. Federal law does not permit regular military troops from engaging in domestic law enforcement, but National Guard troops, who are under command of the governor, have no such limitations.

In a National Public Radio interview, Governor Blanco defended her actions and the choices she had made. "You need to understand that we are working in what is essentially a primitive site condition. These conditions make it extremely impossible to do everything that is absolutely essential to be done simultaneously. So we deployed our people in a prioritized fashion. And our goal is to save as many lives as possible. No state, no region is prepared for the dimensions that we have dealt with" (Lehrer 2005).

Governors of several other affected states, in contrast, were considered much more proactive in preparing and implementing their states' relief and evacuation services. In Tennessee, the governor issued an executive order to suspend certain laws and rules in order to provide relief to the victims of Hurricane Katrina as part of the state's Emergency Management Plan. Under state law, the governor is authorized to "suspend the provisions of any law, order, rule, or regulation prescribing the procedures for the conduct of state business or the orders or rules of any state agency, if strict compliance with the provisions of any such law, order, rule, or regulation would in any way prevent, hinder, or delay necessary action in coping with the emergency." Among the applications of these emergency powers is the permission for certain pharmacists to assist evacuees. Emergency powers also allow certain kinds of restricted vehicles to move on interstate highways that they would not normally be permitted to use. Alabama's governor set up an uncompensated care pool that allowed state officials regulatory flexibility in providing medical care for Katrina evacuees.

In Arkansas, the governor issued a state of emergency order in specific jurisdictions that allowed affected counties to tap into emergency response funds to defray purchasing and other costs. This permitted school and city buses to be moved into disaster areas. Governor Haley Barbour set up a Mississippi Hurricane Recovery Fund to serve as the state's central clearinghouse for corporations, organizations, and individuals to make donations for residents who were recovering and preparing to rebuild.

Even though California was more than a thousand miles away from the hurricane's damaging force, Governor Arnold Schwarzenegger activated the state's Office of Emergency Services (OES) to coordinate a response to the Gulf region. The state had experienced more than its fair share of natural disasters, and is accustomed to dealing with a wide variety of emergencies. Working with FEMA, the OES deployed swiftwater rescue teams, urban search and rescue teams, incident support team managers, fire and rescue teams, disaster medical assistance teams, National Guard troops, California Highway Patrol officers, and Department of Forestry and Fire Protection teams.

It might seem as if such steps would be a matter of course, and a part of interstate cooperation. But governors face serious conflicts in determining how to respond to crises, especially when it involves another state. In the case of Hurricane Katrina, virtually all the adjacent states were dealing with problems of their own, including damage from previous and subsequent hurricanes that hit the Gulf Coast region. Some, such as Arkansas, became major relocation sites for those evacuated from other states. Others, including Texas, dealt with Katrina refugees just days before another hurricane hit. Governor Blanco's use of gubernatorial discretion was likely to be criticized no matter what steps she would have taken, given the magnitude of the disaster and conflicts with local and federal officials.

Financial Management

The financial operations of a state rival those of many countries in terms of revenues and expenditures. The determination of how decisions are made is constitutionally restricted, with the power sometimes vested in the governor, and sometimes, in a department-level financial manager. In the latter case, the individual may serve as an independent elected official, or may be required to submit a budget to an appointee of the governor. All fifty states require the election of an independent state treasurer (sometimes called the state comptroller) who is part of the executive branch of government. Some states also have created a legislative finance manager to achieve some degree of checks and balances over the executive office, although the individual is not elected. The structure in the majority of states, however, gives the governor the authority to authorize, and the power to appropriate to the state legislature.

The state budget process is central to the administration of state government. Budgets allocate resources, set policy, review and evaluate policy, and lay the foundation for future planning and program review. Although state practices are fairly similar, a 2004 survey by the National Conference of State Legislatures found that variations occur including whether a state uses an annual or biennial budget cycle, the nature of requirements to balance the budget, whether states are subject to tax and expenditure limits, the nature of requirements to maintain budget reserves (rainy day funds), and whether federal funds are subject to the appropriations processes (National Conference of State Legislatures 2004).

Most states follow the executive budgeting model, where the governor's staff members propose a budget to be submitted to the state legislature. The budget covers the majority of state functions, but does not include the budget for the courts or legislature, because they have their own operating budgets. In some states, the executive budget becomes a starting point for negotiations with legislative leaders, but in others (including Arizona, Colorado, and Texas) the executive budget is, for the most part, disregarded. In Maryland, Nebraska, and West Virginia, the legislature is limited in how much they can increase or decrease budget items. Forty-three state constitutions give the governor the discretion to exercise a line-item veto, allowing the removal of individual programs or "lines" in the budget (National Conference of State Legislatures 2004).

A governor's control over the state's budget is among the criteria for judging whether the executive is constitutionally weak or strong, according to some scholars (Lindstrom and Robar 1996, 45). Discretionary power over budgets is usually the result of the need for flexibility in determining policy direction (sometimes amounting to total discretion with virtually little or no limitations), balanced against legislative control. California state law, for instance, gave governors the authority to make mid-year budget cuts as a spending control strategy until 1983, when the power was withdrawn by the state legislature.

Governors do have some discretion in the expenditure of state funds. In Maryland, for instance, the governor may use the Opportunity Fund to build roads, sewer systems, and other types of infrastructure to attract investment to the state (Bailey and Johnson 2004). In New York, most of the early expenditures in Governor Pataki's implementation of the Clean Air and Clean Water Acts were discretionary. Critics of the administration argued that the public did not receive an annual accounting of the thousands of dollars spent from the state's Environmental and Wildlife Funds (MacClennan 1998). Overall, however, the legislature almost always has the final word in state spending, regardless of the governor's political agenda.

Policy Development and Implementation

Governors have considerable discretion in setting the state's policy agenda, depending upon numerous factors. They are political animals as well as managers, because all fifty states require that the individual be chosen in a statewide election. Governors in the larger states, such as New York, California, and Texas, have national visibility and power because their states are represented by large congressional delegations. This gives them enormous power in comparison to governors in small states such as New Hampshire, Vermont, and Rhode Island.

Beyle (1999) identifies four characteristics that determine the personal power of governors: electoral mandate, position on the state's ambition ladder, personal future, and job performance rating in public opinion polls. In the 2005 ranking, 15 governors were rated as having an electoral mandate (a landslide win of 11 or more points); 16 were identified as having a steady progression on the state's political ambition ladder; all but 13 were early in their gubernatorial term and could run again; and 11 had a job approval rating of over 60 percent. The aggregation of the scores yielded the identity of the governors considered to have the most personal power: West Virginia, Kansas, Colorado, Iowa, Louisiana, Michigan, South Dakota, Vermont, and Wisconsin. Yet it is unlikely that most Americans could identify these same governors by name, because their visibility is lower than most others. Some factor must translate personal power into public approval of the job the governor is doing.

The governor's primary duties involve the development and implementation of public policy. Some actions are statutorily directed, while others serve as a request for a specific course of action. Some states, such as Michigan, include the authority to issue executive orders as part of the governor's power. Executive orders usually detail the specific actions the governor requires to be taken, and the timetable by which they are to be completed, such as a re-organization of a department. Policy agendas are often outlined in the State of the State addresses they give, which outline their priorities. In 2006, governors were optimistic about their states' futures, with 84 percent describing economic conditions as good or improving, and nine pointing to high or near-high employment levels. State budgets were projected to be in balance or with a surplus by 82 percent of the governors (Nodine 2006).

What is perhaps unusual is that although each governor could have chosen from a broad array of policy directions and initiatives, five topics were the center of their speeches: education, health care, economic development, energy and the environment, and taxes. In some ways, the similarities among policy choices might be expected, because issues such as teacher quality and salaries, health and wellness, and business growth are at the heart of many states' futures. But the speeches also could indicate a lack of leadership and innovative thinking, because the solutions proposed showed very little differences. Of the 45 speeches analyzed, 82 percent of governors discussed proposals for tax reduction for businesses or individuals, and 69 percent described initiatives to develop energy resources or to promote energy efficiency and conservation, no doubt a response to the increased costs of gasoline (Nodine 2006).

Given the high level of discretion they each have, why are the policy agendas so uniform? Part of the answer lies in the fact that every governor (with the exception of New Hampshire and Vermont, where the term of office is two years) must run for office every four years. From the moment the governor steps into the statehouse, the mobilization of re-election forces begins, and the policy clock begins ticking. This provides governors with a short window of opportunity to move forward with their own policies, and as a result, many make only incremental changes in the overall policy agenda of their state. They may describe their work in terms of new directions, new initiatives, or new programs, but in reality, governors can only tweak the way they approach issues.

The Web site for Wyoming's governor, for example, identifies eight policy areas that are the focus for his administration: agriculture, economy, energy, environment, government, health care, people, and wildlife. In contrast, the policy focus for several governors in states with large urban centers includes crime and public safety. Wisconsin's governor launched his POWER initiative in 2006, with the acronym translated as Promoting Our Wisconsin Energy Resources. The governor noted that Wisconsin was leading the way in energy independence, a claim made by a half dozen other governors as well.

One of the difficulties that governors face is that policy is often driven by events they cannot control, thus limiting their discretion to decide what they want on their own agendas. In 2006, West Virginia Governor Joe Manchin signed new mine safety legislation that had been passed unanimously by the state's legislators. Manchin had not made mine safety an important part of his gubernatorial agenda, nor had the legislature. But the deaths of 14 miners in two incidents over a one month period forced the issue onto the state's agenda after widespread publicity put pressure on officials to take action. The governor said that the new bill, which required better communications, tracking devices, underground oxygen supplies, and faster emergency responses, would help prevent tragedies like the two that had killed the miners. "We want to be the benchmark everyone looks to when they mine," the governor told relatives of those killed at the bill's signing ceremony. "The sacrifice you all have made will change mining in this country" (Helber 2006).

Of course, there are some exceptions where a governor has tried to carve out new issue territory. For instance, the governor of Colorado convened a statewide summit meeting as part of his Initiative on Responsible Fatherhood in 1996. A gubernatorial task force spent six months identifying the causes and possible solutions around the problem of father absence, producing a blueprint for a state agenda and recommendations for immediate action. Oregon's governor signed an executive order in 2003 that created an advisory group that produced the Oregon Strategy for Greenhouse Gas Emissions the following year. In both of these cases, the governor was attempting to put his personal agenda forward in a way that distinguished his administration from other governors.

Public Safety

California Governor Arnold Schwarzenegger's decision not to grant clemency to Tookie Williams was analyzed in the Introduction to this book as an example where gubernatorial discretion literally can be a life or death matter. Public safety issues are highly visible, widely publicized, and extremely emotional, making decisions especially difficult no matter which course of action is chosen.

Illinois Governor George Ryan was the subject of international attention when he stopped the execution of inmates on death row in January 2000. The governor declared a moratorium on the use of capital punishment until a commission he appointed studied the issue. The commission's report, issued in April 2002, identified numerous ways errors, arbitrariness, and prejudice can influence capital punishment decisions (Fellner 2002). Governor Ryan's "deep reservations" about the system did not necessarily mean he wanted an end to the death penalty, but he did react to a system that he believed took away innocent lives. His action was an abrupt change from other administrations' policies.

Former California Governor Gray Davis, who was defeated by Schwarzenegger, took the opposite approach in a 2002 case involving Robert Rosenkrantz. Rosenkrantz had been convicted of second-degree murder in 1985 and sentenced to 17-years-to-life in prison after he shot a former high school classmate who had exposed him as a homosexual. He was 18 at the time he committed the crime, and while in prison, he became a model prisoner. He earned a college degree and had received several offers of post-release employment after studying computers in prison. When he became eligible for parole, gay activists and state legislators lobbied for his release, and he was granted parole by the state's Board of Prison Terms in 1999.

Shortly after taking office, Davis told a reporter that any inmate serving time for murder in California was not going to get out during his watch. "If you take someone else's life, forget it" (Chiang 2002). Davis then implemented what many called a "no parole" policy and vetoed Rosenkrantz's release. A coalition of religious groups, law enforcement officials, and the trial judge in the Rosenkrantz case filed a brief urging the court to order his release, arguing that Davis' action was a violation of California law and due process guarantees under the constitution. A judge ordered Rosenkrantz freed, ruling that the governor's policy was unlawful and that the prisoner was being confined beyond his lawfully set parole date. Governor

Davis appealed the ruling to the state Court of Appeal, which upheld the lower court judge, noting that Davis had violated a 1988 proposition approved by voters that gave the governor the authority to overturn parole decisions involving convicted murders. The law requires the governor to read the parole board's report and issue a timely, written decision. Davis appealed the lower court's decision to the state's Supreme Court, contending that his power to block parole was absolute and is similar to his power to grant clemency to spare a condemned inmate's life. In his appeal, he asked the Supreme Court to clarify his authority.

Prior to the Rosenkrantz case, Davis reviewed 140 murder cases where an inmate had been granted parole by the Board of Prison Terms. He vetoed parole in all but two cases, and sent 11 cases back to the board for full review. The two exceptions involved women serving sentences for murder who said they had been victims of battered-woman syndrome. But he had also denied parole for other women who also said they had been battered by the men they killed. Davis' predecessor, Governor Pete Wilson, had allowed 68 murderers to be paroled by not taking action on the board's recommendations (Chiang 2002). In support of their brief seeking Rosenkrantz's release, a group led by the American Civil Liberties Union noted that, "Every court that has ruled on [these] cases has determined that there is no evidence supporting a denial of their parole and that they are not a threat to society. The Supreme Court must act, because [Rosenkrantz] will not get a fair hearing in light of Governor Davis' no parole policy" (ACLU 2002).

In the final ruling on the case, the court supported the governor, upholding his veto of Rosenkrantz's release. The chief justice held that the governor was only required to show that there was "some evidence" to support denial, the same standard required to uphold a denial by the board itself. The facts cited by the governor, he said, were sufficient to meet that standard (Ofgang 2002). Lawyers for Rosenkrantz said that the governor had disrupted the state's parole system, calling it "totally broken." But a criminal prosecutor who wrote a brief in support of the governor said the case involved the governor's exclusive powers. "If the electorate doesn't like what he's doing," he said, "then they have the last word" (Chiang 2002).

Veto Powers

Every state constitution makes provision for the governor to veto legislation, part of the system of checks of balances that also exists at the federal level. Although President George W. Bush did not use his veto power during the first six years of his administration, governors are much more likely to do so. There is usually some constitutional requirement that the governor take action on a bill within a prescribed amount of time, although governors also may use their discretion by not signing a bill at the end of a legislative system, called a *pocket veto*. Timing can be important, as was the case when Colorado Governor Bill Owens vetoed 18 bills on the Friday of the Memorial Day weekend in 2006, including several controversial proposals. He could have chosen to issue the veto messages the following week, but his choice of when to take action was considered politically calculated because the veto package received much less publicity due to the holiday.

Veto power is important to a governor's relationship with the state legislature, especially when the governor represents a different party than that controlling the statehouse. Between January 2003 and June 2006, for instance, Arizona Governor Janet Napolitano, a Democrat, vetoed a record number of bills sent to her by the Republican majority in the legislature. On one hand, observers believe that conservatives viewed the more than 110 vetoes as a reason to support a different candidate in the 2006 gubernatorial campaign, turning out in opposition to her stance on issues such as putting more National Guard troops along the Mexican border, creating a waiting period for abortions, and making it tougher for patients to win lawsuits against emergency room doctors. But others saw the vetoes as a show of force during Napolitano's first term, because she held a commanding lead in public opinion polls and had a high voter approval rating. The legislature was unable to override the vetoes, which one Republican consultant said was the mark of savvy, calculated politicians (Scutari 2006).

Veto powers also give a governor the opportunity to quash legislation believed to be vague or unnecessary. In Vermont, the governor vetoed a 2006 bill that would have added gender identity or expression to the state's nondiscrimination law, stating that he believed transgender people were already protected under existing law. New Hampshire's governor vetoed a bill that would change election laws that tied voter eligibility to their car registration. An individual whose car was registered in another state would be banned from voting at their polling place, as would those whose driver's license was from another state. The governor noted that the bill was unnecessary and would be likely to create confusion and new difficulties for senior citizens who register their cars in states where they have second homes. A similar reason was used by Colorado's governor in vetoing a 2006 bill that would broaden the state's communication piracy laws, saying that while the bill might be required, it was not defined clearly enough.

A governor will often veto legislation that restricts gubernatorial authority. Wisconsin Governor Jim Doyle, for instance, vetoed a Republican bill that would have given the legislature the power to approve off-reservation tribal casinos. Under the current law, off-reservation casino agreements must be approved by the U.S. Bureau of Indian Affairs and the governor. When Doyle, a Democrat, took office, he signed several new compacts with tribes within months after becoming governor, arguing that the new casinos meant more revenue for the state. Republicans filed a lawsuit saying that the governor had overstepped his authority, and the state

Supreme Court agreed. They criticized Doyle because Wisconsin tribes had given heavily to the national Democratic Party, and some of the funds were then allocated to him in the final days of the 2002 campaign. A spokesman for the governor said that the partisan complaints were absurd. "The governor's been clear throughout his administration he opposes this legislation because it doesn't square with federal law and it becomes unmanageable to try to negotiate agreements with 132 legislators" (Richmond 2006).

In other cases, a veto allows a governor to use the power of discretion when issues are highly politicized. Governor Kathleen Sebelius of Kansas vetoed a controversial bill that would have required physicians to inform state officials about late-term abortions, and whether the fetus was abnormal. It would also have expanded the type of additional information doctors would have to report, such as how a woman would have been harmed without the procedure. State law already requires doctors to report the number of abortions they perform each year, and when the fetus is at least 22 weeks old, they must show that it could not have survived outside the mother's womb or that the woman faced death or substantial and irreversible impairment. In vetoing the measure, the governor said that the bill "will force women to provide intimate, sensitive health information to the government. Privacy is a fundamental concern to all Kansans" (Manning 2006).

Other Duties

The responsibilities outlined in the previous sections are not the only ones the governor has, but they are arguably the ones where there is the greatest opportunity for the use and abuse of discretion. In addition to serving as the chief executive, the governor is also a ceremonial figurehead, hosting official visitors and guests. For instance, governors routinely order ceremonial and political proclamations, usually to commemorate special events and occasions. These proclamations often have little substantive value and are largely symbolic in nature. They may also be issued in recognition of an individual.

On May 1, 2006, North Carolina's governor issued proclamations honoring twelve different issues, from Electric Safety Month and Asthma Awareness Month, to Strawberry Month, Motorcycle Safety Awareness Month, and Egg Month. May 1–5, 2006 was also declared Healthy America Week in most states to raise the awareness of the urgent need for Americans of all ages to live healthier, more active lives. Arkansas Governor Mike Huckabee said that he hoped Healthy America Week would give citizens an occasion to highlight healthy habits that would last a lifetime. Tennessee Governor Phil Bredesen used the proclamation to hold a town hall meeting with students to discuss improving student wellness in and out of schools.

The proclamations by these two governors did not result in major policy changes, but did showcase their administration's commitment to the issue.

As managers, governors can use their authority to schedule cabinet meetings, according to the constitutions of 16 states. They may also decide whether they want to transfer their power to another official when they leave the state, even on vacation. In Missouri, for instance, the governor temporarily transferred power to the lieutenant governor on one occasion so that he had the honor of signing a bill that he had previously worked on.

When Governors Challenge the Federal Government

The federal system creates a natural competitiveness among the federal, state, and local governments in terms of power and discretion. In most cases, federal laws supersede those of states.

Some challenges to federal authority are relatively minor, while others have a more substantive effect. For instance, the National Governors' Association (NGA) first established a policy in 1997 that expressed their concern about the impact of post office closings and relocations on communities. The U.S. Postal Service has the ability to override local zoning requirements, which permits it to build new facilities that conflict with plans for growth management, environmental management, or public safety. The association's members urged the federal government to comply with state and local building codes, and to give first consideration to locating federal facilities on historic properties in central cities to help revitalize those areas (National Governors' Association 2006b).

Other challenges have been based on changes in federal laws that impact state governments, especially those related to unfunded mandates and cost sharing. In 2005, for instance, governors expressed "serious apprehension" about provisions in a budget reconciliation bill that would reduce federal funding for child support and child welfare, along with other human service programs. The House Ways and Means Committee included a provision that would reduce the federal match rate for child support administrative costs from 66 percent to 50 percent. The provision also included limitations in eligibility for children in the foster care system and adoption assistance programs (National Governors Association 2005). The challenge was important because it allowed governors to fight the changes as part of a national organization's opposition to the legislation, rather than as representatives of individual states. A governor could, of course, choose to criticize the congressional bill independently, but this mechanism eliminates the potential for being singled out as an opponent of Congress. By choosing which battles to fight and which ones to avoid, gubernatorial discretion provides a convenient way of balancing partisan and policy concerns.

A Governor on the Spot: The Case of Terri Schiavo

Governors attract attention for a number of reasons, some of which are relatively mundane, and others which result in an international uproar. Florida Governor Jeb Bush generated incredible controversy when he used his discretion to become involved in a dispute over the life of a terminally ill patient in his state in 2005. Terri Schiavo was born in Pennsylvania in 1963 and married her husband, Michael, in 1984. In 1986, they moved to Florida where her parents had retired. She experienced cardiac arrest on February 25, 1990, caused perhaps by a potassium imbalance that led to a lack of oxygen in her system, causing brain damage. She was placed on a feeding tube that provided her with nutrition and hydration, and was taken to a skilled care and rehabilitation facility. Michael was appointed as Terri's guardian by a Florida court in June 1990, and over the next few years, she was taken to various rehabilitation facilities for testing and therapy. In 1993, Terri's parents, the Schindlers, tried to get a court to remove Michael as Terri's guardian, due in part, some believe, to a dispute over medical malpractice funds he had been awarded in a case against the physicians who had cared for his wife.

In May 1998, Michael Schiavo petitioned the court to authorize the removal of Terri's feeding tube, despite the fact her parents opposed the move, saying their daughter would have wanted to stay alive. In 2000, a county circuit court judge ruled that Terri Schiavo would have wanted to have the feeding tube removed, and the ruling was upheld the following year by Florida's Second District Court of Appeal. The Schindler family asked for an appellate court rehearing, but that petition was denied, as was a subsequent petition by her parents to the Florida Supreme Court that chose not to review the case. The U.S. Supreme Court also decided not to hear the case, and on April 24, 2001, a judge ordered the feeding tube removed from Terri Schiavo, but it was ordered reinserted after two days. Over the next two and half years, the tube was removed and then reinserted as part of a flurry of legal motions and appeals flooded the court. The case ignited emotional debates worldwide.

On October 7, 2003, Florida Governor Jeb Bush intervened in the Schiavo case, filing a federal court brief in support of Terri's parents in an effort to stop the removal of the feeding tube. A federal court judge ruled that he lacked jurisdiction in the case, and a week later, the feeding tube was removed again for six days. The Florida Circuit Court and the First Circuit Court of Appeal refused to grant a request by "supporters" of the family to direct Governor Bush to intervene in the case. Hoping to have the feeding tube reinserted once again, the Florida legislature passed a bill, "Terri's Law," that allowed the governor to issue a one-time stay of a court order in certain cases. Governor Bush issued an executive order directing the reinsertion of the tube again. In a press conference in the White House Rose Garden,

President George W. Bush praised his brother Jeb's actions and how he handled the Schiavo case.

In the interim, Michael Schiavo filed a state court suit in which he argued that Terri's Law was unconstitutional, and sought an injunction against the reinsertion of the tube. Governor Bush intervened a second time, asking the Circuit Court judge to dismiss the lawsuit, but the court denied the governor's motion. Bush then appealed, seeking the removal of the judge who dismissed his case. By mid-February 2004, the Schiavo case had been the subject of dozens of motions and appeals, and Pope John Paul II even weighed in on life-sustaining treatments for patients in a vegetative state. A judge ruled against Governor Bush, stating that Terri's Law was unconstitutional, prompting still another round of appeals to the Florida Supreme Court, which ruled the law was, in fact, unconstitutional. Governor Bush intervened a third time, filing a motion for a rehearing, which was denied, but then granted the governor's motion that any further action be stayed until the case was decided by the U.S. Supreme Court. On January 24, 2005, the U.S. Supreme Court announced it would not review the Florida Supreme Court's ruling that Terri's Law was unconstitutional, and turned down another request for review seven weeks later. The feeding tube was removed for a third time in accordance with court order. The U.S. Congress intervened on behalf of the Schindler family, and President George W. Bush signed a law calling for the reinsertion of the tube under special emergency legislation.

Governor Bush held a news conference on March 23, 2005 in which he reported that a neurologist claimed that Terri Schiavo is not in a persistent vegetative state, asking the Florida Department of Children and Families to take custody. Still another petition was filed by the Schnidler family before the U.S. Supreme Court, which refused to hear the case for a third time, as did the Florida Supreme Court. Governor Bush finally admitted defeat on March 27, saying he did not have the power to intervene further. The U.S. Supreme Court refused to consider an Eleventh Circuit Court ruling, which appeared to end all further attempts at an appeal. After having her feeding tube removed on March 18, Terri Schiavo died on March 31. An April 12 *Wall Street Journal*/Harris Interactive poll found that most people disapproved of how President Bush, Governor Bush, and Congress handled the issue. Governor Bush re-entered the fray ten weeks later, asking a state prosecutor to investigate the circumstances of Ms. Schiavo's 1990 cardiac arrest, specifically mentioning the time between when she collapsed and when her husband dialed for emergency help.

As this lengthy narrative indicates, Governor Jeb Bush used every type of discretion available to him to intervene on behalf of the Schindler family. What is noteworthy, however, is that rather than relying on an executive order, which was within his authority, Bush used his power by going to the courts and to the state legislature. Whether that intervention was appropriate is not the purpose of this book, but it does show the incredible lengths a governor can go to when trying to influence a policy outcome. The eleven-year battle over Terri's Schiavo's life and death ended in 2005, but the steps taken by the governor are likely to have repercussions long after Bush has left office after two terms in 2006. Conservatives continue to praise the former governor for his actions, while bioethicists are still uncertain what impact the Schiavo case will have on the future of individuals in similar situations.

Discretion and Other State-Level Executives

Although there are some similarities between the federal and state executive branches, there are also substantial differences, depending on which state is being compared. All states have a line of succession should the governor become unable to serve, as is the case between the president and the vice-president. But the duties of state officials, and their level of discretionary power, vary considerably. Forty-two states have cabinets; in eight states the cabinet is authorized in the state constitution, and in sixteen states, they have their primary basis in statutes. The remaining states have cabinets established through tradition, or as creations of the governors. In every state except Florida, the cabinet is made up of individuals appointed by the governor (in Florida the cabinet is comprised of statewide elected officials). Cabinet size varies from 7 in Vermont to 75 in New York, although most have 20 or fewer members. For the most part, these appointees serve as administrative managers and as a liaison from the governor to state departments. This limits their ability to make discretionary decisions, because they serve at the pleasure of the governor and are subject to dismissal at any point in time.

The individual first in line for succession to the governor is the lieutenant governor, a position historically modeled after the state of New York in its 1846 constitution. Seven states do not have a lieutenant governor. State laws require that the individual be popularly elected and preclude the lieutenant governor from holding other offices. In some states, the lieutenant governor's duties are similar to the vice-president of the United States, but there is not always a requirement that the two executives be of the same political party. As in most states, Mississippi's lieutenant governor serves as president of the state senate, and presides over its meetings, casting the deciding vote in the case of a tie. In other states, the position also involves serving as the director of other executive branch agencies, which the vice-president does not do. In Nebraska, for instance, the lieutenant governor serves as chair of the Nebraska Information Technology Commission and as Director of Homeland Security in addition to presiding over the state legislature. Ohio's lieutenant governor is also the state's Development Director, but the office holder serves primarily as the individual responsible for implementing the governor's initiatives, with little personal power.

One of the few state executives with policy discretion is the head of each state's educational system, a position that is popularly elected in 14 states and appointed by a separate board in 21 states. In California, the Superintendent of Public Instruction is popularly elected, although not always popular. In 1879, state legislators called superintendents "mere parasites" and the office "superfluous" and a "waste of money" because the office had cost over $16,000 in a two-year period. Still, the state legislature agreed that the position was a necessary, laborious position of dignity, meriting a salary equal to that of the Secretary of State (Superintendent of Public Instruction 2006). Because the state school's chief is most likely elected by the voters or chosen by a board outside the control of the governor, there is less opportunity for the governor to control education policy in the state. As head of a state's public education system, this official is often involved in controversial decisions over issues such as the content of textbooks, graduation requirements, and teacher certification, although that authority may be shared with local school districts and school boards.

Discretion involves not only the ability to take action, but to defer action as well. In some cases, the latter track puts the state's top school official at electoral risk. Arizona's Superintendent of Public Instruction was heavily criticized in 2006 for his decision involving a man who had voluntarily relinquished his state teaching certificate. In May 2002, the man had quit his job with a school district after admitting to becoming addicted to Internet pornography, some of which involved teenagers. He reapplied for a certificate 16 months later, but withdrew his application when it became clear that his request would be rejected by the state's Professional Practices Advisory Committee. The committee provides an advisory opinion to the state education board. He reapplied again in 2006, testifying that he was "disgusted with my own actions, and the thoughts that I had." He told the school board that he was receiving counseling, that his students did not have access to the computer he used, and that he had been employed at a charter school that did not require state certification. The advisory committee accepted the explanation, and the Superintendent deferred to their decision, explaining that they had done more extensive research. One local newspaper criticized the decision, noting, "We don't know what's more shocking: that a group of professional educators would consider working with a schoolteacher who frequently viewed pornography on his classroom computer until he was caught four years ago, or that an elected superintendent of public instruction would rely on some committee's judgment, instead of his own common sense, about the standards that should apply for those who seek state teaching certificates" (Horne, Board Failed 2006).

Most state executives have authority only over their own departments, and may have little interaction with other officials, either elected or appointed. Some positions are related to specific professions, but they may have limited statutory power. After the 1965 Watts Riots in Los Angeles, the popularly-elected Insurance Commissioner was faced with hundreds of millions of dollars in claims for property damage, and business owners began to complain that insurance companies were refusing to issue policies or cancelling existing ones. But the Insurance Commissioner responded that he was unable to help the businesses because he did not have that type of regulatory authority over private insurance companies in the state. By intimating that he was powerless to take action, the commissioner also avoided any controversy over actions he did not take in resolving the situation.

State Boards and Commissions

One area of study that has received less attention when it comes to managerial discretion is the role played by some state boards and commissions. Governors have the authority to create (and sometimes dismantle) topic-related bodies that represent specific interests, or may have licensing functions. When the boards have broad policymaking power, appointments by the governor become considerably more important. Controversial appointments and wide ranging rulemaking authority have increased both the influence and the scope of board powers over time.

Montana, like most states, has a state-level agency charged with implementing environmental statutes, including those promulgated at the federal level but delegated to the states. Its Department of Environmental Quality (DEQ) has, as one of its divisions, a seven-member Montana Environmental Review Board (MERB) whose members are appointed by the governor to four year terms. Although the Board, created in 1995, has no rulemaking powers, it does have the authority and duty to adopt all rules to implement state and federal laws including the Clean Air Act, water quality fees and standards, public water supply and sewage systems, facility siting, mega-landfills, solid waste management plans, hearings on motor vehicle wrecking facilities, and radioactive materials. When the state legislature enacts new environmental laws, MERB sets the rules that tell DEQ how to implement those laws as well as hear appeals of DEQ decisions. Other environmental programs are administered by various state agencies, including lakeshore protection, the federal Superfund program, infectious waste and integrated waste management, slash disposal, and the regulation of herbicides and pesticides. Still, its discretionary authority to implement some of the state's key environmental laws makes it extremely powerful.

When Montana Governor Brian Schweitzer started his term in 2005, he had the opportunity to appoint four new members to the MERB. His appointees differed considerably from his Republican predecessors, and included a county commissioner who was also an attorney and had served as a watchdog over a mining operation, and another who had served on local air and water pollution control boards. A third new member was the director of the Blackfeet Tribe Fish and Wildlife Department, and the fourth was a University of Montana hydrologist who was a member of several environmental groups. They replaced a lobbyist for mining, railroad, and industrial interests, and a campground owner whose husband was a former chief of staff to one of the state's Republican senators. Shortly after the four new members were appointed by the governor, a fifth member who had been appointed by a Republican governor decided to resign, citing her frustration at working with the new majority.

Those active in environmental organizations, who had believed that the MERB had failed to address many of the state's needs in the past, welcomed the governor's new appointees, hoping that the board would make significant changes that could strengthen Montana's water and air quality regulations. Several, including the Montana Environmental Information and Information Center, and the Northern Plains Resource Council, were already involved in efforts to have MERB set mercury standards for coal-fired power plants and a petition to force mining companies to restore water quality to state standards within two years of completing mining operations (Peters 2006).

New York's State Board of Parole has an even more daunting task: reviewing the records of felons seeking parole to determine whether they should be released. Although the responsibility leads to controversy in many states, it is especially acute in New York because of the governor's agenda. A 2006 study by the *New York Law Journal* found that in fiscal year 1992–1993, the state released 23 percent of the prisoners eligible for parole who had committed murder, attempted murder, kidnapping, and arson, or what the state terms *A-1 felonies*. During 2004 to 2005, only nine prisoners, or 3 percent, were released. The study points to one major difference in explaining the change: the election of Governor George Pataki in 1995. The Republican governor replaced Democrat Mario Cuomo, and had run on a "get tough on crime" platform. Pataki replaced all of Cuomo's appointees to the parole board, and quickly sent a message about how they should perform their duties. The study found that, "Governor Pataki's appointees to the New York State Board of Parole have evidently used their broad discretion to implement a gubernatorial policy to keep violent felons behind bars as long as possible, notwithstanding the recommendations of sentencing judges guided by a different and more lenient legal, political, and legislative framework" (Caher 2006).

Defense attorneys believe the parole board has gone far beyond its constitutional authority, and one contends that the parole board is acting as a second sentencing court, imposing its own sentence in place of the sentence imposed by the judge. Citing a multitude of examples, the study found that inmates sentenced to indeterminate terms, such as 15-years-to-life, were facing parole barriers matching those sentenced to 25-years-to-life or more. For those whose upper limit on their sentence is life, parole is totally subject to the positions taken by the board.

By law, parole is a possibility, not a guarantee or reward for good behavior, and an inmate has no legal expectation of securing parole release. Moreover, the parole board has broad discretion in making its decisions. While the board is required to take into consideration a number of factors—such as the seriousness of the crime and the inmate's rehabilitative effort—it can place any weight on those factors and need not explain itself (Caher 2006).

While it is within the parole board's authority to use whatever standards it chooses, the change in governors has dramatically changed the fate of inmates who have repeatedly requested parole. One man who has served more than 30 years on a 25-years-to-life sentence for three murders has completed numerous rehabilitation and vocational programs while in prison. He says he does not know what else he can do to obtain release from what he believed was a legislatively defined sentence. Another, who committed murder in 1978 and also received a 25-years-to-life sentence, has been denied parole eight times and is now 72 years old. One other felon, who plea bargained a term of 15-years-to-life for murder in 1983, expected to be released after 15 years or so. But as the study notes, he had the misfortune of coming up for parole when government attitudes about early release had changed. He has been denied release four times since Pataki took office despite having served 23 years in prison.

The parole board's supporters point to the fact that it would be expected that the governor's appointees would share the executive's criminal justice philosophy. One state official notes, "The governor's focus as a matter of public safety is to make sure that people convicted of violent crimes serve the longest possible sentences." Another official notes that since Pataki took office, new crimes by parolees have decreased and the number of parolees returned to prison on new felony convictions has dropped 48 percent. But critics charge that the parole board is retroactively imposing their beliefs on inmates who were sentenced long before Pataki was elected. "The parole commissioners are playing a role they are not supposed to play," says the wife of one parolee. "They are re-sentencing in effect. They are playing a judicial role" (Caher 2006).

It is expected that gubernatorial appointees reflect not only the values of the individual who chooses them but also societal norms, which shift over time. As public opinion changes, the attitudes of public officials swing back and forth as well. When voters perceive that those they have elected are unresponsive to those changes, they have the opportunity to vote that individual out of office. But for political appointees, such as those selected to sit on the New York Board of Parole, there is no way the public can register approval or disapproval. The legacy of their decisions lasts years beyond the shelf life of the governor.

CHAPTER 4

Managerial Discretion at the Federal Level

On September 8, 1974, President Gerald R. Ford made a decision that would become a defining moment in U.S. history. In a nationally televised speech from the Oval Office, the President somberly announced that he was signing Proclamation 4311 granting a pardon to former President Richard M. Nixon.

> "As President, my primary concern must always be the good of all the people of the United States whose servant I am. As a man, my first consideration is to be true to my own convictions and my own conscience. My conscience tells me clearly and certainly that I cannot prolong the bad dreams that continue to open a chapter that is closed. My conscience tells me that only I, as President, have the constitutional power to firmly shut and seal this book" (Ford 1974).

On June 17, 1972, five men, including the security director for the Committee for the Re-Election of the President, were arrested on charges they had broken into the headquarters of the Democratic National Committee at the Watergate office building in Washington, DC. Two other men with close ties to President Richard M. Nixon were linked to the break-in, and later indicted by a federal grand jury. As their trial began, five of the defendants pleaded guilty, and soon after, the remaining two were convicted. One of the men wrote a letter to the trial judge saying that perjury had been committed during the trial and that others had been involved in the Watergate incident. Several White House aides subsequently resigned, as did the U.S. Attorney General. The White House counsel, cooperating with federal prosecutors, testified before the Senate Watergate Committee that President Nixon was participating in a cover-up of the break-in within a few days of the burglary. In July 1973, Nixon, who had taped virtually every conversation held in the Oval Office, refused to give the Senate committee the tapes that could potentially implicate him in the cover-up. Seven former presidential aides were indicted in connection with the Watergate cover-up in March 1974; Nixon was named as an unindicted co-conspirator.

On May 9, 1974, the House Judiciary Committee began impeachment proceedings against the President, and in July, the U.S. Supreme Court ordered Nixon to surrender the White House tapes to a special Watergate prosecutor. Later that month, the House committee voted 27 to 11 to approve an article of impeachment that charged Nixon with obstructing justice, and two other articles of impeachment followed. Transcripts of the Nixon tapes revealed that the President had ordered the Federal Bureau of Investigation to drop its investigation of the Watergate break-in, fearing that it would reveal the involvement of his re-election campaign. After being told by three Republican members of Congress that he had little chance of avoiding impeachment, Nixon resigned as president on August 9, 1974 and Vice President Gerald Ford immediately took the oath of office.

One month later, in his Oval Office speech, Ford explained why he had decided to grant a pardon to Nixon.

> "The facts, as I see them, are that a former President of the United States, instead of enjoying equal treatment with any other citizen accused of violating the law, would be cruelly and excessively penalized either in preserving the presumption of his innocence or in obtaining a speedy determination of his guilt in order to repay a legal debt to society. But it is not the ultimate fate of Richard Nixon that most concerns me, though surely it deeply troubles every decent and compassionate person. My concern is the immediate future of this great country" (Ford 1974).

There was a national outcry against Ford after the speech, and he has been criticized for decades for his decision. Constitutional scholars agreed that the President had exercised his discretion legally, but political analysts said that Ford had acted rashly out of sympathy for his friend. Ford may have believed that the pardon would allow the nation to heal, but he undoubtedly underestimated the political backlash that followed. Voter anger was believed to have contributed to Ford's loss to Jimmy Carter when he ran for election on his own in 1976.

In 2001, Caroline Kennedy, daughter of the late President John F. Kennedy, presented Gerald Ford with the Profiles in Courage Award, named after her father's book. Kennedy called Ford a man who demonstrated that, "politics can be a noble profession." Her uncle, Senator Edward Kennedy, said that although he had criticized Ford at the time of the pardon, history had proven Ford right. "I would be less than candid, indeed less than human, if I didn't tell you how grateful—how profoundly grateful—Betty and I are for this recognition. Indeed, the award committee has displayed some of its own brand of courage" (Cable News Network 2001).

Previous chapters of this book have dealt with managerial discretion at the local and state levels, identifying many similarities in how decisions are made by mayors, city and county managers, governors, and their executive staff. At the federal level, the structure is much the same, but the impact of decisions is likely to be more widespread and significant. A city manager's decision on whether to enforce an ordinance banning homeless people from sleeping in a local park, for instance, affects fewer individuals than a decision by the federal Secretary of Health and Human Services to terminate a program for low income housing nationwide. Although Gerald Ford's decision to pardon Richard Nixon directly affected only one man who was not a violent criminal, it still had repercussions for decades.

The president's responsibilities include serving as manager-in-chief, with the authority to determine both policy and the individuals who implement policy. This chapter begins with an explanation of how the president's managers are selected through the appointment process, followed by a discussion of the use of managerial discretion in dealing with emergency situations, executive orders, and the president's use of discretion in foreign affairs and intelligence gathering.

Presidential Appointments

The framers of the Constitution were uncertain how to specify the level of discretion the president would be given in appointing members of his administration, and attempted to choose from several scenarios. One faction at the constitutional convention, led by James Madison, wanted to give the Senate appointment power to ensure that decisions would be made by a small group of enlightened members of society. Another group of delegates believed that by allowing the president to make his own appointments, one person could be held accountable for errors or problems.

The resulting document used a hybrid approach that gives the president the authority to nominate appointees, who must then be confirmed by the Senate. In *Federalist 76,* Alexander Hamilton noted, "One man of discernment is better fitted to analyze and estimate the peculiar qualities" of appointees, while being mindful that Senatorial approval "would be an excellent check upon a spirit of favoritism in the President" (Hamilton et al. 1982).

The appointment process is found in Article II, Section 2 of the U.S. Constitution, and requires almost all appointments to be confirmed by a majority vote of the Senate. Nomination of an individual is the first official step in the process, but the route to confirmation begins long before the president submits a name to the Senate. After each presidential election, Congress (alternating between the House and the Senate) publishes the "Plum Book," known officially as the *United States Government Policy and Supporting Positions.* It lists all non-competitive positions in the executive branch, whether filled or vacant, that the president has the authority to fill. The sheer number of presidential appointees (perhaps as many as 8,000) requires the development of a team to screen and evaluate potential members of the administration, including those considered part of the Executive Schedule, Senior

Executive Service, and Foreign Service (although federal law limits many of these positions to career appointments), and Schedule C positions (non-competitive jobs because of the confidential or policy-determining nature of the position's duties), among others.

There are no constitutional requirements that the president must explain why a person has been nominated, and historically, the reasons have not always involved an individual's level of expertise. Under the spoils system, discussed in the Introduction, political patronage was more often than not the reason why someone received an appointment. Other factors guiding contemporary presidents include "a blend of comfort, ideology, loyalty, competence, long-time service, and integrity" (Campbell 2001).

Often unmentioned, however, is whether the nominee is "confirmable." While the nominee is thoroughly vetted through more than 50 pages of applicant information as well as financial disclosure documents, background checks, interviews, and other clearance procedures, the second stage of the appointment process—confirmation—is highly politicized. Appointees expect to be grilled by members of Senate committees, must suffer through minute examination of their political and personal records, and realize that even the most minor juvenile transgression is likely to be exposed. In addition, the media has made nominees fair game for innuendo and speculation about their worthiness to join the public service, making the prospect of enticing someone to volunteer for such treatment less and less likely.

It has long been argued that the presidential appointment process is ineffective, as one scholar testified at a Congressional hearing:

> "In the early 1980s, I helped to write a book called *America's Un-Elected Government* that complained about some of the flaws in the presidential appointments process. Watching the travails of the Reagan administration as it sought to get its appointees in place, it was hard then to imagine that things could get much worse. But in retrospect that seems like almost a golden age for presidential appointments. The average Republican appointee was confirmed and in place in a little over 5 months. That was about twice as long as it took the Kennedy appointees to get into place" (Mackenzie 2001).

Despite the criticism about the appointment process, there is little disagreement that the president, as the chief executive in charge of the vast federal bureaucracy, must also look for persons with strong managerial skills. Beyond their political acumen, executive branch managers are "more than just leaders of bureaucracy. They are also key controllers of what agencies do. They push the president's orders downward into the federal bureaucracy, oversee the execution of the laws and represent their departments and agencies on Capitol Hill" (Light 1999, 519).

Judicial Appointments

It would be difficult to argue that one type of appointee is more influential than another, but judicial appointees are especially scrutinized for their legal record as well as their expertise because they serve for life. Of the 156 nominations to the U.S. Supreme Court between 1789 and 2005, 35 were not confirmed by the Senate, representing 30 individuals (some persons were nominated more than once). According to a report by the Congressional Research Service, confirmation failed for many reasons, including: opposition to the nominating President, the nominee's views, or the incumbent members of the court; senatorial courtesy; perceived political unreliability of the nominee; perceived lack of ability; interest group opposition; and fear of altering the balance of the Court. When the Senate has failed to confirm a nominee (11 were rejected by a vote of the full Senate), the president has the option of re-nominating the person, and five of the 30 were later re-nominated and confirmed (Hogue 2005).

One scholar divides Senate confirmations into three historical stages. Between 1922 and 1955, members of the Senate seldom questioned nominees, and most appointees were approved without substantial debate. From 1955 to 1967, the Senate Judiciary Committee routinely posed questions to the nominee, who appeared before the committee as a part of the confirmation process. From 1987 on, the Senate has made confirmation hearings "occasions for conflict and grandstanding" (Katzmann 1997, 19).

The nomination of one Supreme Court justice was so controversial that it spawned a new verb, to *bork* someone, defined as destroying a judicial nominee through a concerted attack on his character, background, and philosophy. Robert Heron Bork was a native of Pittsburgh who had served as a Marine, been a private attorney and law professor, and was Solicitor General of the United States before returning to private practice. In 1981, he was nominated by President Ronald Reagan to fill a vacant seat on the U.S. Court of Appeals for the District of Columbia Circuit, and received Senate confirmation. President Reagan nominated Bork to the U.S. Supreme Court on July 1, 1987 to replace Justice Lewis F. Mumford. The Senate debate over confirmation was protracted and personal, with the judge's video rental history becoming part of the controversy over his nomination. Several organizations aired television commercials urging senators to vote against confirmation, while others felt he was too blunt and partisan. On October 23, the Senate rejected the nomination on a vote of 42 to 58. Bork resigned from the Court of Appeals, and Reagan's nomination of Anthony Kennedy was subsequently confirmed.

It is arguable whether Reagan could have foreseen the controversy over Bork, or if the nominee had been appropriately scrutinized by Reagan's aides before the nomination was even made. What is important about the controversy is that many scholars believe the Senate hearings had a chilling effect on future judicial nominees. Basic judicial competence was no longer a satisfactory standard, nor was a nominee's adherence to the president's ideological values. Partisan affiliation is often not an issue, but how a potential justice rates on the liberal–conservative spectrum now is important, especially on issues such as abortion and others that might potentially come before the court. While most recent nominees have declined to comment on purely hypothetical circumstances, they are still asked about controversial topics to determine not only what they say, but how they say it. Those perceived as being evasive, unfamiliar with the law, or simply unpopular have a difficult road ahead.

Thus, while the constitution appears to balance the authority for judicial nominations between the president and the legislative branch, the level of discretion presidents once had has clearly been reduced in the last few decades as Congress has become more partisan and ideological. Underscoring that observation, the proportion of nominations to defeats is much higher for the Supreme Court than for any other position to which the president makes appointments (Campbell 2001).

Other Presidential Appointments

While the controversies over judicial nominees have limited the scope of presidential discretion, other nominees who serve more as managers than policymakers have usually benefited from Senate deference. Some senators take their role in the confirmation process literally in belief that the constitutional prescription of "advice" to the president is only that task. Others recognize that the majority of the president's other appointments are relatively routine, and that at most, the individual is likely to serve no more than eight years, the length of two presidential administrations.

Studies of executive appointments provide an opportunity to compare the differences among various types of appointees and the presidents who nominate them. Democratic presidents, for instance, are more likely to nominate women to senior administrative positions requiring Senate confirmation. Of President Jimmy Carter's more than 1,000 nominations, nearly 18 percent were women, but under President Ronald Reagan, fewer than 12 percent of his 2,300 appointees were female. George H. W. Bush raised the number to nearly 20 percent, but his successor, Bill Clinton, more than doubled it to 42 percent. Once a position in the president's cabinet becomes available, there are clear differences in the time interval between the nomination and confirmation, especially when departments are compared among one another longitudinally. Nominees to be Secretary of Labor, Commerce, and Attorney General tend to take the longest to be nominated and are almost the longest at being confirmed. Cabinet positions that take the shortest amount of time to fill are usually at the Department of State, Treasury, and Education (Campbell 2001).

In the area of foreign policy, presidents are typically given wide discretion in awarding ambassadorial positions, often because of a tacit agreement that the person serves a ceremonial, rather than policymaking, role. As part of his reform-oriented agenda, President Carter established a Presidential Advisory Board on Ambassadorial Appointments in 1977. Although he had the power to appoint the board's members, the goal was to professionalize the ambassadorial ranks by seeking additional information on both career and non-career appointees. Carter hoped to avoid some of the controversy that had occurred when previous administrations had nominated ambassadors who were perceived as political payoffs, or unqualified for other reasons.

Under the appointment board, the Department of State was asked to furnish information about the nominee's qualifications, although the executive order was very vague in identifying what factors qualify a prospective ambassador. The language referred only to the requirements of particular ambassadorial posts, evaluation criteria, and information regarding the potential nominee, along with "other information the board deems appropriate in order to render an informed judgment concerning a prospective nominee's qualifications and suitability" (Carter 1977). When he became president in 1981, Ronald Reagan promptly revoked Carter's executive order, abolishing the board altogether.

Since that time, appointments to ambassadorial positions have increasingly been subject to confirmation hearings by the Senate, with only a handful avoiding the process or not obtaining confirmation. When it has appeared that an ambassador might not win confirmation, presidents have several tools at their disposal. James Hormel, an heir to the Hormel food fortune, had been nominated by President Clinton as ambassador to Luxembourg in 1997. Prior to the nomination, Hormel had served as dean of the University of Chicago School of Law, was a member of the U.S. delegation to the United Nations Human Rights Commission in Geneva, and was previously confirmed by the Senate to serve as a member of the U.S. delegation to the U.N. General Assembly session in 1996. The Senate Foreign Relations Committee approved the nomination in the first stage of the confirmation process, but Republican leaders in the Senate refused to allow the nomination to come to a floor vote.

Hormel, who is openly gay, was attacked by conservative organizations that accused Clinton of giving Hormel, "a government-sanctioned platform to advance the gay agenda." The executive director of the Traditional Values Coalition accused the nominee of being, "a purveyor of smut" and of "cheering on child molesters and transvestite nuns" (Cable News Network 1999a). Although it appeared Clinton had sufficient Senate votes to have Hormel confirmed, he chose instead to use his recess appointment privilege, a constitutional mechanism that allows a president to make an appointment in order to maintain continuity in administrative government when

Congress is not in session. Recess appointments are technically temporary and expire at the end of a Senate session, and they have become increasingly common. Ronald Reagan made 240 recess appointments; George H. W. Bush made 77; Bill Clinton made 140; and George W. Bush made over 110 recess appointments during his first term as president.

The high point in the opposition's discontent with Bush administration appointees was in December 2004, when he was faced with disapproval of several of his second term nominees, including Alberto Gonzales (later confirmed as Attorney General in February 2005), Harriet Miers (nominated as a justice to the U.S. Supreme Court but later withdrawn from consideration), and John Bolton as ambassador to the United Nations.

Bolton, nominated in March 2005, was considered an unexpected choice for the position even though he had considerable experience in working at the Department of State, with the U.S. Agency for International Development, and as Undersecretary of State for Arms Control and International Security. In the latter position, he was responsible for implementing the president's policies for preventing weapons proliferation. Democrats attempted to thwart Bolton's confirmation through a filibuster; Republicans threatened a "nuclear option" by requiring a vote on the president's nominees to consist of a simple majority instead of three-fifths of the Senate, a move that would have had system-wide ramifications. Although Bolton had made it past the Senate Foreign Relations Committee, criticism from within the President's own party stalled debate on the Senate floor. When Congress went into summer recess, Bush appointed Bolton to the position, which is temporary until 2007.

Crises and Managerial Discretion

Presidential scholars give great weight to political resources and their importance in agenda-setting and policymaking. Each chief executive enters office with predetermined checks and balances, but decisions are also shaped by individual attributes, especially those related to a president's ability to acquire political capital. The facts that the president is selected in a nationwide election and is constantly seen on television give him more leverage to act in a discretionary manner subject to constitutional and political realities (Neustadt 1990, 237). However, while having nationwide visibility is a political asset, it is not everything. Most observers would agree that information, expertise, public approval, and professional reputation are critical in providing the executive with the ability to take discretionary actions.

Presidents must also rely upon other actors within the executive branch, and must depend upon their ability to make instantaneous decisions during periods of crisis. Many important choices related to foreign policy crises are made by the Joint Chiefs of Staff, who not only have experience but technical information related to security issues immediately at hand. Other types of crises depend upon established executive branch agencies and their staff, a factor that became extremely apparent after the terrorist attacks on the World Trade Center on September 11, 2001.

Aside from war and other armed conflict, the federal government has been a somewhat belated crisis manager, especially during disasters. For the first 160 years of American history, the United States had no general policy or agency to deal with disasters, human-caused or natural. This is not because of a lack of opportunity; catastrophes occurred regularly in the emerging nation. The New Madrid Earthquakes (1811–1812), the Chicago Fire (1873), the Johnstown Flood (1889), the Galveston Hurricane (1900), the San Francisco Earthquake (1906), and other twentieth century disasters caused billions of dollars in damage by today's standards. Between 1803 and 1947, Congress issued 128 specific acts expressing sympathy for the events, and occasionally provided some token financial assistance (Platt 1999).

Responsibility for rescues, repair, and reconstruction, however, was left to local governments, working in conjunction with churches, community groups, and less often, state governments. After the lower Mississippi River broke through levees in 1927, spreading floodwaters over 20,000 square miles, the governors of the six affected states pleaded to the federal government for assistance, the first time when federal policy to deal with a disaster on such a large scale was created. But for the most part, that aid took the form of major infrastructure projects such as dams, undertaken by the Army Corps of Engineers, and not direct financial assistance to victims.

It was not until 1950 that the federal government became deeply involved in reducing the impact of disasters on communities and local residents, with passage of the Federal Disaster Relief Act. A series of hurricanes in the 1950s, the 1964 Alaskan Earthquake, devastating hurricanes along the Gulf Coast in the 1960s, and earthquakes in the 1970s made federal control a necessity as the damage figures became far more than state or local governments could absorb. But legislation also made clear that federal aid was to supplement, not replace, other assistance.

The Federal Emergency Management Agency (FEMA) was established by President Jimmy Carter's executive order in 1979, partially in recognition of the morass of agencies that had become involved in disaster response. These included the Army Corps, the Reconstruction Finance Corporation, Bureau of Public Roads, and the Department of Housing and Urban Development, to name just a few. His policy centralized disaster management until the 1980s, when FEMA was assigned responsibility for "integrated emergency management" during the Reagan administration. Under that policy, FEMA was expected to handle almost every imaginable crisis, from ice storms and wildfires to nuclear war. During the Clinton administration, FEMA was once again retooled to limit its responsibility to domestic natural hazards (Platt 1999).

Defining disaster has become an artful enterprise, identified partly in fact and partly in carefully crafted legislative language in Public Law 100-707. The 1950 statute has been amended to read,

> "'Major disaster' means any natural catastrophe (including any hurricane, tornado, storm, high water, wind driven water, tidal wave, tsunami, earthquake, volcanic eruption, landslide, mudslide, snowstorm, or drought), or, regardless of cause, any fire, flood, or explosion, in any part of the United States, which in the determination of the President causes damage of sufficient severity and magnitude to warrant major disaster assistance under this Act to supplement the efforts and available resources of states, local governments, and disaster relief organizations in alleviating the damage, loss, hardship, or suffering caused thereby."

In 1974, disaster was redefined under Public Law 93-288 with the creation of a new category of presidential declarations authorized for emergency, defined as, "any occasion or instance for which, in the determination of the president, federal assistance is needed to supplement state and local efforts and capabilities to save lives and to protect property and public health and safety, or to lessen or avert the threat of a catastrophe in any part of the United States." However, the distinction between an "emergency" and a "major disaster" has never been clearly specified, and most presidential declarations have been designated as "major disasters." About two thirds of the requests for a disaster declaration were granted by the president between January 1, 1953 and August 19, 1994 (Platt 1999, 19).

The Government Accounting Office (now known as the Government Accountability Office) responded to the need for some parameters on executive discretion in its 1981 study of disaster declarations. After reviewing 31 gubernatorial requests for disaster assistance, the GAO concluded there was "a lack of consistency in the quality and methods of assessments and lack of knowledge as to FEMA's methods of evaluation that creates doubt as to whether the federal government is only providing supplementary assistance and whether each request is judged in a fair and equitable manner" (U.S. Government Accounting Office 1981).

In response, FEMA prepared draft rules that would reduce federal disaster relief expenditures by using a complex formula that included a state deductible and a decrease in the federal cost share from 75 percent to 50 percent. The proposed regulations garnered considerable opposition by members of Congress and local government officials, and the changes were withdrawn from consideration. In 1988, the Robert T. Stafford Disaster Relief and Emergency Assistance Act even went a step further by prohibiting the use of any formula or scale to deny disaster assistance to an area. The statute effectively gave FEMA officials unbridled discretion in determining how much aid was not only required, but desirable (Platt 1999, 19–20).

During congressional hearings on the military's role in dealing with disasters in February 2006, Senator Joe Lieberman of Connecticut told the Senate Committee on Homeland Security and Governmental Affairs that there were both practical and constitutional implications to consider. Calling the Defense Department's response to Hurricane Katrina, "as passive as most other agencies," Lieberman criticized the military's situational awareness and said the Pentagon was hesitant to move necessary assets unless they were requested. When Deputy Secretary of Defense Gordon England saw pictures of Katrina's damage on television, he concluded that troops and equipment needed to be deployed immediately without the normal paperwork. But Lieberman also said, "the federal government appeared to be operating on the fly, and the roles of the military—National Guard and active duty—appear to have been part of a response that was cobbled together as the week went on. In the end, the lack of a plan led to unnecessary confusion, unnecessary bureaucratic struggles, and more human suffering than should have been" (Lieberman 2006).

Lieberman's questions about the role of the military in the management of disasters were not new. Interest increased in the aftermath of the September 11 terrorist attacks. Even though local responses in New York were considered heroic, on a larger scale, there continued to be skepticism about national preparedness. One observer noted, "State and local governments criticized the federal government for talking tough on terrorism but failed to write checks." For their part, some federal officials had long criticized some state and local officials for failing to take emergency planning seriously enough (Kettl 2004, 71).

Although it is unlikely that the military will take on the duties of law enforcement officers in any upcoming disaster, it is certain that their managerial roles will be considered in light of what happened after the Hurricane Katrina disaster. Some officials, such as Undersecretary England, used their own discretion in deciding to send in federal troops, while others appear to have sat on the sidelines. In public organizations where the chain of command is extraordinarily powerful, such as the U.S. military, crisis management may be left to the manager-in-chief.

The President and Executive Orders

While presidential discretion is partly a function of political resources, the most visible manifestation of that power is in the discharge of constitutional responsibilities. Discretion exists in so many forms and at varying degrees, but it is arguably more contested in applications of the doctrine of executive privilege and use of executive orders. Even after Congress's attempt to check the president's war-making powers, generally, the president retains considerable discretion in the conduct of foreign policy.

Much has been written on executive orders and directives (Mayer 2000; Cooper 2002; Howell 2003), and presidential determinations are issued under statutory authority and directed to government officers. An executive order has the same force of law after thirty days if Congress fails to nullify it. That implies much discretionary power enabling presidents to ignore aspects of the doctrine of separation of powers because the orders are not ratified by Congress. Executive orders are dictatorial powers originally intended for national emergency situations such as war.

Most scholars observe that executive order authority derives from the constitutional provision in Article II, Section 3 empowering the president to "take care that the law be faithfully executed." However, these are laws already passed and not laws created through the Executive Order. Some commentators question the validity of discretionary powers exhibited in issuance of those orders, while others contend that executive orders are based on existing statutes or the president's other constitutional responsibilities. These orders are primarily issued to establish executive branch agencies, to modify bureaucratic rules or actions, change decision-making procedures or give substance and force to existing statutes.

What seems to account for their proliferation is a philosophical position taken from John Locke's treatise on government. In Locke's formulation, the president should be permitted to exercise as much discretion as possible—even if it means contradicting the law—or the public good in times of dire emergencies. Locke defined this act of discretion as a *prerogative*. The principal idea was to ensure that the good of society be preserved during tough times. Without discretionary power, the executive would not act to defend public interests. In some situations, legislators are not able to foresee and provide suitable laws as required, leaving the executor of laws the power to act accordingly. The theory also stipulates that the legislature frequently provides vague language in statutory provisions, allowing the executive considerable leeway at the policy refinement and implementation stage.

Because the potential for abuse is strong, the Supreme Court has been drawn into the constitutional debate, ruling that it is up to Congress to protect itself. Part of the concern is that the executive branch of the government has grown in both size and power, perhaps encroaching on Congressional legislative powers. What Congress does is to ensure that there is sufficient public awareness of policies implemented through executive orders.

Presidential lawmaking by executive order has grown with the modern presidency. In principle, presidents are not supposed to legislate, but the executive power necessitates some degree of de facto lawmaking. Clearly, this power is not unlimited. When Harry Truman seized the steel industry in order to head off a threatened strike that would have hindered the execution of the Korean War, the Supreme Court ruled Truman's executive order was illegal. More recently, a federal district court struck down Bill Clinton's executive order regarding permanent strikers' replacements, a decision the administration chose not to appeal. There has been a trend in recent years for presidents to be increasingly vague about the legal basis for their executive orders (Bartlett 2001).

By all measures, the lack of specificity in statutory provisions makes it harder for Congress and the courts to determine the legal basis for presidential actions. Furthermore, claims of constitutional authority do not lend themselves easily to legal scrutiny unless reviewed by the Supreme Court.

Examples of presidential use of executive orders in lieu of Congressional context abound in history. For example, one of the most described uses of managerial discretion at the presidential level was Andrew Jackson's forceful removal of law-abiding Cherokee off their ancestral lands. The Cherokee fought the illegal eviction in the U.S. Supreme Court and won. Nevertheless, Jackson, using discretionary power, defied the Court's ruling and removed members of the Cherokee nation from their homelands; over 4,000 Cherokees died on the infamous "Trail of Tears." Another example of discretionary power was Abraham Lincoln's suspension of many fundamental constitutional rights during the Civil War. His actions included closing down newspapers opposed to wartime policies and imprisonment of dissidents. Lincoln suspended the right of *habeas corpus*. His justification for those drastic actions was to preserve the Union.

In 1917, Woodrow Wilson failed to persuade Congress to arm U.S. vessels plying hostile German waters before the United States' entry into World War I. When Congress balked, he invoked the policy through an Executive Order. Franklin Delano Roosevelt issued Executive Order No. 9066 in December 1941 to round up thousands of Japanese residents in the United States for internment into concentration camps. Their property was confiscated; most Japanese Americans never were compensated for their losses. It is instructive that both Lincoln and Roosevelt's actions were during wartime decisions.

Most recently, President George W. Bush issued numerous executive orders pertaining to homeland security, the war against al-Qaida terrorists, and the changes in information and communication technology, all reflecting the socio-political realities of the new millennium. Among the most notable are Executive Order 13234, which established the Presidential Task Force on Citizen Preparedness in the War on Terrorism, and Executive Order 13200, which created the President's Information Technology Advisory Committee.

Executive Privilege as Discretion

Just as executive orders have no basis in the Constitution, the concept of executive privilege is extra legal as well. Typically, executive privilege is used by a president who refuses to provide information or documents related to the administration.

Often, the refusal is based on the grounds of national security and secrecy, although those reasons are subject to considerable interpretation. Some historians and legal scholars believe that the doctrine of separation of powers is the source of executive privilege, because it implies that the Executive Branch has the privilege to resist encroachments by the legislative and judicial branches. Others contend that executive privilege does not exist at all because it was not included by the framers as part of their intent in writing the Constitution.

President George Washington was the first to rely upon executive privilege in 1796 when he refused to comply with a request by the House of Representatives to provide documents related to the signing of the Jay Treaty with England. Washington's reasoning was that, because the Constitution gives only the Senate the power to ratify treaties, there was no reason why the House should be seeking the documents. He later turned the documents over to the Senate.

Another early case involved President Thomas Jefferson, who was asked to produce documents sought by the defense counsel in the trial against Aaron Burr for treason. The U.S. Supreme Court, in an opinion written by John Marshall, commanded Jefferson to comply even though Jefferson said that release of a letter he purportedly held would endanger public safety. In ruling that the president could not be excluded by the law granting Burr due process in court, Marshall said that only the court could determine whether in fact public safety was at risk, not the Executive Branch (Dorf 2002).

The case that gave new definition to the concept of executive privilege is the one behind the incident described at the beginning of this chapter involving President Richard Nixon. As part of the Watergate investigation in 1974, the Supreme Court considered whether Nixon could claim that the privilege existed for documents not related to national security. Nixon contended that he did not have to comply with the special prosecutor's subpoena for the tapes made in the Oval Office. Although he did not admit that the tapes implicated him in any criminal wrongdoing, Nixon said that government officials would not be able to speak or write honestly if they knew those documents or tape recordings were not private. Public dissemination of confidential information was certainly an issue, the Court ruled, but executive privilege was not absolute. The government's interest in prosecuting criminal actions must be balanced against confidentiality, and in this situation, the Court ordered Nixon to release the tapes. Nixon complied two weeks later, and then resigned as president four days later.

Subsequent claims of executive privilege have not been as controversial as the one involving Nixon, but they have been contentious in different ways. President George W. Bush signed an executive order in 2001 that rescinded another signed by President Ronald Reagan implementing the 1978 Presidential Records Act. Under the Bush order, former presidents could claim that under the executive privilege doctrine, they could withhold certain papers and materials produced during their administration. The discretion about what to withhold lies totally with the former president, who may, in effect, lock up whatever materials are chosen.

Subsequent issues have broadened the doctrine in ways even the Supreme Court may not have envisioned. In 1993, the constitutional question was whether executive privilege applied to discussions between the president and persons outside of government. First Lady Hillary Rodham Clinton had served as chair of a healthcare reform panel during her husband's administration, and the group's meetings had been private. The Association of American Physicians and Surgeons had contended that under the Federal Advisory Committee Act, the panel's meetings must be open to the public if the person is not an officer or employee of the government. The U.S. Court of Appeals managed to sidestep the issue by deciding that the First Lady was in fact an officer or employee of the government, so she was not required to abide by the open meeting statute. Otherwise, the court might have had to determine whether the meetings ought to have been open and deliberations disclosed, even though they involved a non-government First Lady and any other government officials who were part of the executive branch (Dorf 2002).

In another Clinton administration action in 1996, the U.S. Department of Justice was asked to determine the applicability of executive privilege to deliberations regarding the assertion of privilege. At issue was whether documents reflecting and constituting deliberative communications within the White House Counsel's Office and between that office and the Department of Justice relating to their advice and recommendation about executive privilege the president was asserting were, in themselves, privileged. President Clinton had been issued a subpoena from the House Committee on Government Reform and Oversight, and he had asked his advisors whether he was required to answer the congressional request. The Acting Assistant Attorney General relied on the ruling in the Nixon case, stressing that the separation of powers makes executive privilege fundamental to the operation of government. According to his letter of opinion, "A president and those who assist him must be free to explore alternatives in the process of shaping policies and making decisions and to do so in a way many would be unwilling to express except privately" (Schroeder 1996).

Executive privilege was also claimed in 2002 when Vice President Dick Cheney refused to provide the Government Accounting Office (GAO) with information about meetings held with Cheney's National Energy Policy Development Group. The GAO is non-partisan, but is considered a part of the legislative branch of government because it reports to Congress. The Comptroller-General, who heads the GAO, had simply asked for a list of the names of the participants in the meetings, rather than the content of any discussions that were held, which might not be covered under case law. More importantly, it is unclear whether the privilege also extends to the vice president, rather than just to the president.

The administration of George W. Bush also attempted to claim executive privilege in March 2004 when the President's National Security Advisor, Condoleezza Rice, was called to testify before the National Commission on Terrorist Attacks, better known as the 9/11 Commission. Rice initially contended that executive privilege allowed her to refuse to testify before the legislative commission as part of the separation of powers doctrine, but she later was compelled to do so. It is unclear whether the use of executive privilege is being constitutionally expanded to cover those within the entire Executive Office of the President, or whether courts will continue to deal with the issue on an ad hoc basis. Managerial discretion is also a concern when other agencies are concerned.

The Power to Veto

Most of this book focuses on discretion that is exercised through the use of power that is enumerated in constitutions or statutes by managers. When the president acts as the chief manager of the government, he has some discretion in deciding how to handle policy issues formally brought to him by Congress. In the debate over the U.S. Constitution, the framers were aware of the need to give the president a check on congressional power. As part of strategy for balancing out the authority of any one branch of government, one of those powers is found in Article I, Section 7 of the Constitution. This section gives the president the power to veto any bill passed by Congress, but also limits his ability to do so. Constitutional amendments, for instance, cannot be subject to a presidential veto. A president has 10 days (excepting Sundays) to act upon a measure that is presented. Although it is not well known, the president also has the power to refer the bill to the head of a department within the federal government with jurisdiction over the subject matter for investigation and a report. Ideally, the report helps the president to reach a decision about whether to approve it. If approved and signed, a messenger informs Congress, and the bill is designated as enrolled.

If the president decides to veto a bill, it is sent back to the House or Senate (wherever the bill originated) along with a message stating the reasons for the veto. Either body then has the choice to refer the measure to a standing committee, table it for possible consideration at a later date, or order that it be considered on a specific date. Members may also move to reconsider the bill immediately, which requires a two thirds vote of the chamber where the bill first originated. When a president chooses not to approve a bill within the ten-day period but also chooses not to exercise veto power, it becomes law without presidential approval.

Since the founding of the federal government in 1789, 36 of the 43 presidents have exercised their veto authority a total of 2,551 times, according to the Congressional Research Service. Congress has overridden these vetoes on 106 occasions. Presidents have vetoed 80 appropriations bills, and Congress has overridden 12 of those vetoes. Prior to 1960, most of the vetoes were over private bills—legislation that would benefit a single individual or company—which were almost never overridden. George Washington vetoed two bills; his successor, John Adams, did not veto any during his term, nor did Thomas Jefferson. By the time Andrew Jackson became president, vetoes were used much more frequently, with Jackson vetoing 21 measures, and Ulysses S. Grant adding 45 more to the total. The record for most vetoes belongs to Presidents Grover Cleveland (414) and Franklin D. Roosevelt (635). Not since Millard Fillmore (1850–1853) has a president served a full term without exercising the veto power and not since Thomas Jefferson (1801–1809) has a two-term president left office without vetoing a bill (Kosar 2006).

Considerable literature exists on the topic of presidential vetoes and why they are—or are not—used. Robert Spitzer's study, for instance, calls the veto power the "touchstone of the American presidency" (Spitzer 1988). "The general presumption in the literature about vetoes and overrides is that the actors involved are always focused on legislative outcomes. It is assumed that all actors have as their primary goal the realization or the blockage of some legislative proposal and that defeat is costly (in terms of public, institutional, and/or political prestige)" (Conley and Kreppel 2001). Some scholars contend that the president is now less able to influence roll call votes in Congress because of the nature of divided government, where the president and legislature are of different political parties. Others believe that the strategic use of an implied veto serves as a way of persuading members of Congress to vote one way or another (Deen and Arnold 2002).

A study of the administration of George H. W. Bush, for instance, found that he exercised 162 "public" and 39 "private" veto threats during the 102nd Congress. Of the 162 public threats, 69 percent involved bills categorized as "minor," as were 95 percent of bills threatened by private veto threats, defined as those that were never reported in the national media. Eleven of the 162 public veto threats were used against bills considered "highly salient," including two related to the issue of abortion. Still, researchers conclude that the Bush administration was involved most often in highly complex negotiations behind the scenes, rather than the highly charged rhetoric often associated with the threat of a veto (Conley 2003).

Use of a presidential veto is not without cost, however. While presidents may exercise the veto as a constitutional use of presidential power, doing so in the public eye may lead voters to the conclusion that he is unable to persuade members of Congress to agree with his position. Inter-branch confrontation also leads to "blame game" politics between the White House and Capitol Hill. Reneging on a veto threat might result in some form of electoral retaliation if they are perceived as bluffing.

Perhaps the most controversial element of the veto power in contemporary administrations has been the proposed line item veto, which would allow a president to rescind specific spending or tax legislation that has been passed by Congress. At least 11 presidents have sought this authority to give them discretion over spending bills when they were wrapped into other, larger measures. President George W. Bush supported the Line Item Veto Act of 2006 that would give him the power to "rein in wasteful spending, reduce the budget deficit, and improve accountability," consistent with the Constitution. Ten years earlier, Congress had enacted the Line Item Veto Act of 1996, which was declared unconstitutional by the U.S. Supreme Court in 1998 (White House 2006a).

In July 2006, George W. Bush exercised his veto power for the first time during his previous five and a half years in office. At issue was a proposed expansion of the use of embryonic stem cells in medical research. Both the president and members of Congress had been actively lobbied to pass legislation that would end what amounted to a chokehold on researchers seeking cures for diseases like dementia, Parkinson's disease, and spinal cord injuries. Polls showed that the vast majority of Americans, perhaps as many as three fourths, supported this research, as did celebrities such as Michael J. Fox and Mary Tyler Moore, and many political figures including former First Lady Nancy Reagan. Despite majority approval in both the House and the Senate, Bush acted upon his personal belief that the research was unacceptable. In an announcement in the East Room of the White House where Bush was surrounded by *snowflakes* (children who were the product of embryos that had been surgically implanted in women where a couple had been infertile), the president said that the researchers should not be allowed to treat the embryos as "spare parts."

Bush had signed 1,130 bills before invoking the veto, an action that was interpreted in several ways. Some observers believe that he was continuing to shore up his conservative base before the 2006 congressional elections, hoping to energize campaigns in several key states including Missouri. Others theorized that the president was following his long-held personal beliefs that linked the use of embryonic stem cells to the abortion debate. A spokesman for the conservative Heritage Foundation said, "This is a highly charged moral issue that does not lend itself to legislative compromise. It is easier to negotiate and split the difference on highway bills, spending bills, than a core moral issue like the use of federal funds for stem cell research" (Benedetto and Stone 2006). It is likely that the president's decision to use his veto power will be one of the enduring legacies of his administration, and an example of how discretionary decisions can acutely affect the lives of millions of Americans with the single stroke of a pen.

From the perspective of presidential discretion, Bush was able to preserve his *policy reputation,* a term used to describe whether Congress is aware of the president's position prior to a vote. In this instance, it was clear that Bush had no intention of trying to accommodate or compromise with Congress.

Discretion within Executive Branch Agencies

The presidency as an institution is internally complex, with numerous organizational units. In addition to the vice president, the 15 members of the president's Cabinet, and their respective departments, the Executive Office of the President (EOP) includes the Council of Economic Advisors, Council on Environmental Quality, Office of Administration, Office of Management and Budget, Office of National Drug Control Policy, Office of Science and Technology Policy, the President's Foreign Intelligence Advisory Board, the U.S. Trade Representative, and the White House Office. Within the White House Office are the Domestic Policy Council, Homeland Security Council, National Economic Council, Office of Faith-Based and Community Initiatives, Office of the First Lady, Office of National AIDS Policy, Privacy and Civil Liberties Oversight Board, USA Freedom Corps, White House Fellows Office, and the White House Military Office. Under the administration of George W. Bush, Cabinet-level rank has also been accorded to the Administrator of the Environmental Protection Agency, Director of the Office of Management and Budget, Director of National Drug Control Policy, and the U.S. Trade Representative (White House 2006b).

The EOP has experienced considerable expansion, growing from one executive office unit in 1924 to six in 1939 under President Franklin Roosevelt. By the end of President Harry Truman's administration in 1952, there were nine units, and ten during the second term of President Dwight Eisenhower (1958); it dropped to eight in 1962 under President John F. Kennedy, and then bounced up to twelve in 1968 under Lyndon Johnson. The Nixon administration, often accused of running "the Imperial Presidency," increased the EOP to its highest level of 17 units in 1971, and this number dropped again to 11 under Presidents Carter and Reagan. After a brief increase from 12 to 14 under President George H. W. Bush, the number dropped back to 12 during the Clinton administration.

With so many organizational entities charged with carrying out the president's orders, it is expected that the managers of the units, from the cabinet secretaries on down, would be able to exercise much discretion in their operations. The president expects his appointees to be loyal to his vision, but there is also the realization that the agencies and offices cannot be micromanaged from the Oval Office. Three cases illustrate how managerial discretion has been interpreted: the Environmental Protection Agency, the Central Intelligence Agency, and the U.S. Department of Justice.

The Environmental Protection Agency

President Richard Nixon seized the opportunity to ride the wave of environmental activism that began with the enactment of the National Environmental Policy Act in 1969 and the first Earth Day on April 22, 1970 by establishing the Environmental Protection Agency (EPA). As an independent agency, the EPA was not given Cabinet-level status, but its administrator was appointed by the president. Calling the 1970s "the environmental decade," Nixon used this opportunity to harness control of the momentum that had developed to shape policy for the next several years.

In February 1970, for instance, he called upon Congress to pass a new air pollution statute, beating congressional Democrats to the punch on making the environment their own issue. Subsequent legislation passed during the Nixon administration dealt with water pollution, solid waste management, pesticide use, dumping of waste into oceans and coastal waters, and endangered species. More importantly, however, Nixon's appointment of William Ruckelshaus as administrator of the EPA made clear that future environmental policy would be controlled by the executive branch and not by the environmental community. Still, Ruckelshaus was able to cobble together a staff of bureaucrats from other agencies and a few scientists, and during its first sixty days, the EPA brought five times as many actions as the agencies it inherited had brought during any similar period. Ruckelshaus initiated a strong program that went after corporate polluters, especially those accused of illegal sewage discharges, establishing the EPA's credibility for enforcement (Landy et al. 36). The reputation continued under the next administrator, Russell Train, who took over in 1973, and his successor under President Carter, Douglas Costle.

Initially, the EPA's budget reflected the national sentiment (and public opinion polls) that showed the nation's desire for cleaning up decades of pollution. In 1973, the agency's operating budget was about $500 million and by 1980 it had increased to $1.3 billion. The initial 7,000 employees hired in 1971 when the agency began operating nearly doubled by 1980, in part a reflection of Congress's continued support for the environment. But when Ronald Reagan took office as president in 1981, the EPA's direction changed dramatically under a series of administrators who followed a different policy agenda. With a strong electoral mandate, Reagan decided to change national policy by controlling the EPA's leadership, weakening the authority of established professionals in the agency, and reducing its budget.

His appointee as EPA administrator, Anne Gorsuch, had been a Colorado state legislator but had little direct managerial experience. Her friend, fellow Coloradan James Sanderson, had worked with a Denver firm that represented development and energy interests and conservative Republican supporter Adolph Coors. Her chief of staff, John Daniel, had been a lobbyist for the Denver firm, Johns Mansville, a manufacturer of asbestos products. The White House filled the rest of the EPA team with a trial lawyer for Exxon, the dean of engineering at New Mexico State University, a public relations specialist who had worked for Reagan when he served as governor of California, a paper industry lobbyist, and conservative lawyers. Not one of the staff had worked at EPA's Washington headquarters, and only Daniel had ever worked for EPA. Several key positions as assistant administrators were not filled for months, hampering the agency's abilities to fulfill vital functions. The agency was also reorganized to put political appointees in positions above career staff (Landy et al. 1994, 246–248).

Reagan made another decision that de-emphasized the environment by not appointing the EPA administrator to the Cabinet Council on Natural Resources, eliminating Gorsuch from key decisions involving environmental legislation such as the Clean Air Act. Under Executive Order 12291, Reagan also required all proposed new rules, including those involving environmental protection, to go through the Office of Management Budget for review and possible revision. The importance of the change was that it enabled the Reagan administration to determine if the cost of a proposed rule was greater than the expected benefit, a concept that characterized the administration's approach to regulatory reform. The idea was best expressed by Reagan himself, who had vowed he would get the government off the back of the nation's businesses.

To reduce that burden, one of Gorsuch's initial actions was to abolish the EPA's Office of Enforcement and its staff was relocated to various offices. Between 1980 and 1982, the number of cases that the EPA referred to the Justice Department declined by 50 percent (from 200 to 100) and the number of enforcement orders issued by the agency dropped by one third. Efforts at deregulation also included shifting responsibility from the federal level to the states, giving them increased discretion and reducing federal oversight. During that same period, the agency's budget declined from $701 million to $515 million, about the same level it had started with a decade earlier, even though the EPA's responsibilities had increased as a result of new legislation. Between 1981 and 1983, the agency's staff declined by nearly a quarter and many veteran employees simply resigned, more than forty percent left in less than a year (Landy et al. 1884, 250).

By the time she was forced to resign because of a scandal within the agency in 1983, Gorsuch had completely changed the agency from one that had taken an active role in promoting environmental protection and enforcing rules and statutes to one that had lost its most valuable and experienced staff and had almost no funds to operate its key programs. She had followed President Reagan's policy agenda, virtually dismantling the EPA through managerial decisions that were almost unknown to most of the public. When Ruckleshaus returned for a second time as EPA administrator, he was charged with reviving the agency, but at that point, the damage had already been done.

Since that time, a new battle has developed within the EPA over how much science should be considered in making policy decisions on key environmental issues. A series of case studies has shown that many choices have been made on the basis of incomplete or misleading data that have been used to support one policy choice over another. For instance, academic studies used to determine air quality standards for lead (especially that found in gasoline) were bundled up and then applied to lead found in drinking water, even though standards are developed by two different compartments within the agency. Another drinking water program that focused on arsenic in drinking water had initially made recommendations based on skin cancer studies. A new study showed that there might also be a danger from internal cancer. But when there was an unfounded rumor that the scientist involved with the study might have changed his mind after all, the staff recommended that the agency pursue additional research rather than revising the arsenic drinking water standard. In still another incident, the EPA used an unpublished report on cost-benefit analysis created by the Centers for Disease Control as part of a new regulation dealing with lead and copper contamination of drinking water. A later version of the report reduced the relationship of the benefits by a factor of three, but it was never published (Powell 1999).

These incidents could be viewed in two ways. On one hand, it could be argued that they represent the efforts of an agency to do its work under reduced resources and insufficient lead time, and tasks requiring a great deal of interpretation. On the other hand, some might argue that the EPA consistently uses its discretion in determining what scientific information it wants to use, or not use, which shapes policy decisions. Regardless of which argument seems more compelling, the mere fact that the agency has the ability to make those kinds of choices underscores the importance of managers and the roles they play in administering federal programs.

The Central Intelligence Agency

After the September 11, 2001 terrorist attacks, the Central Intelligence Agency (CIA) was faulted for not doing enough to stop the attacks by communicating directly with other federal agencies and coordinating its intelligence gathering with other governments. The public likely will never know whether the criticism is warranted because of the secretive nature of the agency's work, but questions about how information is gathered continue today. Although the CIA does not conduct intelligence gathering within the United States, in 2006, revelations about access to the records of domestic telephone and Internet service providers put pressure on another executive branch bureau, the National Security Agency (NSA). This agency does conduct domestic surveillance and other intelligence activities, and the public frequently confuses the two.

The CIA was created by President Harry S. Truman in 1947 with the signing of the National Security Act. The statute charged the director of the agency with coordinating the nation's intelligence activities and correlating, evaluating, and disseminating information that affected national security. Congress has oversight powers over the agency's program through the Senate Select Committee on Intelligence and the House Permanent Select Committee on Intelligence. The Act also created the position of Director of Central Intelligence (DCI) who manages the CIA, provides advice on intelligence matters to the president, and serves as the head of the entire U.S. intelligence community. In 2004, the law was amended by the Intelligence Reform and Terrorism Prevention Act, providing for a Director of National Intelligence (DNI) who assumed some of the roles previously fulfilled by the DCI, and a separate Director for the CIA. Under the current structure, the CIA director reports to the DNI. At the operational level, the CIA is managed as an office within the executive branch, with the president appointing both the DNI and the director of the CIA with the consent of the Senate. Because the agency's day-to-day operations and budget are secret, the CIA has more discretion than nearly any other part of the U.S. government.

Since September 11, changes have been underway to reduce the power of the CIA in some areas. The DNI now coordinates 16 intelligence agencies, and provides the president with daily intelligence briefings, a task that previously was the responsibility of the CIA director. The DNI must also deal with intelligence officials within the Department of Defense (DOD), who maintain their need for autonomy in order to provide tactical support for soldiers in the field. Some critics in Congress believe that the system has created a parallel system of intelligence gathering, even though the DOD controls an estimated 80 percent of the nation's intelligence budget through the operation of the new Defense Joint Intelligence Operations Center. CIA officials have attempted to convince the military that the agency needs access to the DOD's raw data to analyze potential threats, but there are signs that the department's secretary is unwilling to give up his discretion to CIA officials (McManus and Spiegel 2006).

The CIA is authorized to collect information through human sources and other means, but it does not have any police, subpoena, or law enforcement functions, and it does not function as an internal security agency. It is responsible for performing other functions and duties related to intelligence that affect national security as directed by the president or the Director of National Intelligence. The CIA's activities include research, development, and deployment of technology, and it also serves as an independent source of analysis on security-related topics. The structure of the agency includes a deputy director, who must also seek Senate confirmation, an executive director who manages the CIA on a day-to-day basis, and directorates of intelligence, science and technology, and support. Additional responsibilities are delegated to the National Clandestine Service, the Center for the Study of Intelligence, which maintains the agency's historical materials and supports the study of intelligence gathering as a discipline, the Office of General Counsel, and the Office of Public Affairs (About the CIA 2006).

The authority to dictate the CIA's tasks rests with the president, who has the discretion of permitting information gathered by the agency to be used by the intelligence committees of both the House and the Senate. Journalist Bob Woodward noted that the important requirement is that presidential actions must be consistent with the executive branch responsibilities spelled out in the Constitution (Woodward 1987, 72). In the post–Cold War environment, the CIA's mission is also to deal with potential attacks and terrorist threats, anticipate threatened disruptions of international oil supplies, and prevent the theft of trade secrets from U.S. businesses (Kessler 1994). The agency also predicts short-term military threats and operates a warning system to protect the United States and its allies.

The National Security Act also established the National Security Council (NSC), which was placed in the EOP as part of the 1949 reorganization plan for the executive branch. The NSC is chaired by the President, and its regular attendees are the Vice President, the Secretary of State, the Secretary of the Treasury, the Secretary of Defense, and the Assistant to the President for National Security Affairs. The Chairman of the Joint Chiefs of Staff is the statutory military advisor to the Council and the Director of the CIA is the Intelligence Advisor. The president's chief of staff, counsel to the president, and the assistant to the president for economic policy are invited to attend any NSC meeting, and the attorney general and the director of the office of management and budget are invited to attend meetings pertaining to their responsibilities (National Security Agency 2006).

Two aspects of managerial authority within the CIA warrant specific consideration. First, the CIA director carefully controls how the agency's budget (an estimated $5 billion per year) is to be spent with very broad discretion and little oversight. Most programs the agency funds and implements are considered secret and involve covert activities. The amount of money spent on intelligence is not intrinsically sensitive, although it may be controversial. Even the amount of money spent on personnel or on construction is classified, so neither members of Congress nor the public has a way of knowing if the funding levels change from year to year, as is the case with other executive branch departments. But the DNI notes that efforts are being made to remake "a loose confederation into a unified enterprise" by controlling the intelligence budget to nudge the separate agencies toward greater collaboration (McManus and Spiegel 2006).

Until recently, information about intelligence spending has been hard to come by, although one CIA veteran said in 2005 that the national budget for all intelligence agencies was $44 billion. The budgets had been deeply held secrets until 1997, when the Project on Government Secrecy of the Federation of American Scientists sued to obtain statistics on budgets under the federal Freedom of Information Act. The CIA director at the time released the budget figure of $26.6 billion, with $26.7 billion in 1998. Since 1999, however, the agency budget has remained classified, with courts upholding the need for secrecy. Officials have argued that disclosing the spying budget would create pressure to reveal more spending details, and that the information could aid the nation's adversaries (Shane 2005).

Congress, however, has attempted to flex its oversight muscle by approving language in the 2007 fiscal budget that would call on the president to make public what the national intelligence program costs each year. The Senate Select Committee on Intelligence also directed the DNI to study the "advisability" of publicly disclosing the budgets for each agency and to report back to the Committee. The vice chairman of the Committee said, "We have taken steps to reassert Congress' constitutional role as a check and balance to the Executive Branch," calling the requirement a "step toward greater transparency and accountability that is long overdue and will allow for a more informed debate on the priority of intelligence programs" (Pincus 2006). Similar efforts by the Senate have been blocked by the White House in the past.

The existing classification of national security information is governed by two executive orders, E.O. 12958, issued by President Clinton in 1995, and E.O. 13292 amending Clinton's order, which was issued by President George W. Bush in 2003. Information related to intelligence sources and methods are governed by both statutes and by regulations issued by the Director of National Intelligence (Kaiser 2006). Bush's executive order includes a uniform system for classifying, safeguarding, and declassifying national security information, including information related to international terrorism. The system includes three levels of classification:

- *Top Secret:* Information that, if disclosed by unauthorized persons, reasonably could be expected to cause exceptionally grave damage to national security;
- *Secret:* Information that, if disclosed by unauthorized persons, reasonably could be expected to cause serious damage to national security;
- *Confidential:* Information that, if disclosed by unauthorized persons, reasonably could be expected to cause damage to national security.

The executive order also identifies the persons with authority to classify the information as the president, vice president, agency heads and officials designated by the president in the *Federal Register,* and U.S. government officials delegated this responsibility. The last category is limited to the minimum required to administer the president's order, and all delegations of original classification authority must be in writing. Those delegated classification authority must undergo training including how classified information is to be safeguarded (Executive Order 13292 2003). Bush's action restricts the classification of information to a small group of individuals, and provides no guidance on how the classification system is to be implemented to determine what kind of breaches really do pose a danger to national security. This implies virtually total discretion, because there is latitude in interpreting what might be a potential danger.

The Department of Justice

On Saturday, May 20, 2006, fifteen agents from the Federal Bureau of Investigation (FBI) raided the Washington, D.C. office of Louisiana congressman William Jefferson, entering his Rayburn House Office Building suite at 7:15 PM and leaving the following day at 1 PM. Jefferson, a Democrat, was part of a 14-month investigation that accused him of accepting bribes as part of a high-tech business promotion in Africa. Jefferson had received a subpoena nine months earlier to provide some of his papers and had refused to do so, saying he did not want to incriminate himself. Two men had already pleaded guilty to bribing Jefferson, and the government was close to an indictment. The day after the raid, an 83-page affidavit was unsealed in which allegations were made that the FBI had videotaped Jefferson taking $100,000 in bribes, and that they had found $90,000 of the money stuffed inside a refrigerator freezer in the congressman's apartment. Jefferson held a news conference in which he said he could not comment further, but that he would do so at the appropriate time. "There are two sides to every story; there are certainly two sides to this story," he said (Eggen and Murray 2006).

Republicans, who had repeatedly been battered by allegations of impropriety within their own party, had initially seemed smug about Jefferson's problems with the FBI. But after the raid, called the "Saturday Night Massacre" by some pundits, members of both parties leaped to defend Jefferson and to denounce the FBI's action. No office of a sitting member of Congress had been raided in U.S. history, and current members were aghast that it had happened to one of their own. In addition, the FBI had refused to allow the House General Counsel to witness the search. The U.S. Attorney General, Alberto Gonzales, told a news conference, "I will admit that these were unusual steps that were taken in response to an unusual set of circumstances" (Eggen and Murray 2006).

Congress was not satisfied. House Speaker Dennis Hastert issued a statement in which he noted that the actions of the Justice Department in seeking and executing the search warrant used in the raid raised important constitutional issues. "Insofar as I am aware, since the founding of our Republic 219 years ago, the Justice Department has never found it necessary to do what it did Saturday night, crossing this Separation of Powers line, in order to successfully prosecute corruption by Members of Congress. Nothing I have learned in the last 48 hours leads me to believe that there was any necessity to change the precedent established over those 219 years." Former House Speaker Newt Gingrich called the raid, "the most blatant violation of the Constitutional Separation of Powers in my lifetime," urging President Bush to discipline or fire "whoever exhibited this extraordinary violation" (Eggen and Murray 2006).

Other members of Congress took immediate action to deal with the constitutional issues. The House Judiciary Committee held a hearing on May 30 in which witnesses were asked to testify whether the incident constituted "reckless justice" that trampled the Constitution. One legal scholar noted, "If it were an act of impulse by some rogue FBI agent, it could be excused. However, this was an act of premeditation, ordered with the direct knowledge and approval of Attorney General Alberto Gonzales. For that reason, it can be neither ignored nor tolerated if the balance of the tripartite system is to be maintained" (Turley 2006). Another witness, calling the raid, "an overzealous exercise of executive power," demanded an explanation for what appeared to be a lack of judicial respect, but targeted the Justice Department and the FBI. "The American People should be deeply concerned that a decision to conduct a raid on Congress was made consciously and evidently at high levels inside the Justice Department and the FBI. Press reports indicate that this was no casual decision but a conscious decision to act in an unprecedented way" (Walker 2006).

Not every observation about the raid was negative, however. In an editorial in the *Houston Chronicle,* the blame for what happened was placed on the shoulders of Congressman Jefferson for failing to obey the subpoena. The newspaper also commented on the fact that, "the same Congress that has done little to stop warrantless surveillance of Americans' communications cannot reasonably claim special privileges protecting it from searches duly approved by a judge." U.S. Senator John Warner of Virginia was one of the few who said that members of Congress should be treated no differently than any other citizen when it comes to criminal matters, a sentiment, according to the *Chronicle,* that was undoubtedly in agreement with most Americans (Under the Law 2006).

What remained unanswered, however, was whether the raid represented a constitutional use of discretion by the Department of Justice and its staff, or whether the action stemmed from the overly broad use of power by the president as manager of the agencies involved, including the Capitol Police, who were instructed to give the agents access to the office. When questioned, White House spokesman Tony Snow noted, "We are hoping that there's a way to balance the constitutional concerns of the House of Representatives with the law enforcement obligations of the executive branch" (Eggen and Lengel 2006).

In each of these three case studies, does the buck truly stop at the president's desk, as President Truman promised? Should the chief executive be held personally responsible for actions taken on his watch, even when he has no direct control of the managers working for the executive branch? In most situations, cabinet officials, agency directors, and other administrators have been expected to fall on their swords in order to protect the chief executive. Rarely has a president admitted that someone who has been appointed within the administration is not at fault, preferring to allow the individual in question to fade away quietly. While pointing at discretion as a necessary tool on the one hand, the other hand might be pointing a finger of blame instead at someone perceived to have erred. It is a part of the nasty business of politics, especially at the federal level, where the stakes are so high. Those entering the public service are expected to understand that fact implicitly. When the U.S. Supreme Court ruled against protections for government whistle blowers in a May 2006 decision, the message was clear: keep problems to yourself and away from the boss.

CHAPTER 5

Discretion and Managerial Accountability

On April 12, 2002, two Greenpeace activists in an inflatable rubber speedboat climbed aboard the commercial vessel *M/V Jade* three miles off the U.S. coast near Miami. They were protesting the importation of illegally harvested mahogany from the Brazilian Amazon, and believed the ship carried 70 tons of the wood. Wearing shirts that were printed with "Greenpeace Illegal Forest Crime Unit," they attempted to unfurl a banner reading, "President Bush: Stop Illegal Logging" but were arrested by the U.S. Coast Guard before they could do so. The activists were detained and two months later were sentenced to time served, one weekend in jail. Greenpeace had approved the peaceful protest and had expected that the activists would be arrested, according to the executive director of Greenpeace USA (Berry 2004).

A moratorium on Brazil exporting mahogany has been in effect since October 2001; in 2000, the United States received more than 70 percent of Brazil's mahogany exports. Greenpeace argued that the Bush administration had little desire to enforce the law, and that they had evidence that the *Jade* unloaded the 70 tons of mahogany in Charleston, South Carolina. The initial indictment stated that the Greenpeace activists had boarded the ship based on erroneous belief about the contents of the shipment. The controversy over the illegal harvesting of rare wood is just one part of the story.

In July 2003, the U.S. Department of Justice filed criminal charges against the entire Greenpeace organization, using an obscure 1872 law that had been last used in 1890 in *United States v. Sullivan*. The statute was meant to protect seamen against *sailor mongers,* that is, women of ill repute who were rowed out to boats about to disembark in port. Using liquor and prostitution, they tried to lure the sailors to their boarding houses when the men came ashore. The law was focused on the proprietors of the boarding houses, and forbade the unauthorized boarding of any vessel about to arrive at its destination. The indictment on charges of criminal conspiracy and illegal boarding made by federal prosecutors in Miami was because Greenpeace authorized the boarding of the *Jade,* a charge the organization admitted was true. Because Greenpeace is a corporation and cannot serve any time in jail, the potential sentence would be to place the organization on probation, requiring the group to report its activities to the government and jeopardizing its tax exempt status. If convicted of the crime, a misdemeanor, the group could also face a $10,000 fine (Liptak 2003).

This case is believed to have been the first federal indictment to target an entire advocacy group for its protest tactics, and it generated a storm of protest from non-governmental organizations. The director of the National Community Relations Division of the American Friends Service Committee noted that their group, along with Greenpeace and other advocacy organizations, "enable the American people to speak truth to power, through ideas and action, including civil disobedience— essential ingredients of a living democracy." The president of People for the American Way was even more direct. "Permitting the selective prosecution of a group like Greenpeace merely because the government disagrees with their point of view would irreparably harm the free speech rights of all Americans. Protecting the right to disagree with the government is what the First Amendment is all about. Indeed, it is profoundly patriotic to engage in peaceful dissent when you think the government is wrong" (Greenpeace 2003). The Bush administration also received more than 65,000 e-mail messages and faxes in protest to the Attorney General's actions.

Legal experts compared the prosecution to the efforts by state prosecutors in the South to harass the National Association for the Advancement of Colored People (NAACP) in the Civil Rights struggles of the 1950s and 1960s. One legal scholar noted, "There is not only the suspicion but also perhaps the reality that the purpose of the prosecution is to inhibit First Amendment activities," while another said, "it has a chilling effect" on First Amendment rights (Liptak 2003).

Greenpeace asked the federal court judge for a jury trial, and the motion to do so was granted, with the trial set for May 18, 2004. The prosecution presented its evidence but before the defense could continue, the judge directed the verdict in favor of Greenpeace, holding that there was insufficient evidence of the charges to allow the case to proceed to a jury. A spokesperson for the U.S. Attorney's Office stated in response to the verdict that the Department of Justice would remain "undeterred in prosecuting those persons who illegally attempt to board ships at the Port of Miami or otherwise threaten port security" in light of the September 11 terrorist attacks on the U.S. in 2001 (Berry 2004).

Despite the outcome, group leaders voiced concern. Julian Bond, chair of the NAACP, said that, "This prosecution is a strong reminder that we can never let our guard down, that Americans' indispensable right to civil disobedience requires our constant vigilance" (Greenwatch 2004). Greenpeace leaders, who had called the case a turning point in the history of American dissent, gave a brief commentary from the courthouse steps in Miami. "America's tradition of free speech won a victory today, but our liberties are still not safe. The Bush Administration and its allies seem bent on stifling our tradition of civil protest, a tradition that has made our country stronger throughout our history" (Greenwatch 2004).

The prosecution highlighted another important issue related to discretion and managerial accountability involving the federal government. Did Attorney General John Ashcroft and his staff at the Department of Justice overstep their authority in pursuing the charges against Greenpeace, especially because their case was based on an archaic statute that had not been invoked in over a hundred years? If so, what mechanisms are in place to protect citizens and groups against potential violations of the law?

Public managers, it has been stated, function in an ambiguous and contradictory environment. Many administrators have been found wanting, and are often blamed for taking actions with far-reaching consequences. In part, the problem of discretion emanates from the need to have a delicate balance between the politically doable and administratively rational actions. Public management scholars have always known that every act of managers is a "seamless web of discretion" (Denhardt 2004, 46).

While a major portion of this book has been devoted to discussions about unique decision-making processes, the question that begs an answer is, "just how much discretion should be left to public managers?" Indeed, all democratic political systems grapple with "establishing a consensus on a coherent approach to administrative discretion" because they all face "the issue of determination of the degree of administrative discretion they are willing to grant in matters of public policy" (Jreisat 2002, 91). By responding to this question, this chapter puts into perspective some elements of discretion that often go unnoticed. A determination of just how much discretion should be exercised will benefit those wishing to have a deeper meaning of the parameters of public management, especially questions of responsibility and accountability.

Responsibility and Accountability

Philosophy

There are several ways of conceptualizing managerial discretion within the public sector. One step is to examine managerial actions against the principles of accountability and responsibility. The fundamental issue is to accept discretion as a given, but to hold public managers accountable for their actions. All public managers, including the president, can face lawsuits and are not above the law. Cooper notes that the "suit against President Richard Nixon and some of his aides tested the boundaries of executive immunity at the national level and established the basic rules about obligations of public officials in tort at all levels" (Cooper 2004, 208-9). Responsibility, therefore, includes a formal legal perspective, which is the idea of following the general will of the public or, more precisely, the electorate. In this context, managers are ultimately responsible to their employers: the people. This is not so much about "we the people" in the sense that a democracy caters to the majority most of the time. Managerial decisions therefore must have a broader meaning to include accountability. The classic ways of inviting reflection can be found in the works of Carl Friedrich (1940) and Herman Finer (1941).

Friedrich thought accountability would best be resolved by outside oversight or internal management controls. Also, managerial responsibility would be assured internally through professionalism and/or professional standards and codes of ethics. This would entail the use of internal checks and balances within a specific agency. Friedrich favored greater discretion at the agency level, noting that managers must have specific skills to enable them make better and more competent judgments as they solved organizational problems.

On the other hand, Finer argued that administrative responsibility could only be maintained externally through legislative or popular controls. External checks and balances were the only way to ensure the subordination of managers because internal power of control would ultimately lead to corruption. In Finer's view, some form of electoral or legislative review was the only possible way to avoid abuses of discretion.

Neither Friedrich nor Finer adequately address the question of political managers who must be politically competent regardless of the controls imposed internally or externally, because both types of control could fail. Could managers be guided by some other force? This leads us to think in terms of the possibility of looking not so much at the agency's confining structures but at the manager's own sense of responsibility and accountability, in terms of having an inner sense of duty.

Kevin Kearns (1995) offers some insights on how this sense is an indicator of accountability. It involves answering to a higher authority—legal or organizational—for one's action in society at large or within one's organization. This narrow definition of accountability draws a very clear distinction between two fundamental questions. First, to *whom* is the organization or individual manager accountable? Second, for *what* is the organization or individual manager responsible? Both questions deal with professional responsibility and obligation. As discussed earlier, the law is often vague or poorly worded, forcing managers to make on-the spot decisions about policy actions. Ambiguous laws are not limited to legislative directives. The president is often no less vague than Congress. Angus MacIntyre (1996) is concerned with the fact that it is difficult to enhance the democratic accountability of bureaucrats who have too much discretion. He takes from Theodore Lowi the idea that if Congress or any other legislative body cannot be precise, then it should not legislate. One of the reasons why legislation is not precise is because the amount of information and time available to legislative bodies are inadequate to prepare a well-informed piece of legislation.

One example is the Healthy Forests Restoration Act (HFRA) of 2003. Congress had considered reforms of U.S. Forest Service policies related to wildfires and public participation in policy decisions in 2001 and 2002; the fire season, along with massive infestations of insects, provided additional momentum for change. President George W. Bush proposed his Healthy Forests Initiative on August 22, 2002, and gathered considerable support, especially among Western legislators. Congress moved swiftly, holding hearings on the Healthy Forests Reform Act the day after the bill was introduced. But partisan bickering and the pressures of the 2002 midterm elections caused efforts to stall, and the legislation failed to get Senate approval.

Efforts to pass reform continued into the 108th Congress, as competing bills were quickly introduced. Another version of the HFRA was introduced in the House in April 2003, and passed to show they were responding to the 2002 fires before the 2003 season began. So there was minimum debate. But the discussion in the Senate was much more protracted and contentious, involving the referral of the House bill. Numerous witnesses were called to committee hearings and new Senate versions were introduced. Attempts at legislative compromise continued into late September without much success. But as major wildfires consumed California and other Western states in late October 2003, Senate members abandoned their deliberations, quickly tabling discussion and their own bills. With no time to spare while the fires burned down thousands of structures and lives were lost, the Senate approved the House bill, despite concerns about its cost and impact.

Congressional Discretion

The social and economic heterogeneity of the electorate tends to cause legislators to find language that is vague and that accommodates as many groups and interests as possible. Of course, language is not infallible. In fact, managerial discretion is often given by Congress only to be used as a criticism of bureaucracy later.

An illustration of this phenomenon occurred after the February 1, 2003 breakup of the Columbia Space Shuttle that killed all seven astronauts on board. Early speculation on the cause of the accident focused on a piece of foam that broke away from the spacecraft's external fuel tank, striking the underside of the shuttle. The damage may have led to abnormal temperature readings and the eventual breakup of the craft.

Less than two hours after the accident, Sean O'Keefe, administrator of the National Aeronautics and Space Administration (NASA) began the process of convening the Columbia Accident Investigation Board (CAIB). He appointed retired U.S. Navy Admiral Hal Gehman, Jr. to serve as chairman of the commission by 5:00 PM the same day. The CAIB was directed to issue its report to O'Keefe, and to operate out of offices at the Johnson Space Center in Houston, but not on the center's property, to insure its independence. The members gathered in Texas on February 10, and the board was divided into three sub-boards dealing with material and management, operations, and technical and engineering issues. Congressional leaders commended O'Keefe for the speed and openness with which the agency shared information with Congress, the media, and the public.

But critics argued that even though O'Keefe acted properly in bringing the board together, there was concern that CAIB was instituted as a non-independent board controlled by NASA. Congressional Democrats sent a letter to the president requesting that the charter of the board be changed to require the CAIB to report directly to the White House and to Congress, rather than to O'Keefe. Other members of Congress demanded that the composition of CAIB, commonly referred to as the Gehman Commission, be changed by adding more scientists and engineers to the mix of military and civilian government employees.

O'Keefe repeatedly defended the board's independence from NASA in the first Congressional hearing on the space shuttle disaster, but also stressed that he was willing to comply with any changes Gehman felt were necessary so the commission could conduct its investigation without undue influence from NASA (Berger 2003). In order to avoid having the White House convene its own commission to study the accident, O'Keefe added an engineering professor who was a former Secretary of the Air Force, and a retired chief executive officer of an energy services firm. Those appointments were insufficient, Congressional members said, so O'Keefe added three experts on space science and space policy, including a Nobel Prize laureate and a former astronaut (American Academy for the Advancement of Science 2003).

What took place with O'Keefe's actions as NASA administrator is typical of the Congress-giveth-and-Congress-taketh-away process, where legislators initially want a manager to take charge and make decisions they are unwilling or unable to make, followed by criticism of those actions. Managers must try to balance between using the discretion they have been given while still recognizing the political forces at play. Kenneth Ashworth (2001) described how this works in real life as he wrote about the challenges he faced in working for the government. "A large portion of your time as a public servant will be spent on dealing with politicians, trying to convince them of policy initiatives or changes you have found to be needed. And part of your experience will include being kicked around or being on the receiving end of abuse from elected officials, most of it mild but some probably quite severe." To explain why this happens, Ashworth wrote,

> "Politicians have needs we bureaucrats don't have. They need to impress their voters and the pleaders for special treatment and satisfy supplicants for exceptions and favors. We bureaucrats can be obstacles to those needs because favors, exceptions, and special pleaders are the bane of our existence. To us these kinds of people are asking us to be unfair and to treat themselves and other citizens unequally. To the politician, this represents a chance to do a favor, to make someone indebted to them, to create the potential for some future trade they may need in order to move something on their agenda" (Ashworth 2001, 2, 11).

Judicial Review

Another mechanism used to make managers accountable is judicial review, which can be used to monitor discretionary decisions. Judicial review of managerial actions can provide administrative agencies with the necessary direction to accomplish their statutory mandates by assisting in designing the standards Congress, state legislatures, and local councils may have failed to provide in the original legislation, which created the specific administrative function (Ludd 1986).

The Americans with Disabilities Act of 1990 (ADA), which has been called the most important civil rights act in U.S. history, was enacted by Congress despite what some believe was a lack of knowledge about disability policy issues. Depending upon who is speaking, the estimate of people with a disability may range from 25 to 60 million (Zola 1993, xvii). This number is vitally important because the cost and scope of services needed to end discrimination depends largely on how many people with disabilities are served by the law. Similarly, the statute prohibits discrimination against an individual with a disability, but leaves vague the precise meaning of the term. The language in the U.S. Code states that a person with a disability is someone who has a "physical or mental impairment that substantially limits one or more of the major life activities of such individual." The U.S. Department of Justice (DOJ), one of the federal agencies with the authority to issue regulations interpreting the meaning of the law, has attempted to figure out what Congress intended. The Attorney General began with the regulations developed by the Department of Health, Education, and Welfare (HEW), adopted in interpreting the 1977 Rehabilitation Act amendments. In its regulations, codified at 28 C.F.R. Section 36.104, designed to guide agency actions, DOJ adopted the HEW language, which defined a *physical or mental impairment* as, "any physiological disorder or condition, cosmetic disfigurement, or any anatomical loss affecting one or more of the following body systems: neurological; musculoskeletal; special sense organs; respiratory, including speech organs; cardiovascular; reproductive; digestive; genito-urinary; hemic and lymphatic; skin; and endocrine."

The HEW regulations also included a commentary stating that the agency did not attempt to set forth a list of specific diseases or conditions that would comprise the impairments because it is impossible to develop such a list that is comprehensive. However, a representative list included in the commentary mentioned, "such diseases and conditions as orthopedic, visual, speech, and hearing impairments, cerebral palsy, epilepsy, muscular dystrophy, multiple sclerosis, cancer, heart disease, diabetes, mental retardation, emotional illness . . . drug addiction and alcoholism."

In 1980, the president transferred the authority for implementing and enforcing the Rehabilitation Act provisions to the DOJ, and the agency adopted the HEW regulations as well as the commentary. The agency used the same definition for what constitutes a disability, and developed regulations to determine the meaning of the second prong of the ADA, that the disability "substantially limits" the person in a major life activity. An illustrative, non-exhaustive list of major life activities included functions such as "caring for one's self, performing manual tasks, walking, seeing, hearing, speaking, breathing, learning, and working." A legal memo issued in 1988 by the acting Assistant Attorney General, Office of Legal Counsel, added that another significant life activity included procreation and intimate personal relations.

In 1998, the U.S. Supreme Court faced a key question in reflecting on what Congress intended in enacting the ADA. Randon Bragdon, a Maine dentist, refused to fill a cavity for Sidney Abbott because her intake form indicated that she was HIV positive. Although she had no outwardly visible signs of HIV, Bragdon told Abbott that he would treat her in a hospital setting so that he could take "extra precautions" even though he never had admitting privileges at a hospital and never explained what those extra precautions might be. Abbott filed an ADA claim, and after making its way through the legal system, the Supreme Court agreed to hear the case. The 5 to 4 ruling in favor of Abbott agreed that she was covered by the ADA, noting that the DOJ had not included HIV in its adoption of the HEW conditions because the illness was not determined to be related to AIDS until 1983. They agreed that asymptomatic HIV was sometimes a disability under the ADA, so that people without visible symptoms can claim protection of the law. However, the court's ruling did not say that HIV is always a disability under the ADA; in this instance, Abbott was entitled to protection because the illness substantially limited one of her major life activities—reproduction—meeting a second standard for coverage. Abbott had decided not to have children after she became infected with HIV because of the risk of passing the virus on to others, and the risk of infection to both her sexual partner and her child.

Without judicial review and interpretation of the ADA, Sidney Abbott would not have received the protections against discrimination the statute offers. The Supreme Court also noted that reproduction and the sexual dynamics surrounding it are central to the life process itself, opening the door for gay men, seniors, and children to be protected as well. The ruling gave the Department of Justice, and other agencies charged with implementing the ADA, additional guidance on how the law applies, limiting their discretion in some ways. But the case was not a "loss" for the DOJ; it is more a clarification of the agency's role that strengthens accountability.

Judicial mediation is also valuable when Congressional control is lacking, as is the case with the U.S. Citizenship and Immigration Services, now under the Department of Homeland Security. The agency, previously called the Immigration and Naturalization Service, has been widely criticized for its use of discretionary decision-making in dealing with the increasingly controversial issue of immigration. In 2006, mass protests occurred across the United States as immigrants and their supporters rallied against the federal government's crackdown on undocumented workers and their families, prompting an even sharper response. President Bush announced that he would bring 6,000 National Guard troops to help secure the U.S. border with Mexico, further incensing human rights activists. As one author noted:

> "Finally, the U.S. government's immigration policies have involved arbitrary and prolonged detention for immigrants who face deportation. The 1996 Illegal Immigration Reform and Immigrant Responsibility Act mandated that the Immigration and Naturalization Service detain without bail all immigrants facing removal for criminal offenses, even minor criminal offenses committed years ago for which the immigrants had already fulfilled their punishment, until receiving the final judgment on deportation. This mandatory detention provision led to the indefinite detention of legal residents facing removal, and these immigrants were denied the same due process rights as U.S. citizens" (DeLaet 2006, 74).

As a nation of immigrants, managerial decision-making involving federal agencies elicits major press coverage. Immigration issues are at the core of American political and administrative discourse. The Elian Gonzalez case is a great illustration of the interplay between political exigencies and managerial discretionary power. It also exemplifies the need for judicial review of agency actions to ensure accountability.

Elian Gonzalez and Discretion in Immigration Cases

Refugees are people who flee their own country for fear of political persecution. Many seek asylum in countries that are willing to accommodate them so long as the individuals respect the laws of the new land. The right to seek protection and asylum is respected in the Universal Declaration of Human Rights, a treaty adopted by United Nations member countries. Many refugees return to their countries of origin after they are assured of peace and security. Usually, it is after oppressive regimes embrace democracy and human rights.

In 1999, 5-year-old Elian Gonzalez left Cardenas, Cuba in a 17-foot aluminum boat with 14 other people, including his mother. Their goal was to reach the United States and stay permanently. He is reported to have suffered a great deal to reach the shores of the United States. At one point, Cuban patrol boats tried to capsize the boat, but the group held up Elian and for some unknown reason, the patrol boats gave up the pursuit. On Thanksgiving Day 1999, their boat capsized in rough seas after a fuel tank burst and caught fire. Thirteen people drowned, one of whom was Elian's mother. For a few days, the boy was alone at sea, clinging to an inner tube three miles off the coast of Florida, where he was rescued by fishermen. The rescuers handed him over to officials of the Immigration and Naturalization Service (INS), who took him to a hospital and then placed him in the custody of his great uncle, Lazaro Gonzales.

Three days after his son was rescued, Elian's father, Juan Miguel Gonzalez, filed a complaint with the United Nations to get attention to his demand that the boy be returned to Cuba and placed in his custody. Attorneys for Elian's family in Miami then filed a request that he be granted political asylum in the United States. On behalf of the minor, Lazaro submitted an asylum application to the INS, but the application was denied. According to the INS, it was not up to Lazaro to file application forms for the boy. The INS regarded Elian's father as the only adult legally entitled to file an application on Elian's behalf.

On January 5, 2000, the INS notified Lazaro that Elian would be sent back to Cuba to be reunited with his father. Lazaro was enraged. He filed a legal action in federal court to stop the INS from sending the boy back to Cuba. INS Commissioner Doris Meissner told reporters that the agency's decision was "based on facts and the law. This little boy, who has been through so much, belongs with his father" (CNN 2000). Elian's relatives filed suit to have Lazaro declared the boy's guardian, and a judge granted their motion. But Attorney General Janet Reno told the Gonzalez family that their suit would have to be filed in federal court. This was followed in March 2000 by a court ruling denying the request for political asylum, while the U.S. Department of State made arrangements for Elian's father and other close relatives to come to the U.S. The government contacted Cuban officials and initiated efforts to have Elian's father, who was divorced from Elian's mother, arrive in the United States.

On April 6, 2000, Gonzalez arrived in Washington DC, where he was hosted by the Cuban Interests Section that represents the Cuban government because Cuba did not have a full-fledged embassy in the United States. The case received front-page media coverage throughout the country. It polarized the Florida community in an unprecedented fashion. Many Cuban-Americans supported Lazaro's cause and argued for the retention of Elian in the country. However, there were dissenting voices across America who posited that the bond between a father and a son was greater than the purported freedom that Elian would enjoy in the United States. The situation was also immersed in the 2000 presidential campaign's politics. While President Bush supported the INS and the Attorney General's actions, Democratic nominee Al Gore said he would support legislation that would allow Elian to stay in the United States until the family's lawsuit was resolved.

Lazaro and his supporters seemed comforted when the courts agreed to hear the case. On April 19, 2000, the 11th Circuit Court of Appeals issued an injunction order preventing the INS or anyone else from removing Elian from the United States. The court held that Elian was entitled to stay in the United States while the courts decided whether or not he could pursue his claim of asylum. The Court agreed to adjudicate the case regardless of the fact that Elian was a minor and at that time did not have parental consent. The belief then was that nothing in the law mandated applicants for asylum to be of a prescribed legal age. It was unclear whether a case like this warranted Elian to be represented by an adult. However, the court worried that the INS had already placed Elian in the care of his great uncle. That did deter the INS from espousing the fact that Lazaro's custody was a temporary measure. Indeed, the INS went ahead and petitioned the 11th Circuit Court to order Lazaro Gonzalez to give Elian to INS to be transferred to his father's care. The Court maintained the status quo.

The INS argued that it had conducted extensive interviews with Juan Gonzalez and determined beyond doubt that he was Elian's father. Moreover, Gonzalez convinced the INS that he had a close and continuous parental relationship with his son. He provided extensive documentation about his son's schooling and medical history as well as social records demonstrating the family bonds. The INS did not find any reason to believe that Elian's father was a danger to his son. The INS also invoked international law that elevates family reunions above other considerations. The agency rejected the idea that three lawyers hired by the Cuban-American community in Miami as well as his great uncle were Elian's legal custodians. According to the INS, only his father Juan Gonzalez would "speak" for his son.

On April 22, 2000, just three days after the court ruled in favor of the family's request to block his return to Cuba, federal agents physically seized Elian from his uncle's home and placed him in his father's custody in the United States. His father was already in the country at an undisclosed location. Perceptions about the INS's handling of the case varied. Some members of the public praised the government agency for its bold action. Others were outraged by the "commando-style" operation to remove Elian from Lazaro's house. Some members of Congress argued that the INS overstepped its authority and violated the Fourth Amendment prohibition against illegal searches. It seemed that there was a problem interpreting the discretionary powers enjoyed by the INS. Generally, the INS is closely associated with the Department of Justice and the Attorney General is by law the final arbiter over immigration issues. The higher courts seemed to recognize that fact when, on June 1, 2000, the 11th Circuit Court of Appeals upheld the INS decision to turn down the asylum application on behalf of Elian. Finally, on June 28, the U.S. Supreme Court closed the case and ordered Elian returned to Cuba with his father. Just hours later, Juan Gonzalez and his son arrived in a jubilant reception in Cuba.

For Elian's handlers to establish his claim of asylum, he would have had to prove he could not return to Cuba because he had a "well-founded fear of persecution on account of race, religion, nationality, membership in a particular social group, or political opinion." However, universal cultural norms about family bonds would make it difficult to prove this claim because he was a minor and his father was a bona fide Cuban willfully living in his homeland. Since 1959, when revolutionaries under Fidel Castro overthrew the regime after years of guerilla warfare, Cuba had embraced a socialist ideology. The Cuban government did not permit Elian, his mother, and the others to leave the island. This was not the first time Cubans had attempted to cross into the U.S. by sea, and in fact, many Cubans had done so. Some have been successful while others never made it or were simply apprehended and sentenced to jail. There are stiff penalties for Cubans who are arrested and returned to Cuba after failing to enter into the United States. Importantly too, Elian and the others would have violated the immigration laws of the United States by entering without legal permission from the United States government. Notwithstanding the facts of the case, the law permits refugees who seek asylum to be allowed into the country. They may also qualify for citizenship if they are not criminals and have met other requirements.

Since the 1960s, many Cubans have been granted asylum in the United States because they proved that they would be persecuted for their political beliefs if they returned to the island nation. The communist victory led to a flood of professional and middle class refugees to the United States, where they established large Cuban communities in Miami, Tampa, and in New York. In 1980, Castro's government allowed over 125,000 Cubans, including some with mental illnesses and criminals, to leave during the Mariel Boat Lift. Another large influx to the United States occurred in 1994, when about 30,000 refugees sought to enter the country on homemade rafts. After that, the INS stopped all Cubans (and those from other nations as well) found in the water and sent them back to Cuba, while those who reached land were allowed to stay.

Those policies have become increasingly controversial since the U.S. Coast Guard began actively turning rafts and boats away. In 1999, for instance, anti-Castro groups charged that Guardsmen had sprayed refugees with powerful water jets and pepper spray. Human rights organizations also questioned the INS definition of "reaching U.S. soil," asking whether the agency had discretion over whether that included a wet beach or aboard a U.S. Coast Guard cutter if rescued. Fleeing Cubans have generally benefited from good will on the part of the American people and government. In fact, under the Cuban Readjustment Act, refugees who arrive on American shores and remain in the United States for 12 months are eligible for an immigration Green Card, which could mean permanent residence and then American citizenship.

At issue is the Attorney General's use of discretion. Janet Reno made a managerial decision to send Elian back home to Cuba. A political choice might have been to exercise discretion and allow Elian permission to be in the country, and provide his father visas to visit him. This might have been acceptable to the Cuban-American community in Florida whose votes Reno would have liked to have when she sought public office later in her career. Yet, the overriding concern, as a manager in the Clinton administration, was to uphold the law to the strictest standards possible. The Attorney General, as chief law enforcement officer in the administration, took the difficult choice of making a decision based on what she construed to be in the interest of both the boy and U.S. democratic legal processes.

Discretion and Democracy

Scholars continue to wonder how much discretion is appropriate to democracy. Finding the right balance of discretion serves the democratic ideals enshrined in the Constitution. When it becomes necessary to exercise discretion, managers are faced with questions of accountability and responsibility. Overall, accountability refers to a wide spectrum of public expectations and decision standards that are used to judge the performance, responsiveness, and even ethical content of public manager's actions.

The point is not to dwell so much on the contextual questions of managerial discretion. As Douglas Morgan noted, perhaps we can overcome the problems associated with discretion by focusing our attention on ways of making managerial discretion serve the ends of democracy better (Morgan 2004). Because we cannot possibly measure the amount of discretion that best serves our democracy, the tendency is to use ethical yardsticks that are part and parcel of the larger administrative enterprise. Political dynamics remain the core arena where discretionary decisions play out and must therefore be the target for intervention. In other words, managerial discretion falls squarely in the realm of political exigencies and therefore it is the political rather than the legal and technical spheres where efforts at containing abuses of discretion are best confronted.

From a policy formulation and implementation standpoint, discretion provides managers with the flexibility to respond to the innumerable different needs and desires of unique subdivisions of their clientele. Managers provide services often under circumstances that could not have been foreseen by legislators to be incorporated into a general congressional act. The concern is that the elimination of discretion would reduce the ability of managers to overcome the many political obstacles to implementation and would eliminate a major portion of government's capacity for responsiveness. However, they can also abuse the discretion allowed them whenever there is a limit to the enabling laws.

While it is not practical to list all possible forms of abuses of discretionary power, some typology has been attempted for ease of analysis. For example, Martin Shapiro notes that abuses of discretion manifest in several forms including situations in which officials have: (1) done things they should not have done; (2) not considered what they should have done; (3) given improper weight to things they should have considered; and (4) made decisions without sufficient evidence (Shapiro 1994a, 503).

The task for good public management is therefore to eliminate or reduce the abuses. However, emphasis on external controls and accountability reduce managers to Weberian-style management while an emphasis on internal control and responsiveness incorporates politics into administration. The challenge is to find a balance between the managerial and political roles at all levels of government.

A solution offered by Kenneth C. Davis (1969) is the formalization of discretion. Davis recognizes both the necessity and the danger of discretion. Because discretion is unavoidable, he calls for a balance. What is required, according to Davis, is discretionary power that is neither excessive nor inadequate. This may be derived through a formalization process of confining or controlling, structuring, and checking discretion by fixing boundaries and keeping managerial actions within them. Confining may come externally from the legislature, and managers may sometimes have to seek broader boundaries to initiate programs and make other staff decisions. The more likely case, however, is that discretion will be delegated too broadly. The manager can then personally develop the standards, principles, and rules formalizing discretion by stating publicly how the legislative intent is to be interpreted regarding distribution, regulation, and enforcement.

Davis' eighteen ways to control discretion emphasize the importance of encouraging openness and criticism in decision-making processes. With openness, he observed, goes opportunity for criticism by outsiders. Internal criticism, by itself, can be an effective and valuable tool in controlling discretionary power at all levels of government. He noted, "Experience proves that such official criticism, especially when publicly made by a person of high prestige, can be a powerful control" (Davis 1965, 82).

Once the public manager establishes the boundaries of discretion, the task is to structure discretion, to regularize it, to organize it, to produce order in it. The purpose of structuring is to control the manner of the exercise of discretionary power within the boundaries. The responsibility for formalization through structuring is placed upon the manager, who will clarify and regularize governmental activity through open plans, rules, and policy statements. Rulemaking remains a powerful component of confining discretion.

Rulemaking

Colin Diver (1983) identifies three dimensions of rules: (1) transparency, (2) accessibility, and (3) congruence. In Diver's opinion, a rational rulemaker will use words with well-defined and universally accepted meanings within the relevant community. The manager will want rules to be "accessible" to the intended audience, that is, applicable to concrete situations without excessive difficulty or effort. The manager will care about whether the substantive content of the message communicated in words produces the desired behavior. For a rule to be transparent, it must mean the same thing to everyone who reads it. Vagueness is at odds with transparency and concerns managers in policymaking processes.

A rule is congruent when it states what the law it implements intended, nothing more, nothing less. To Diver, threats to congruence are "overinclusiveness" and "underinclusiveness." These conditions occur when the rule includes persons, things, or activities that should not be included or excludes those that should be included. Simplicity is achieved when there are few steps and relatively little information needed to determine the applicability of and establish compliance with a rule. Complexity is the threat to simplicity. If transparency is always correlated closely with accessibility and congruence, this would present no difficulty. However, the reality is quite different. Thus, tradeoffs among these three values are unavoidable, and courts must be more sensitive to these tradeoffs (Rosenblum 1972).

Cornelius Kerwin (2003, 3), borrowing from the Administrative Procedure Act, defines a rule as the whole or part of an agency statement of general or particular applicability and future effect designed to implement, interpret, or prescribe law or policy. At the managerial level, the responsibility of developing rules may lie in the hands of a task force or work group (Kerwin 2003, 135). Rules are by-products of the deliberations and votes of elected representatives, but they are not themselves legislation. They are products of the bureaucratic institutions to which we entrust the implementation, management, and administration of our law and public policy (Peters 1993; West 1985). The rules issued by departments, agencies, or commissions are law, and they carry the same weight as Congressional legislation, presidential orders, and judicial decisions. Bureaucratic institutions are vested with all three governmental powers established in the Constitution. Through a device called delegation of authority, government agencies perform legislative, executive, and judicial functions. It is significant that agencies are the sources of rules, because it means rulemaking is subjected to the external and internal influences that have been found to affect decision making in our public bureaucracies.

Kerwin identifies three categories as a way of classifying rules. The first category consists of legislative and substantive rules. These are instances when, by congressional mandate or authorization, agencies write what amounts to new law. These rules bind the agency and the public and must be developed in accordance with mandatory procedures. Legislative rules prescribe law and policy. The second category consists of interpretive rules. These occur when agencies are compelled to explain to the public how it interprets existing law and policy. Because they are advisory in nature, interpretive rules can be developed in any way the agency sees fit, but they are generally published in the *Federal Register.* The third category is procedural rules that define the organization and processes of agencies. These rules inform the public how they can participate in a range of agency decision-making including rulemaking.

One of the agencies that is deeply involved in procedural rulemaking is the U.S. Forest Service (USFS) in the Department of Agriculture. In the early 1990s, members of Congress had complained that the procedures the agency was using to include the public in decision making were flawed and needed to be revised. They believed that existing regulations caused delays that hurt the timber industry and other forest interests; other critics said the existing procedures did not sufficiently involve the public. They sought changes that would result in strict timelines for filing public comments and for administrative appeals of projects. In 1993, the USFS published proposed regulations dealing with these issues, which took the form of changes to the *Code of Federal Regulations* that became effective in 1994. President Clinton then ordered more revisions to USFS procedures dealing with public participation, and a new rule was adopted just two days after the 2000 presidential election.

As one of the first actions of his new administration, George W. Bush had sent a memorandum to executive departments and agencies announcing a review of all new and pending regulations that had been proposed under President Clinton, including the new procedures that had been adopted by the USFS. The appeals procedures the agency had proposed and adopted were stopped, as if they had never taken place. After review, Bush administration officials ordered the Forest Service to develop still another set of rules dealing with public participation and administrative appeals. This time, reflecting the Bush administration's direction, the USFS proposed rules that gave them considerably more discretion that was designed to make forest planning more efficient, reduce costs by eliminating procedural detail, and give more flexibility to local managers (Vaughn and Cortner 2005).

One aspect of the proposed procedural rules relating to public review and comment was controversial enough that the Forest Service abandoned it early on. Upon taking office in 2001, President Bush had initiated a set of government reform efforts, collectively known as the President's Management Agenda (PMA), "to make the Federal government more results-oriented, efficient, and citizen-oriented." One element of the PMA was Expanding Electronic Government, composed of a suite of 24 cross-agency projects to modernize and integrate information technology. Congress followed up with passage of the E-Government Act of 2002.

While the administration was encouraging use of the Internet as part of the regulatory process, the Forest Service attempted to move in the opposite direction, responding to an unprecedented 2000 campaign by environmental groups and their members in support of a new rule governing roadless areas. It is estimated that the agency received 1.6 million public comments, with critics noting that the majority of them were mass e-mails and pre-printed postcards. The barrage was sufficient to convince the USFS to use e-mail filters that sometimes rejected citizen comments, and to propose a new rule that would ban form letters, check-off lists, pre-printed postcards, or other similar duplicative materials from being considered. After months of criticism that this amounted to an inappropriate use of the agency's discretion in how it handled public participation, the Forest Service abandoned the plan (Vaughn and Cortner 2005, 187–188).

Rulemaking is an important tool in limiting the power and discretion of all managers. While acknowledging that some discretion is essential if the administrative process is to operate effectively, efficiently, and fairly, Kenneth Davis concluded that our systems are flooded with excessive discretionary power that needed to be checked. Rules, even when unwritten, set limits on the authority of public officials in all areas of work. It exposes officials to scrutiny from the public.

Another strategy, *checking*, means simply that a legislative body or citizens should check managers' decisions against known policy standards as a protection against arbitrariness. Managers might also check each other's standards as a strategy for limiting abuse of discretion. While checking may originate from external sources, the most usual checking authority is a superior office such as a council or state legislature. In the case of the president, the ultimate superior bodies are Congress and the Supreme Court, acting on behalf of the Constitution's intent of shared powers and national interest.

The Changing Managerial Climate

Managerial practices have shifted at all levels of government. Talk of new public management elicits great interest among contemporary administrative pundits. Managers are supposed to be aware of the need to *de-bureaucratize,* that is, work with less but achieve more. Managers are expected to be customer-friendly and to steer rather than row their agencies. Managers, whether elected or appointed, need to be responsive to virtual processes and embrace changing technological environments including greater openness in decision making. They must also confront squarely the realities of a changing global economy. Public managers cannot wait for globalization to come to them; they are required to prepare for its essence and manifestations locally. The 2004 and 2006 election campaigns were replete with accusations of job outsourcing and loss of jobs at the expense of local firms. Debates on tax reforms did not leave out the specifics of these linkages. Providing tax incentives to companies that create jobs locally was a persistent theme in the political rhetoric associated with both presidential and nationwide elections.

Even local governments are not spared the new dimensions of public administration. To better understand their changing roles in the unfolding circumstances, it is appropriate to discuss limitations on managerial discretion. The concern is that managerial discretion not be abused, especially when policy makers persistently promote a specific ideology in policymaking and implementation. Arguably, the place of ideology in influencing policy choices and subsequent decision-making merits continued discussion.

Contemporary Ideological Influences on Discretionary Policymaking

Chapter 4's discussion of discretion at the federal level provided examples of various ways in which the president exercises discretion. One of the major influences on the president is his ideological commitment, and how it affects the way in which decisions are made. The two major ideologies prevalent in U.S. politics are the neoliberal and neoconservative models.

Neoliberalism as a moral and social philosophy is a set of economic policies that advocates less government in domestic governance and free markets at the international scene. Neoliberalism rejects positive government intervention in the economy and supports privatization in achieving social objectives.

On the other hand, *neoconservatism* is generally understood to denote an ideological persuasion that opposes "big government." Neoconservatism is opposed to the radical left and is generally in support of the aristocratic elite. While conservatism is basically characterized by deep opposition to centralized political power, the differences between the new and old forms are perhaps more visible in terms of the proliferation of influential think tanks and their control of contemporary public policy agenda. The power of neoconservatives in the U.S. political system has grown in recent years, especially after the end of formal communism. Old conservatism gained impetus in the 1930s, through opposition to the New Deal. On its part, neoconservatism, vehemently opposed the Great Society projects.

The starting point is to recognize that presidential appointees are "more than just the leaders of bureaucracy and are key controllers of what agencies do" (Light 1999, 519). As one scholar argues, a number of political executives enjoy greater ability to influence policy direction because of the strength of their personalities. The degree to which the president defers to their expertise and prerogatives is a function of several variables including the importance of their department, the salience of the issues they handle to the president's agenda, and ties with key electoral constituencies (Campbell 1993, 384).

The basic point is that the degree of ideological commitment results in higher forms of policy consensus over key public issues. That the nation's policy decision-making trajectory is heavily influenced by such long-term inclination toward an ideological school is well established. Once the ideological apparatus is established, it becomes institutionalized and difficult to change. More profoundly, an ideology may control policy formation mapping and shape the executive and managerial level appointment processes. As March and Olsen pointed out, institutions are organizational mechanisms that are relatively invariant in the face of turnovers of individual members (March and Olsen 1984, 741). Of importance to this analysis is the party systems, which in a democracy such as the United States, have established networks with socioeconomic institutions and embrace ideological positions that they bring to the policymaking table.

Administrators and managers committed to implementation of policy programs with heavy ideological leanings are more willing to use their discretion to support those programs. Besides, the lesser the ideological distance between the executives and members of Congress, the greater their discretionary authority and ability to force bureaucratic compliance, in vital public policy areas including fiscal matters (Krause 2000). An investigation of the relationship between long run appointments of both neoliberal and neoconservative managers and executives and their impact on policy outputs shows a linear pattern.

When an elected president seeks to promote a specific ideological agenda, there is likelihood that the administration's policy choices are restricted or confined to attaining policy goals that mirror the president's ideological platform. Arguably, a chief executive with considerable political capital will seek to advance the causes for which he was elected. Of course, federal executives are both elected and careerists (Aberbach and Rockman 2000, 54). One key question is whether chief executives, especially presidents, appoint public officials who promote an ideological agenda. Understanding the connections between ideology and presidential appointments, especially federal executives, gives us a sense of the process and how it shapes discretionary decision-making processes. Presidents Bill Clinton and George W. Bush provide examples of presidents' ideological strands. Considerable scholarship has been published that analyzes presidential appointments and appointment strategies (Carter 1994; Weko 1995; Heclo 1977; Mackenzie 1987).

Clinton as Liberal

Was Bill Clinton an ideologue? Numerous conservative news outlets depicted President Clinton's appointees to federal courts and civil service as "liberals." Yet, there were also opinions that Clinton won the election against President George H. W. Bush in part because he embraced a middle of the road, *New Way* approach in his service as chief manager of the federal government.

A number of academics consider the majority of Clinton's executive and judicial appointees as firmly in the middle of the road. In an important study of judicial appointments, the liberal rating was derived from analyzing the court decisions made in three types of cases: criminal, civil rights and liberties, and labor and economic regulation (Stidham et al. 1996). Sentiments that Clinton's appointees were in the moderate mainstream group were widely shared among several observers of the administration's conduct. Most Republicans, including Senate Judiciary Committee Chairman Orrin Hatch (R-Utah), believed Clinton's appointees were too liberal (Schoenberger 1996). But was he speaking with reference to judicial nominees or all appointments in general?

President Clinton's civil service and Senior Executive Service (SES) appointees were mostly careerists. Maranto attributes this to the fact that the Democratic Party had been "long absent" from the presidency and therefore "he had relatively few experienced Democrats to call on for appointments" (Maranto 2004). Before his election to office, Republicans held the White House for 20 of the previous 24 years, meaning that Clinton had to appoint executives who would seek gradual changes in light of the middle-of-the-road agenda of the New Democrats. Clinton's first administration had campaigned on the platform of broad ideals rather than an ideological and programmatic agenda (Warshaw 1997, 181). Clinton's administration was certainly not a modern "New Deal" platform, which Republicans since 1936 have proclaimed to be against their core vision of governance, especially government responsibility and the place of individuals' liberties and rights (Sutton 2002, 203).

Clinton had very little experience in Washington DC and therefore had to depend on appointees whose professional disposition was moderate, at the very least. His campaign agenda mirrored the ideals formulated by the centralist Democratic Leadership Council and its think tank, the Progressive Policy Institute (PPI). Clinton also successfully cast his campaign as a referendum of the new against the old rather than liberals versus conservatives (Reske 1997).

Perhaps Clinton's appointment of Republican William Cohen as Defense Secretary is illustrative of his desire to emphasize pragmatism rather than promoting an ideological agenda. Clinton was basically acknowledging the suggestion that, "defense careerists are ideologically closer to Republican appointees" (Maranto 2004). Although "liberal leaning" Leon Panetta of California was head of the Office of Management and Budget (OMB), he was generally a moderate, as was Robert Robin, a Wall Street investment banker who headed Clinton's National Economic Council (NEC). The same argument can be made for his nomination of Senator Lloyd Bentsen (D-Texas) as Treasury Secretary. Bentsen had been Chairman of the Joint Economic Committee and had voted for tax cuts in 1980 and 1991.

Clinton was also concerned with the appointment of a diverse body of public executives. Clinton's diversity agenda strongly promoted a balance of ethnic, gender, and geographic (EGG) considerations. Clinton's appointees are summed up well in a description of the crucial second-tier managerial staff that included assistant secretaries, undersecretaries, and deputy secretaries. Shirley Warshaw observed, "The primary criterion for appointment was that these nominees meet the EGG test. Political philosophy was not considered to any significant degree" (Warshaw 1997, 184).

Beyond diversity, Watson points out that Clinton's cabinet appointees were defined more by their educational credentials than any other variables (Watson 1993). As *Washington Post* analyst Al Kamen observed, the appointees were pragmatists rather than ideologues (Kamen 1993).

In the realm of foreign affairs, Clinton's administration was criticized by neoconservatives for reducing military expenditures and lacking a clear sense of moralistic idealism. One of the galvanizing issues was the removal of Saddam Hussein from power in Iraq and condemnation of China's policy toward Taiwan. The 2000 election of George W. Bush represents a different experience in terms of the administration's ideological orientation.

The Neoconservative Political Agenda

In contemporary political history, the effects of the first Republican takeover at the turn of the 20th century, beginning with Theodore Roosevelt (1901–1908) and continuing with William Taft (1909–1912), Warren Harding (1921–1924), Calvin Coolidge (1925–1928), and Herbert Hoover (1929–1932), were periods in which remnants of the Puritan ethic, especially the notion of invoking the city on the hill moralism, drove the U.S. culture. When a Democratic president, Woodrow Wilson, broke the Republican stretch in 1912, he also embraced some form of moralism, albeit internationally, through "going to war to defend freedoms and democracy." Regardless of the Republican Party's pretense to domestic moralism, its core constituencies were more concerned about personal moral behavior than problems of social justice and economic inequality. It is in the area of social justice and economic security that Democrats, especially under Franklin D. Roosevelt's (FDR) leadership, that these concerns became a permanent feature of the policy discourse. FDR's presidency is generally considered to be the beginning point of the modern presidency, and most significantly, the high point in the rise of public bureaucracy. It is then that the country witnessed an expansion of government programs.

Conservatives saw the growth in public programs as a direct challenge to their fundamental beliefs in creating a social order that would preserve their advantages. But one must not necessarily assume conservatism was an all-Republican idea. To the contrary, in the South, conservatives participated in national political life in the 1930s within the framework of the Democratic Party because of traditional reasons. Parts of the South had rejected moderate Republicanism based on Lincoln's Emancipation Proclamation. For a short while, they also supported FDR's New Deal to the extent that the government assisted farmers during the economic distress of the 1930s. By 1960, a significant number of Protestant conservatives campaigned against John F. Kennedy's election, perhaps because he was Catholic. The shift to conservatism and its contemporary form can be traced to the consolidation process beginning with Senator Barry Goldwater's campaign in 1964 as a candidate for all Christian conservatives.

The "ultraconservative" Ronald Reagan, an associate of Goldwater, more than any recent Republican leader gave conservatism its current form. The waves of conservatism as a movement in American politics were boosted first by Barry Goldwater's campaign and Ronald Reagan's ascendancy to the presidency in 1980, and Newt Gingrich's efforts to capture the House in 1994. Conservatives took over the GOP in 1974, and they were energized by the Equal Rights Amendment bill and the 1978 government threat to increase regulation of religious schools. For his part, Ronald Reagan aggressively embraced key conservative values and sought to overhaul the system, including reducing the role of the government, cutting taxes, and returning services to local governments (Warshaw 1997, 111). Certainly, Richard Nixon's moral failures with Watergate did not go down well with conservatives, but he and other Republican political leaders, governors, and mayors appointed individuals who embraced the newer forms of conservatism (*neo-cons*).

The Nixon administration nominated ideological conservatives to head agencies, including the Office of Economic Opportunity (OEO), in an attempt to modify the Great Society and War on Poverty initiatives that were the bedrock of the Lyndon B. Johnson administration's Democratic agenda. Similarly, the Reagan administration tapped into its pool of conservatives to manage public agencies and departments (Light 1999, 520). Richard Nixon's record on dismantling the Great Society was legendary. Most authors believe he misused his executive discretion by ordering the Office of Management and Budget (OMB) to impound more than $40 billion in appropriated funds from programs he did not like (Patterson 2004, 419).

Two other recent Republican Party administrations, those of Gerald Ford (1974–1976), and George H. W. Bush (1989–1992) lost re-election to Democrats Jimmy Carter and Bill Clinton (Norquist 1993; Barker 1994, 6). Most analysts observe that the two Republican leaders did not energize the core Christian Right base. Pundits contend that the two did not implement enough conservative policies that would endear them to the massive block of the now highly organized Christian Right. More specifically, newer assessments reveal that their records in implementing conservative public policies did not match those of Ronald Reagan and now, George W. Bush. Perhaps, President George W. Bush has propelled the conservative agenda to newer and unprecedented heights.

One of the conundrums between the impacts of these Republican administrations is the congruence between policy managers' neoconservative values and their policy implementation strategies. On balance, evidence suggests that most public policy managers in the neoconservative tradition structure their discretionary actions on a neoconservative agenda.

Policy neutrality at the level of policy management is explicable, for the most part, within an ideological framework. Any explanations for policy management, especially when discretion is applied, therefore can be considered to be consistent with maximization of a conservative ideological agenda. Such is the nature of policy formulation and implementation in a political environment pregnant with ideological fervor.

The rage on the political right has resulted in the emergence of a radically anti-government and populist conservative agenda (Crothers 2003). Neoconservative militias have called for a rollback in government services and tax cuts while embracing militarism abroad. Previously, they coalesced around a strong anti-communism globalist agenda. The conservatives saw big government as the major threat to their traditional religious and economic values. In their new social movements, the Religious Right and Christian Coalition quickly became a force to reckon with at both national and local levels. By and large, the 1994 Republican takeover of Congress was, in part, their success. The Christian Coalition supported the Republican Party's Contract with America and added its own Contract with the American Family that sought to control local education, parental rights, family-friendly family relief, and privatization.

Many public service managers appointed by the Bush administration have embraced a neoliberal agenda. When managers hold an explicit ideological agenda, members of the public, who are key stakeholders in agency outputs, must expect policy outputs that mirror those values consistent with managerial and executive ideological dispositions. Such managerial outlooks confer benefits to groups that embrace similar values. At the same time, groups outside the ideological mix regard discretionary actions by those policymakers to be broadly countervailing, even though democratically legitimate.

In theory, if the broad majority is conservative, then managerial and executive policies emanating from the political system would not pose a major acceptability challenge. However, when the population is divided in two roughly equal blocks, then discretionary actions bent toward formulating and implementing a largely ideological agenda might maximize certain values disproportionately to the detriment of fundamental rights of a sizeable population. Managers bear a large share of those costs to the larger society.

Although it has been argued that executive and managerial power can be constrained and checked within the democratic apparatus, administrative theory still regards individuals as ultimately accountable for their actions. Administrative responsibility and accountability as important values still predict consequences for ideologically-driven public executives and managers, especially when their discretionary policy actions produce actions that in the long run produce more risks and costs to society. Ideally, managerial actions should leave no one behind. In more technical language, policy guidelines that embrace Pareto criterion are preferred, for the most part, within bounded rationality. *Pareto criteria* assume that those policy decisions made will leave no one worse off and at least some members of society in better social conditions than prior situations.

If managerial and executive embrace of an ideological agenda leads to performance that is either consistent or inconsistent with higher ethical values and/or higher costs to society, the policies might be reasonably interpreted to be inconsistent with broader societal good. Therefore, policy formulation and implementation should be, in large, measure-guided. While the convergence of interests, operating in a deeply divided society, must be potentially embedded in an ideological framework, most policy outcomes should increase the potential for larger societal benefits. This is the balancing act that policy managers must grapple with as they exercise discretion.

The impact of managerial ideological decision-making is bound to have some detrimental effects of entrenched ideological policymaking in general. Sufficiently high levels of conservatism in policy orientation do not reduce the risk of political backlash when an opposing highly-charged ideological administration takes over. Discretion is at the political margins of policymaking. Managerial policy actions that are sufficiently sensitive to the "other" side stand a better chance of successful implementation, especially in a mature civil service that embraces principles of Weberian neutrality. However, managerial and executive actions that stand out as being thickly biased lead to long run performance discrepancies.

There are many examples to show the short run performance of a sample of administrative and managerial discretionary policy leadership in recent conservative administrations. Consistent with prior studies, sample policy steering and leadership have biased impacts on public policy outputs. This pattern is consistent with value maximizing motives of any ideologically biased administration.

At the higher levels of public policy management, conservative takeovers yield policy outcomes that in the short run are at odds with populations that do not share conservative ideological orientations. Simultaneously, the policy outcomes produce outcomes favored by those with similar values. Perhaps this is common sense and expected in a less than perfect democracy. The theoretical issue, however, is that policy administrators and managers designing and implementing policies around an ideology are likely to narrow their choices and drive public policy in a linear direction, thus, to a large extent, constraining discretion. It may be that this is another way of recognizing Augustus Jones' finding that appointees who do not favor a specific policy choice are less enthusiastic implementing it (Jones 1991). The poignant question would be, would a self-identified conservative implement liberal policies?

Bush as Conservative

President George W. Bush's strong credentials as a neoconservative have been evident in his appointments. Arguably, his form of conservatism superseded Ronald Reagan's in terms of the role played by the Religious Right. Bush was aired on national TV claiming that he was a "born again" Christian and that "the hand of God was guiding the affairs of this nation" (Kengor 2004; Aikman 2004; Singer 2004).

While the late Ed McAteer's Religious Roundtable, his protégé Jerry Falwell's Moral Majority, Pat Robertson, and other evangelical groups and individuals backed Reagan's 1980 presidential campaign, their role was not as entrenched as under George W. Bush (Montgomery et al. 1996). In the 2000 election, Bush won more than 79 percent of voters who described themselves in exit polls as members of the Christian or Religious Right. The Religious Right more forcefully blessed George W. Bush's campaigns in 2000 and 2004, taking advantage of new technologies to mobilize believers to fight against the "unholy" Democrats. Ironically, the modern rise of the Religious Right began in 1976 when Jimmy Carter was president (Peterson 2002). In fact, some conservative Christians helped elect Carter in the same year but turned against him when he promoted what proved to be socially moderate policies.

The rewards for the Christian Right's support were enormous. First, through his Faith-Based Initiatives, the President channeled federal monies to religious organizations that provide a host of public services. Because Congress had stalled the Faith-Based Initiatives Bill, President Bush issued two executive orders embedding offices for faith-based agencies across the government in various departments, including Health and Human Services, Housing and Urban Development, Labor, Justice, Education, Agriculture, and the Agency for International Development (USAID).

Second, he appointed Christian conservatives to policy management positions in the federal bureaucracy. Several of these appointments had managerial oversight in key regulatory boards. Others enforced agendas often without consultation with vital bureaucratic expert bodies or—worse—without adequate public scrutiny. An example is that of Eric W. Treene, who was installed at the Justice Department as special counsel for religious discrimination. Treene, who was litigation director at the Becket Fund for Religious Liberty, a public interest law firm, was endorsed by conservative religious activists (Duin 2004).

Another example is Bush's appointment of Creationist George Deutsch to the National Aeronautics and Space Administration (NASA) Public Affairs office. As a Public Affairs Officer, part of his role was to provide liaison for scientists to interview with the media. His role with others in the NASA public relations and affairs office is to ensure that public information products are well written and appropriate for the intended audience. However, he had no role regarding the content of the information to be provided to the public and could not change the scientific or technical data.

Deutsch tried to prevent NASA scientists from speaking publicly about the divide between creationism and evolutionary theories. NASA policy has always been to present scientific findings without religious overtones. Although individual scientists employed by NASA can present personal views outside their official area of expertise in non-official capacities, they are required to clearly state that their views are individual and ask to be quoted as such. He eventually resigned after allegations about lying on his resume (Revkin 2006). Deutsch was just one among hundreds of

Bush administration officials who sought to attack scientifically-determined social policies, including limiting funding for cloning and stem cell research, regulating science that supports abortion, and embedding creationism in public schools.

Conservatism blends well with creationism because it supports elements of Social Darwinian thought that individuals are self-interested but capable of altruism toward family and friends. Furthermore, Social Darwinism confirms the view that "individuals have inherently unequal abilities and that these inequalities are likely to be greatest in the personality traits, such as intelligence and ambition, that are related to acquiring property" (McGinnis 1997, 7). As John McGinnis noted, "Conservatism will certainly be easier to integrate with evolutionary biology" (McGinnis 1997). These values, in the structural content of policymaking, play an important role in the use of managerial discretion.

Policymaking in the education sector informs the political socialization processes more profoundly. The issues associated with school curriculums, and especially the debate about creationism, has continued to challenge elected and appointed policymakers. On the surface, it might not appear to be an issue of substance. Yet, appointments of conservatives have affected the science–religion policy debate in an unprecedented way. The scientific community has been at odds with appointees of the neoconservative bent who signaled that evolution was unprovable. While promoting the concept of Intelligent Design (ID), neoconservatives have sought to control Boards of Education and to force teachers to offer an alternative explanation to Darwinian evolutionary theory.

Neoconservatives introduced ID discourses after, "their defeat in court and inability to introduce creationism into schools as a viable, alternative theory to evolution" (Cravatts 2006). For example, in 1987, a Supreme Court case against the State of Louisiana rejected the state's attempt to insist that creationism be taught equally with evolution. In *Malnak v. Yogi,* the court saw creationism as a religiously based interpretation of reality and not a scientific endeavor. Critics of the ID school point to the separation of religion from state activities, specifically, the Constitution's First Amendment's establishment clause. The court's summary of the Louisiana case, *Edwards v. Aguillard,* noted, "The Establishment Clause limits the discretion of state officials to pick and choose among them for the purposes of promoting a particular religious belief" (Cravatts 2006, 5).

Another noteworthy example of a political appointment supported by the conservative religious establishment was that of Paul Bonicelli to be the deputy director of the United States Agency for International Development (USAID), an important agency in matters dealing with foreign aid and the promotion of democracy. Bonicelli's main credential was that he had been a Republican staffer on the International Relations Committee in the House of Representatives. He also served as dean of academic affairs at Patrick Henry College, a Christian fundamentalist institution in rural Virginia whose motto is, "For Christ and Liberty."

In 2002, President Bush had appointed Bonicelli and Janice Crouse of the ultraconservative Concerned Women for America to be a part of the American delegation to the United Nations Children's Conference. Bonicelli was expected to play a central role in promoting biblical values in U.S. foreign policy, and was among the numerous appointees with conservative credentials to serve in foreign policy implementation. Apparently, out of his concern that the Senate might battle over the confirmation of his nominee to the position of U.S. representative to the United Nations, Bush named John Bolton while Congress was in recess. Critics of the administration viewed the recess appointment as a strategy for overriding the Senate's wishes. This is not unusual, as presidents have often used their recess appointment power for political reasons (Hogue 2005a, 1).

From a Constitutional perspective, recess appointments are within the president's powers. The Constitution, in Article II section 2, Clause 3, notes that the "president shall have power to fill up all vacancies that may happen during the recess of the Senate, by granting commissions which shall expire at the end of their next session." According to a Congressional Research Service (CRS) Report for Congress, the purpose of a recess appointment was to "allow the President to maintain the continuity of administrative government through the temporary filling of offices during periods when the Senate was not in session, at which time his nominees could not be considered or confirmed" (Hogue 2005a, 1). Filling vacancies, in the language of the courts as seen in *Staebler v. Carter* (1979) and *Mackie v. Clinton* (1993) has been interpreted broadly to mean that the "president would make appointments to any position that becomes vacant prior to the recess and continued to be vacant during the recess, as well as positions that become vacant during the recess" (Hogue 2005a, 3).

The frequency of appointments varies with contingencies and presidential styles. For example, Ronald Reagan appointed 240 individuals during recess time, George H. W. Bush, 77, Bill Clinton 140, and George W. Bush made 110 recess appointments during his first term (Hogue 2005a, 2). Technically, at the end of the session, the appointee has to either leave office or stand for formal confirmation in the Senate. This did not happen in the case of Bolton, who served through December 2006. Bolton had a long standing record of lack of respect for the United Nations and international law, and his conduct was also a subject of intense discussion, particularly because he "is suspected of using National Security Agency wiretaps to investigate rival diplomats in the intelligence field" (CNN 2005).

Paul Wolfowitz, a Bush nominee as president of the World Bank during a period of European and Third World disquiet, was a student of Leo Strauss, a former political science professor at Chicago University and the father of neoconservatism.

Many critics saw Strauss as a fascist thinker, advocate for elitist schemes, and hater of democracy. Strauss was considered an advocate of the tyranny of the wise and supporter of traditional and religious loyalties (Dennis 2005). On the other hand, Wolfowitz's supporters regarded him as a visionary intellectual while his detractors considered him an "ambitious ideologue" (Baker 2005).

The appointment of Paul Hoffman, a deputy assistant secretary at the Department of Interior, may not have been big news. Yet, in several ways, it fits into the pattern described above. Hoffman had previously run the Chamber of Commerce in Cody, Wyoming and was an aide to fellow Wyoming resident, Vice President Dick Cheney. Hoffman was responsible for revising the basic management policy of the National Park System. He is reported to have rewritten several National Park policies to "allow the sale of religious merchandise," and "remove from the policy document any reference to evolution or evolutionary processes." His policy mission, contrary to National Park Service rules, therefore included "doing everything possible to strip away a scientific basis for Park management" (Wilkinson 2005).

There were other important dimensions of President George W. Bush's appointment of conservatives alleged to have been approved by the Christian Right. Bush named John Ashcroft as Attorney General, much to the chagrin of some liberals and moderate conservatives who in several opinionated forums derided his appointments of neoconservatives to public office (Huberman 2003; Hightower 2004). Ashcroft, considered a religious man, was later replaced by another conservative, Alberto Gonzalez, who was the son of a Pentecostal preacher. During his Senate confirmation hearings, Ashcroft responded to a question from Senator Arlen Specter (R-Pennsylvania) concerning his thinking about a review of the attorney general's discretion, especially the work of Special Counsel, appointed whenever conflict arose. He remarked that he was not sure of what the remedy to standard abuses of discretion were, other than to note that, "This is a delicate arena of the line between the executive and the judicial" (Federal Documents Clearing House 2000). Ashcroft later admitted that the "right oversight by legislative officials is very important." Most commentators regarded Ashcroft's tenure as having been remarkable, especially his prosecution of individuals considered a danger to homeland security. Many regard Ashcroft to have acted in a manner that challenged freedoms and liberties of Americans at unprecedented levels.

Besides Ashcroft, President Bush nominated conservatives to the U.S. Supreme Court. First, he replaced Chief Justice William Rehnquist with John Roberts, Jr., another conservative. Most pundits regarded the failed senate confirmation of White House Counsel Harriet Miers to the Supreme Court as having been influenced by the Religious Right's assessment that she was not conservative enough. Conversely, the nomination and subsequent confirmation of Justice Samuel A. Alito, Jr. to replace retiring Justice Sandra Day O'Connor was seen as a victory for the Christian Right. In 1984, Alito had been a government lawyer in the Reagan administration.

Overall, the expectation was that a neoconservative Supreme Court would give support to policies that are ideologically inclined. This move has not been without challenge. In fact, members of the scientific community have vehemently opposed the administration's tilting of public policies towards promoting an ideological agenda. U.S. scientists have persistently called for restoration of scientific integrity in policymaking.

Conclusions

From this brief discussion of appointments, the case can be made that at the policymaking level, managers in the neoconservative fold use their discretion and authority to promote an ideological agenda. They have attempted to shape policy in at least two important ways: first, by redefining public values and promoting actions that reify conservatism. Second, they provide a new level of public recognition of conservative agendas in all aspects of public policymaking, including undermining the scientific basis for policymaking, by embedding religious doctrine in the formulation and articulation stages. As in the past, the conservative administration utilizes managerial and executive discretion to its fullest in directing agency goals.

To the extent that elected and appointed officials set policy goals, their discretionary actions will continue to reflect their ideological biases. However, to the extent that bureaucrats wish to implement policies in a neutral way, tensions will ensue (Reeves 1986, 119). Thus, just how much discretion is possible at the managerial and executive level is also a function of the ability of the bureaucracy to bridge the gap created by ideologically-tilted policy structures and decision processes. In the new millennium, no doubt, the policy environment is governed by presidential leadership whose ideology informs policy decisions in all three branches of federal government.

Presidents as managers have a large number of decisions to make. Writing in the 1830s, Alexis de Tocqueville argued that the American president could not even prevent a law from being passed. He had to cooperate with Congress to make sure that laws were enforced. A century later, Franklin D. Roosevelt made the presidency a powerful entity. Under Roosevelt, the president was the foremost ruler of the country. As manager, the president continues to be responsible for faithfully executing the laws of the land. How he executes laws is the realm in which discretion can be best understood. Presidential use of executive orders is one instrument that gives the impression that presidents are using the resources they have to make discretionary decisions. If there is public perception that an executive order has created a situation that compromises public interests, then the specific order as an instrument of discretion is questioned.

The Elian Gonzalez case discussed in this chapter illustrates the difficulties of balancing politics and discretionary power. The Attorney General's decision was based on the letter of the law, executing the law of the land on behalf of the executive. Both moral and political considerations were incorporated in Janet Reno's decision, the most fundamental being to return a child to his biological father. This value weighed far more than political exigencies, showing solidarity against Cuba's lack of democracy and the plight of fleeing refugees. While the case is specific to federal issues, it demonstrates the broader interplay of discretion and management that can affect managers at all levels of government.

At both state and local levels, too much discretion is detected whenever the number of lawsuits and general public discontent about officials' conduct increases. Public dissatisfaction in an official's use of discretion will be readily spotted in local media coverage. Much like the president, state governors and mayors, especially those in strong mayor frameworks, use executive orders to pass a host of discretionary measures. Still, they enjoy similar powers to make appointments and reorganize government operations as they deem fit. Local officials, especially school administrators, must often deal with the delegation of managerial discretion. Just how much can state and local governments take?

It might be useful to note that in the case of school violence described in Chapter 4, federal laws are often at odds with school district regulations. Many experts in the realm of education favor flexibility in dealing with cases of school violence but the overriding public interest in the matter brings it to national focus. This is a question for experts in American federalism. It would mean having a precise measure of what the proper role of state and local governments should be. Having answered that part, the next stage is to find answers to the use of the *residual* powers at the state and local government levels. Obviously, these are issues of state and local specificity. The challenge is to understand the factors that shape localized discretionary policy choices, especially electoral politics. Managers making discretionary choices at the margins are most likely to do so with party politics in mind. The degree of inter-party competition as well as the rational need to survive an election makes decision actors select choices that are considered more responsive.

The difficulties to be confronted appear to be just how much discretion should managers be allowed? While several authors grapple with this question, the precise answer seems less promising. Discretion in the realm of management seems to fall in the gray area between the legal–rational administrative realities and political realm of pronounced policies. In other words, a manager must make a discretionary decision at the margins of the prescribed law. What pass as strategies to control discretion must still face the harsh realities of the political ecosystem. The political system is, of course, based on values such as equality, fairness, constitutional competence, representativeness, and justice. These are derived from time tested regime values.

Perhaps we can find clues in understanding the more familiar concept of judicial discretion. We know that judges base their decisions on sentencing guidelines as well as facts determined by a competent jury. If a judge's decision is not based on the facts of the case, it is considered as arbitrary. Likewise, in the context of managerial discretion, certain principles must inform decision making. These principles can be drawn from varied sources including a manager's ethicality and integrity. This is the place where public managers, including the president, governors, mayors, city administrators, county managers, and school district heads, exercise leadership in the government system.

Bibliography

Aberbach, Joel D. and Bert A. Rockman. 1976. "Clashing Beliefs within the Executive Branch: The Nixon Administration Bureaucracy." *American Political Science Review 70* (2): 456–468.

1988. "Mandates or Mandarins? Control and Discretion in the Modern Administrative State," *Public Administration Review 48* (2): 607–612.

1995. "The Political Views of U.S. Senior Federal Executives, 1970–1992." *Journal of Politics 57* (3): 838–852.

2000. *In the Web of Politics: Three Decades of the U.S. Federal Executive.* Washington, DC: Brookings Institution Press.

"About the CIA." 2006. U.S. Central Intelligence Agency. [database online]. Available from www.cia.gov (cited May 31, 2006).

Agranoff, Robert. 1990. "Managing Federalism Through Metropolitan Human Services Intergovernmental Bodies." *Publius: Journal of Federalism 20* (1) Winter: 1–22.

Aikman, David. 2004. *A Man of Faith: The Spiritual Journey of George W. Bush.* Nashville, TN: W Publishing Group.

Alaya, Ana M., and John P. Martin. 2002. "Paterson Mayor Accused of Graft, Feds Charge." *The Star Ledger* (January 25) [database online]. Available from www.nj.com/news/ledger (cited January 20, 2006).

Alderson, Michael J., and Brian L. Betker. 2003. "Managerial Discretion Costs and the Acquisition of Capital: Evidence from Forced Warrant Exercise." *Financial Management 32* (Spring): 109–126.

Alessi, Ryan. 2006. "Fletcher Takes Beating in GOP Poll." *Lexington Herald-Leader* (July 16). [database online]. Available from www.kentucky.com (cited July 16, 2006).

Allison, Graham T. 1980. "Public and Private Management: Are They Fundamentally Alike in All Unimportant Respects?" *Proceedings of the Public Management Research Conference,* November 19–20, 1979. Washington, DC: Office of Personnel Management, OPM Document 127-53-1. (February): 27–38.

American Academy for the Advancement of Science. 2003. "Bi-Cameral Hearing on the Columbia Disaster." (April 15) [electronic bulletin board]. Available from www.aaas.org (cited June 24, 2006).

American Civil Liberties Union. 2002. "Religious Groups and Law Enforcement Officials Charge That Governor Davis' 'No Parole Policy' is Unconstitutional." News release (August 8). [database online]. Available from www.aclunc.org (cited May 26, 2006).

Andrisani, Paul J., Simon Hakim, and E. S. Savas. 2002. *The New Public Management: Lessons from Innovating Governors and Mayors.* Norwell, MA: Kluwer.

Applebome, Peter. 1995. "Political Hands Reach for the Schools." *New York Times* (September 17). [database online]. Available from www.nytimes.com (cited January 21, 2006).

Applebome, Peter, and Jeremy Alford. 2005. "History of Corruption in Louisiana Stirs Fears That Aid Will Go Astray." *New York Times* (October 1). [database online]. Available from www.nytimes.com (cited January 26, 2006).

Arpaio, Joe. 2003. "Sheriff Joe Arpaio's Biography." (October 18). [database online]. Available from www.reelectjoe.com (cited May 24, 2006).

———. 2004. "About the Sheriff." (October 18). [database online]. Available from www.mcso.org (cited January 23, 2006).

Ashworth, Kenneth. 2001. *Caught Between the Dog and the Fireplug, or How to Survive Public Service.* Washington, DC: Georgetown University Press.

Bailey, Thomas, and Thomas Johnson. 2004. "Are Economic Development Incentives Blessings in Disguise or Necessary Evils?" [database online]. Available from www.reap.vt.edu/publications (cited July 7, 2006).

Baker, Gerard. 2005. "Paul Wolfowitz: Cold Eyed Ideologue Who Is a Romantic at Heart." *The Times.* (March 18). [database online]. Available from timesonline.co.uk (cited July 8, 2006).

Ball, Howard, Dale Krane, and Thomas Lauth. 1985. "Discretionary Justice at DOJ: Implementing Section 5 of the Voting Rights Act." In *Discretion, Justice, and Democracy,* edited by Carl F. Pinkele and William C. Louthan. Ames: Iowa State University Press.

Banks, Leo W. 2005. "Catastrophe in Care." *The Tucson Weekly.* (June 2). [database online]. Available from www.tucsonweekly.com (cited July 3, 2005).

Barker, Lucius J. 1994. "Limits of Political Strategy: A Systematic View of the African American Experience." *American Political Science Review 88* (1): 1–13.

Barnard, Chester. 1948. *The Function of Chief Executive.* Cambridge, MA: Harvard University Press.

Bartlett, Bruce. 2001. "Executive Orders, Or Rule By Decree." *National Center for Policy Analysis Idea House* (April 14). [database online]. Available from www.ncpa.org (cited May 31, 2006).

Beardsley, Elizabeth J. 2006. "Stumbo Seeks Removal of 2 Judges in Merit System Case." *Louisville Courier-Journal* (March 4). [database online]. Available from www.courier-journal.com (cited May 26, 2006).

Beer, Samuel H. 1993. *To Make A Nation: The Rediscovery of American Federalism.* Cambridge, MA: Harvard University Press.

Bender, Lewis G., and Thaddeus C. Zolty. 1986. "Rapid Growth: Impacts on thePolitics and Administration of Rural Government." In *Rural Public Administration: Problems and Prospects,* edited by Jim Seroka. Westport, CT: Greenwood Press.

Benedetto, Richard and Andrea Stone. 2006. "Bush Rejects Stem Cell Bill With His First Veto." *USA Today* (July 20). [database online]. Available from www.usatoday.com (cited July 21, 2006).

Berger, Brian. 2003. "NASA Chief Insists Columbia Investigation Board Will Be Independent." (February 12). [database online]. Available from www.space.com (cited June 24, 2006).

Berry, Colleen. 2004. "'Sailor Mongering' Resurfaces in Greenpeace Lawsuit." *American Constitution Society* (December 14). [bulletin board]. Available from www.acsblog.org (cited June 23, 2006).

Bertelli, Anthony M., and Laurence E. Lynn, Jr. 2003. "Managerial Responsibility." *Public Administration Review* 63 (3): 259–268.

Beyle, Thad. 1999. "The Governors." In *Politics in the American States: A Comparative Analysis,* edited by Virginia Gray, Russell Hanson, and Herbert Jacob. Washington, DC: Congressional Quarterly Press.

Blood, Michael R. 2006. "Governor Embraces L.A. Mayor's Plan." *Seattle Post-Intelligencer* (April 19). [database online]. Available from www.seattlepi.com (cited May 3, 2006).

Blume, Howard. 2006. "A Savvy End Run on Schools: Villaraigosa Bypasses L.A Voters in favor of Sacramento Fight He Thinks He Can Win." (April 23). [database online]. Available from www.latimes.com (cited June 23, 2006).

Boghossian, Naush. 2006. "Commission Split on LAUSD Takeover Setback for Mayor." *Daily News* (June 11). [database online]. Available from www.dailynews.com (cited June 14, 2006).

Bowdoin College Internet Reviews. 2005. [database online]. Available from www.bowdoin.edu (cited November 24, 2005).

Burke, John P. 1996. "Administrative Discretion and Responsibility: Another Look at Moral Agency and Democratic Politics." Paper presented at the Annual Meeting of the American Political Science Association, San Francisco, (August 29– September 1).

Cable News Network. 1999a. "Clinton Appoints First Openly Gay Ambassador." (June 4). [database online]. Available from www.cnn.com (cited May 30, 2006). 1999b. "From Little League to Madness: Portraits of the Little Shooters, Are U.S. Schools Safe? In-Depth Special." (April 30). [database online]. Available from www.cnn.com (cited June 20, 2006). 2000. "INS Rules Elian To Return To Cuba." (January 5). [database online]. Available from www.cnn.com (cited June 24, 2006).

2001. "Ford Honored for Decision to Pardon Nixon." (May 21). [database online]. Available from www.cnn.com (cited May 29, 2006).

2005. "Bush Should Use Recess Appointments Power Carefully."(July 4). [database online]. Available from www.cnn.com (cited July 7, 2006).

Caher, John. 2006. "Dismantling Parole: Parole Release Rates Plunge Under Pataki's Tough Policy." *New York Law Journal* (January 31). [database online]. Available from www.law.com (cited May 26, 2006).

Campbell, Colin S. 1993. "Political Executives and Their Officials." In *Political Science: The State of the Discipline,* edited by Ada W. Finifter. Washington, DC: American Political Science Association, 383–406.

Campbell, Colton C. 2001. "The Politics of Presidential Appointments: A Thorny Business." *White House Studies 1* (2): 167–184.

Caputo, David A., and Richard L. Cole. 1977. "General Revenue Sharing: Its Impact on American Cities." *Government Finance* (November): 24–33.

Carrington, Keith Bevon. 1999. "Administrative Discretion in Public Agencies: The Case of Civilian Review of Police." (PhD. Diss., Rutgers University-The State University of New Jersey).

Carroll, Susan, and Daniel Gonzalez. (2005). "Napolitano Taps Disaster Funds for Border Counties." *The Arizona Republic* (August 16). [database online]. Available from www.arizonarepublic.com (cited November 27, 2005).

Carroll, Susan, and Judi Villa. 2005. "Arizona Wants Feds to Deport Criminals." *The Arizona Republic* (February 24). [database online]. Available from www.azcentral .com (cited November 24, 2005).

Carter, Jimmy. 1977. Executive Order 11070, Presidential Advisory Board on Ambassadorial Appointments (February 5). [database online]. Available from www .presidency.ucsb.edu/ws (cited May 30, 2006).

Carter, Stephen L. 1994. *The Confirmation Mess.* New York: Basic Books.

Cartier, Genevieve. 2005. "Administrative Discretion as Dialogue: A Response to John Willis (Or: from Theology to Secularization)." *University of Toronto Law Journal 55* (3): 629–656.

Chambers Dennis J., Ross Jennings, and Robert B. Thomson. 2001. "Managerial Discretion and Accounting for Research and Development Costs." (December) Social Science Research Network Electronic Library. [database online]. Available from www.ssrn.com (cited January 12, 2006).

Chang, Kenneth. 2004. "Scientists Say They Were Questioned on Politics." *New York Times* (July 9). [database online]. Available from www.nytimes.com (cited July 9, 2004).

Chen, Yenn-Ru. 2003. "Managerial Risk Taking: The Impact of Executive Stock Options on Managerial Risktaking," (Ph.D. Diss., University of Houston).

Chiang, Harriet. 2002. "Test of Davis' Stance on Killers: Court to Rule on Parole Practice." *San Francisco Chronicle* (October 7). [database online]. Available from www.sfgate.com (cited May 29, 2006).

"County Sheriff: No More Handcuffing Inmates in Labor to Bed." 2006. (April 19) [database online]. Available from www.thepittsburghchannel.com (cited May 24, 2006).

Cho, Seung Theresa. 1999. "The Effects of Increased Managerial Discretion on Top Executive Composition, Compensation, and Attention: The Implication for Strategic Change and Performance." (PhD. Diss., Columbia University).

Conley, Richard S. 2003. "George Bush and the 102nd Congress: The Impact of Public and 'Private' Veto Threats on Policy Outcomes." *Presidential Studies Quarterly* 33 (4): 730–750.

Conley, Richard S., and Amie Kreppel. 2001. "Toward a New Typology of Vetoes and Overrides." *Political Research Quarterly* 54 (4): 831–852.

Cooper, Phillip J. 2002. *By Order of the President: The Use and Abuse of Executive Direct Action.* Lawrence: University Press of Kansas.

Cooper, Phillip J. 2004. *Cases on Public Law and Administration.* 1st ed. Belmont, CA: Thomson Wadsworth.

2007. *Public Law and Public Administration,* 4th ed. Belmont, CA: Thomson Wadsworth.

Cravatts, Richard L. 2006. "Why Intelligent Design Flunks Science and Why It Will Also Fail in Court." *American Chronicle* (April 17). [database online]. Available from www.americanchronicle.com (cited June 20, 2006).

Crothers, Lane. 2003. *Rage on the Right: The American Militia Movement from Ruby Ridge to Homeland Security.* New York: Rowman & Littlefield.

Dankzker, Mark L. 1994. "Requirements for the Position of Municipal Police Chief: A Content Analysis." *Police Studies* 17 (3): 33–42.

1996. "The Position of Municipal Police Chief: An Examination of Selection and Requisite Skills." *Police Studies* 19 (1): 1–17.

Davis, Kenneth C. 1965. *Administrative Law: Cases, Text, Problems.* St. Paul, MN: West.

1969. *Discretionary Justice: A Preliminary Inquiry.* Baton Rouge: Louisiana State University Press.

Death Penalty Information Center. 2006. "Clemency" [database online]. Available from www.deathpenaltyinfo.org (cited July 14, 2006).

Deen, Rebecca A., and Laura W. Arnold. 2002. "Veto Threats as a Policy Tool: When to Threaten?" *Presidential Studies Quarterly* 32 (1): 30–45.

DeLaet, Debra L. 2006. *The Global Struggle for Human Rights: Universal Principles in World Politics.* Belmont, CA: Thomson Wadsworth.

Denhardt, Janet, and Robert B. Denhardt. 2003. *The New Public Service: Serving, Not Steering.* Armonk, NY: M.E. Sharpe.

Denhardt, Robert B. 2004. *Theories of Public Organization.* Belmont, CA: Thomson Wadsworth.

Dennis, Felix. 2005. "The Ultimate Neoconservative." *The Week Magazine* (April 22). [database online]. Available from www.theweekmagazine.com (cited July 7, 2006).

Derthick, Martha. 2000. "Ways of Achieving Federal Objectives." In *American Intergovernmental Relations,* edited by Laurence J. O'Toole, Jr. Washington, DC: Congressional Quarterly Press.

Diaz, Elvia. 2005. "Bill to Cut Migrant Benefits." *The Arizona Republic* (March 25). [database online]. Available from www.azcentral.com (cited November, 27, 2005).

Dillman, David L. 2002. "The Paradox of Discretion and the Case of Elian Gonzalez." *Public Organization Review* 2 (2): 165–185.

Diver, Colin.1983. "The Optimal Precision of Administrative Rules." *Yale Law Journal* 93 (1): 65–109.

Donnison, David V. 1982. *The Politics of Poverty.* Oxford, UK: Robertson.

Dorf, Michael C. 2002. "A Brief History of Executive Privilege, From George Washington Through Dick Cheney." *Findlaw Legal News and Commentary* (February 6). [database online]. Available from www.writ.news.findlaw.com (cited May 31, 2006).

Drake, Frederick D., and Lynn R. Nelson. 1999. *States' Rights and American Federalists: A Documentary History.* Westport, CT: Greenwood Press.

Duin, Julia. 2004. "Faith, Justice and the American Way." *The Washington Times* (May 6). [database online]. Available from www.washingtontimes.com (cited July 7, 2006).

Dunn, Mike. 2004. "City Council Lobbies for Ethics Reform." KYW News Radio. [database online]. Available from www.kyw1060.com (cited September 24, 2004).

Dworkin, Ronald M. 1979. "Is Law a System of Rules?" In *The Philosophy of Law,* edited by Ronald M. Dworkin. New York: Oxford University Press.

Eggen, Dan and Allan Lengel. 2006. "Officials Defend Raid on Lawmaker's Office." *Washington Post* (May 24). [database online]. Available from www.washingtonpost .com (cited May 31, 2006).

Eggen, Dan and Shailagh Murray. 2006. "FBI Raid on Lawmaker's Office Is Questioned." *Washington Post* (May 23). [database online]. Available from www .washingtonpost.com (cited May 31, 2006).

Elliott, Delbert, Kirk R. Williams, and Beatrix A. Hamburg. 1998. "An Integrated Approach to Violence Prevention." In *Violence in American Schools: A New Perspective,* edited by Delbert Elliott, Kirk R. Williams, and Beatrix A. Hamburg. New York: Cambridge University Press.

Ellis, Steven M. 2004. "Gubernatorial Executive Orders under the Michigan Constitution of 1963." [database online]. Available from www.law.msu.edu/library (cited May 26, 2006).

Escobar, Edward J. 2003. "Bloody Christmas and the Irony of Police Professionalism." *Pacific Historical Review* 72 (2): 171–199.

Executive Order 13132. 1999. Federalism. *Federal Register 64* (153) (August 10): 43255–43259.

Executive Order 13292. 2003. Further Amendment to Executive Order 12958, as Amended, Classified National Security Information. *Federal Register 68* (60), (March 28): 15315–15316.

Federal Documents Clearing House. 2000. *Political Transcript* (January 16). [database online]. Available from www.fdch.com (cited July 7, 2006).

Finer, Herman. 1941. "Administrative Responsibility in Democratic Government." *Public Administration Review 2*: 335–350.

Fisher, William. 2005. "Tom Paine: Bush's Newest Crusader." *Theocracy Watch,* (December 1). [electronic bulletin board]. Available from www.theocracy.watch.com (cited July 9, 2006).

Flaherty, Jordan. 2005. "Hurricane Katrina: Crime and Corruption in New Orleans" (October 17). [database online]. Available from www.alternet.org/katrina (cited May 15, 2006).

Ford, Gerald R. 1974. "President Gerald R. Ford's Remarks on Signing a Proclamation Granting Pardon to Richard Nixon" (September 8). [database online]. Available from www.ford.utexas.edu/library/speeches (cited May 29, 2006).

2006. "Revenue Sharing." *Factbook* (May 17, 2006). [database online]. Available from www.ford.utexas.edu/library (cited July 7, 2006).

Freund, Ernst. 1917. *Standards of American Legislation.* Chicago: University of Chicago Press.

Friedrich, Carl J. 1940. "The Nature of Administrative Responsibility." In *Public Policy,* edited by Carl. J. Friedrich and E. S. Mason. Cambridge, MA: Harvard University Press.

Gerhardt, Michael J. 2000. *The Federal Appointments Process.* Durham, NC: Duke University Press.

Giuliani, Rudolph W. 2002. *Leadership.* New York: Miramax Books.

Gonzalez, Daniel. 2005. "Language Gap Grows." *The Arizona Republic* (October 12). [database online]. Available from www.azcentral.com (cited November 24, 2005).

Gortner, Harold, Julianne Mahler, and Jeanne B. Nicholson. 1997. *Organization Theory: A Public Perspective,* 2nd ed. Fort Worth, TX: Harcourt Brace.

Greenpeace USA. 2003. "Groups Demand Ashcroft Drop Greenpeace 'Sailor Mongering' Case, Support Americans' Right to Protest" (December 11). [electronic bulletin board]. Available from www.greenpeace.org (cited June 23, 2006).

Greenwatch. 2004. "Federal Judge Tosses Out Ashcroft Effort to Stifle Greenpeace, Peaceful Protest" (May 20). [database online]. Available from www.bushgreenwatch.org (cited June 23, 2006).

Grodzins, Morton. 2000. "The American System." In *American Intergovernmental Relations,* edited by Laurence J. O'Toole, Jr. Washington, DC: Congressional Quarterly Press.

Hall, Mimi, and Patrick O'Driscoll. 2005. "Border Patrols Growing in Arizona." *USA Today* (March 29). [database online]. Available from www.usatoday.com (cited November 24, 2005).

Hamilton, Alexander, James Madison, and John Jay. 1982. *The Federalist.* New York: Bantam Books.

Hammond, Thomas H., and Jack H. Knott. 2000. "Public Management, Administrative Leadership, and Policy Choice." In *Advancing Public Management: New Developments in Theory, Methods, and Practice,* edited by Jeffrey Brudney, Laurence O'Toole, Jr., and Hal Rainey. Washington DC: Georgetown University Press.

Handler, Joel. 1986. *The Conditions of Discretion: Authority, Community, Bureaucracy.* New York: Russell Sage.

Handler, Joel F. 1992. *The Conditions of Discretion.* New York: Russell Sage.

Hathaway, Josie. 1999. "Mayor Archer Leads His New School Board on the Road to Public School Reform." (April 19). [database online]. Available from www.usmayors.org (cited May 10, 2006).

Heclo, Hugh. 1977. *A Government of Strangers.* Washington, DC: Brookings Institution.

Heilmann, Michael R. 2003. Principals' Perspectives on Discretion and Decision-Making (Masters Thesis, University of Manitoba, Canada.) [electronic bulletin board]. Available from mspace.lib.umanitoba.ca/(May 26, 2006).

Helber, Steve. 2006. "West Virginia Governor Signs Mine Safety Legislation." *USA Today* (January 26). [database online]. Available from www.usatoday.com (cited May 29, 2006).

Hightower, Jim. 2004. *Let's Stop Beating Around the Bush.* New York: Viking.

Hilts-Scott, Shirley. 2001. "Threats and Disruptions at School Not Tolerated." Arizona Department of Education. [electronic bulletin board]. Available from www1.usu.edu/mprrc (cited January 30, 2002).

Hogue, Henry B. 2005a. "Recess Appointments: Frequently Asked Questions." *CRS Report for Congress* (March 15). Washington, DC: Congressional Research Service.
2005b. "Supreme Court Nominations Not Confirmed 1789–2004." *CRS Report for Congress.* (March 21). Washington, DC: Congressional Research Service.

Honig, Bonnie. 2003. "Bound by Law? Alien Rights, Administrative Discretion and the Politics of Technicality: Lessons from Louis Post and the First Red Scare." Paper presented at the Annual Meeting of the American Political Science Association, Philadelphia (August 28–31).

"Horne, Board Failed on Teacher Who Viewed Porn in Classroom." 2006. *East Valley Tribune* (May 26). [database online]. Available from www.eastvalleytribune.com (cited May 28, 2006).

Horner, Robert, George Sugai, and H. Horner. 2000. "A School-Wide Approach to Student Discipline." *The School Administrator* 57 (2): 20–23.

Howard, Tom. 2006. "County Voters to Decide Limits on Obscenity." *Billings Gazette* (May 21). [database online]. Available from www.billingsgazette.com (cited May 22, 2006).

Howell, William G. 2003. *Power without Persuasion: A Theory of Presidential Action.* Princeton, NJ: Princeton University Press.

Huber, John D., and Charles R. Shipan. 2002. *Deliberate Discretion? The Institutional Foundations of Bureaucratic Autonomy.* New York: Cambridge University Press.

Huberman, Jack. 2003. *The Bush-Hater's Handbook: A Guide to the Most Appalling Presidency of the Past 100 Years.* New York: Nation Books.

Hyman, Irwin A., and Pamela A. Snook. 1999. *Dangerous Schools: What We Can Do About the Physical and Emotional Abuse of Our Children.* San Francisco: Jossey-Bass.

Jones, Augustus J., Jr. 1991. *Affirmative Talk, Affirmative Action: A Comparative Study of the Politics of Affirmative Action.* New York: Praeger.

Jowell, Jeffrey. 1975. *Law and Bureaucracy: Administrative Discretion and the Limits of Legal Action.* New York: Dunellen Publishing Co.

Jreisat, Jamil E. 2002. *Comparative Public Administration and Policy.* Boulder CO: Westview.

"Judge Waives Fine Against Elderly Woman Given Jaywalking Ticket." 2006. *San Jose Mercury News* (July 8). [database online]. Available from www.sanjosemercurynews .com (cited July 14, 2006).

Kaiser, Frederick M. 2006. "Protection of Classified Information by Congress: Practices and Proposals," (April 5) *CRS Report for Congress.* Washington, DC: Congressional Research Service.

Kamen, Al. 1993. "Administration Still Walking on EGG Shells." *Washington Post* (April 19): 21.

Karlin, Rick. 2006. "Pataki's Choices for Jobs Languish." *Albany Times Union* (May 22). [database online]. Available from www.timesunion.com (cited May 27, 2006).

Katzmann, Robert A. 1997. *Courts and Congress.* Washington, DC: Brookings Institution Press.

Kearns, Kevin P. 1996. *Managing for Accountability: Preserving the Public Trust in Public and Non Profit Organizations.* San Francisco: Jossey-Bass.

Kellman, Laurie. 2006. "AG Testimony Sought on Capitol Office Raid." *Boston Globe* (May 31). [database online]. Available from www.boston.com (cited May 31, 2006).

Kengor, Paul. 2004. *God and George W. Bush: A Spiritual Life.* New York: Regan Books.

Kerwin, Cornelius M. 2003. *Rulemaking: How Government Agencies Write Law and Make Policy.* Washington, DC: Congressional Quarterly Press.

Kessler, Ronald. 1994. *Inside the CIA: Revealing the Secrets of the World's Most Powerful Spy Agency.* New York: Pocket Books.

Kettl, Donald F. 2004. *System Under Stress: Homeland Security and American Politics.* Washington, DC: Congressional Quarterly Press.

Key, V. O., Jr., 1949. *Southern Politics in State and Nation.* Knoxville, TN: University of Tennessee Press.

Kiel, Dwight C. 1986. "The Modern Foundations of Administrative Discretion: The Pendleton Act of 1893 and the Act to Regulate Commerce of 1887." In *Administrative Discretion and Public Policy Implementation,* edited by Douglas H. Shumavon and H. Kenneth Hibbeln. New York: Praeger.

Kosar, Kevin R. 2006. "Regular Vetoes and Pocket Vetoes: An Overview." *CRS Report for Congress* (July 20).

Kotter, John P. 1993. "Power, Dependence, and Effective Management." In *The Political Environment of Public Management,* edited by Peter Kobrak. New York: Harper Collins.

Kotter, John P., and Paul R. Lawrence. 1974. *Mayors in Action: Five Approaches to Urban Governance.* New York: Wiley and Sons.

Krane, Dale. 1998. "Local Government Autonomy and Discretion in the U.S." National Academy of Public Administration, Standing Panel on the Federal System. [database online]. Available from www.napawash.org (cited May 22, 2006).

Krause, George A. 2000. "Partisan and Ideological Sources of Fiscal Deficits in the United States." *American Journal of Political Science 44* (3): 541–560.

Kua, Crystal. 2006. "Governor Vetoes Bills Restricting Appointees." *Honolulu Star Bulletin* (May 4). [database online]. Available from www.starbulletin.com (cited May 28, 2006).

Landy, Marc K., Marc J. Roberts, and Stephen J. Thomas. 1994. *The Environmental Protection Agency: Asking the Wrong Questions.* New York: Oxford University Press.

Larkey, Patrick. 1979. *Evaluating Public Programs: The Impact of General Revenue Sharing on Municipal Government.* Princeton, NJ: Princeton University Press.

Lazere, Ed. 2001. "Mayor's Housing Initiative Would Provide Little Assistance to Low Income District Residents Facing the Most Serious Housing Needs." (June 7) DC Fiscal Policy Institute. [database online]. Available from www.dcfpi .org. (cited January 30, 2006).

Leidlein, James. 1993. "In Search of Merit: A Practitioner's Comments on 'The Staffing Function in Illinois State Government After *Rutan*' and 'Curbing Patronage Without Paperasserie.'" *Public Administration Review 53* (4): 391–392.

Lehrer, Jim. 2005. "Hurricane Katrina: Louisiana Governor Responds," *NewsHour with Jim Lehrer* (August 31). [database online]. Available from www.pbs.org/ newshour (cited May 27, 2006).

Leys, William S. 1943. "Ethics and Administrative Discretion." *Public Administration Review 4* (Winter): 10–17.

Lieberman, Joseph. 2006. "Military Role in Katrina Response Seemed Cobbled Together." Testimony before the Committee on Homeland Security and Governmental Affairs. U.S. Senate. Second Sess. (February 9). [database online]. Available from www.senate.gov/~gov_affairs (cited May 30, 2006).

Light, Paul C. 1991. *The President's Agenda: Domestic Policy Choice from Kennedy to Reagan.* Baltimore, MD: Johns Hopkins University Press.

1999. *A Delicate Balance: An Introduction to American Government.* New York: St. Martin's.

Lindner, Charles L. 2005. "Governor, Let Tookie Live." *Los Angeles Times* (December 4). [database online]. Available from www.latimes.com/news (cited May 10, 2006)

Lindstrom, Matthew J. and Stephen F. Robar. 1996. "Executive Organization in Arizona." In Zachary A. Smith, ed. *Politics and Public Policy in Arizona.* Westport, CT: Praeger.

Lipsky, Michael. 1980. *Street-Level Bureaucracy.* New York: Russell Sage.

Liptak, Adam. 2003. "Typical Greenpeace Protest Leads to an Unusual Prosecution," *New York Times* (October 11). [database online]. Available from www.nytimes.com (cited June 23, 2006).

Liu, Gaoquan. "Uncertainty, Managerial Discretion and Incentives." Unpublished paper; (August), Department of Economics, University of Pennsylvania.

Loftus, Tom, and Mark Pitsch. 2006. "Fletcher Indicted." *Louisville Courier-Journal* (May 11). [database online]. Available from www.courier-journal.com (cited May 26, 2006).

Long, Norton. 1949. "Power and Administration." *Public Administration Review 9* (Autumn): 257–264.

Loveridge, Ronald O. 1971. *City Managers in Legislative Politics.* New York: Bobbs-Merrill.

Lowi, Theodore J. 1969. *The End of Liberalism: Ideology, Policy and the Crisis of Public Authority.* New York: W. W. Norton.

Ludd, Steven O. 1986. "The Essentiality of Judicial Review: Toward a More Balanced Understanding of Administrative Discretion in American Government." In *Administrative Discretion and Public Policy Implementation.,* edited by Douglas H. Shumavon and H. Kenneth Hibbeln. New York: Praeger.

MacClennan, Paul. 1998. "Pataki's Disappointing Record on Environmental Issues." *Buffalo News* (September 3). [database online]. Available from www.junkscience.com (cited September 29, 2004).

MacIntyre, Angus. 1986. "The Multiple Sources of Statutory Ambiguity: Tracing the Legislative Origins of Administrative Discretion." In *Administrative Discretion and Public Policy Implementation,* edited by Douglas H. Shumavon and H. Kenneth Hibbeln. New York: Praeger.

Mackenzie, Calvin G. 1987. *The In-and-Outers*. Baltimore: Johns Hopkins University Press.

———. 2001. "Presidential Appointment Process: Origin, Development, and Calls for Reform." Testimony before the Committee on Governmental Affairs. U.S. Senate. First Sess. (April 4). [database online]. Available from www.hsgac.senate.gov (cited May 30, 2006).

Madison, James. 1961. *The Federalist Papers, No. 41*. New York: New American Library.

Mannies, Jo. 2006. "Nomination for Ethics Panel Draws Opposition." *St. Louis Post-Dispatch* (April 27). [database online]. Available from www.stltoday.com (cited May 27, 2006).

Manning, Carol. 2006. "Governor Vetoes Abortion Reporting Bill." (May 19). [database online]. Available from www.kansas.com (cited May 28, 2006).

Marando, Vincent L. 1990. "General Revenue Sharing: Termination and City Response." *State and Local Government Review* 22 (Fall): 98–107.

Maranto, A. Robert. 2004. "Bureaus in Motion: Civil Servants Compare the Clinton, G.H.W. Bush, and Reagan Presidential Transitions." *White House Studies* 4 (4): 435–440.

March, James G., and Johan P. Olsen. 1984. "The New Institutionalism: Organizational Factors in Political Life." *American Political Science Review* 78 (3): 741.

Mason, Alpheus T. 1972. *The States' Rights Debate, Antifederalism and the Constitution*. New York: Oxford University Press.

Matheson, Scott M. 1986. *Out of Balance*. Salt Lake City, UT: Peregrine Smith.

Mayer, Ken. 2000. *With the Stroke of a Pen*. Princeton, NJ: Princeton University Press.

McGinnis, John O. 1997. "The Origin of Conservatism." *National Review* (December 22). [database online]. Available from www.nationalreview.com (cited July 9, 2006).

McKenna, Frank, Jr., Philip A. Russo, Jr., H. Kenneth Hibbeln, and Douglas H. Shumavon. 1990. "National Fiscal Policy Changes and the Impact on Rural Governments: CDBG Cuts and the Loss of GRS." *Public Administration Quarterly* 14 (Fall): 324–352.

McManus, Doyle and Peter Spiegel. 2006. "Spy Czar, Rumsfield in a Turf War." *Los Angeles Times* (May 6). [database online]. Available from www.latimes.com (cited June 1, 2006).

Meeks, Brock N. 2005. "U.S. Agency Poised for Big Border Security Operation." *MSN News* (March 29). [database online]. Available from www.msnbc.com (cited November 24, 2005).

Migue, Jean Luc and Gerard Belanger. 1973. *Toward a General Theory of Managerial Discretion*. Quebec, Canada: Group de Recherche Secteur Public.

Milakovich, Michael E. and George J. Gordon. 2004. *Public Administration in America* Belmont, CA: Thomson Wadsworth.

(2007). Public Administration in America, 9th ed. Belmont, CA: Thomson Wadsworth.

"Minutemen Back on Patrol in Arizona; Volunteer Force Regroups amid National Debate Over Immigration." (April 1, 2006). [database online]. Available from www.msnbc.com (cited April 18, 2006).

Misangyi, Vilmos Fosnocht. 2002. "A Test of Alternative Theories of Managerial Discretion." (PhD. Diss., University of Florida).

Mississippi Department of Education. 2001. "House Bill 1609 Education Legislation." [electronic bulletin board]. Available from www.mde.k12.ms.us/ (cited June 8, 2006).

Montgomery, John Warwick, David Kilgour, and C. E. B. Cranfield. 1996. *Christians in the Public Square*. Edmonton, Alberta, Canada: Canadian Institute for Law, Theology, and Public Policy.

Moore, Karen L. 2004. Business Resource Center Newsletter 3 (3) [database online]. Available from www.brc.dc.gov/newsroom (cited March 3, 2006).

Morellee, Erwan. 2004. "Can Managerial Discretion Explain Observed Leverage Ratios?" *University of Rochester Review of Finance* 17: 257–294

Morgan, Douglas F. 2004. "Varieties of Administrative Abuse: Some Reflections on Ethics and Discretion." [database online]. Available from www.eli.pdx.edu (cited September 3, 2005).

Morgan, Douglas F., and John Rohr. 1982. "Administrative Discretion and Bureaucratic Statesmanship: Saving the Public Interest." Paper presented at the Annual Meeting of the American Society of Public Administration, Honolulu, Hawaii (March 21–25).

Morris, Bruce and Donna Wells. 2000. "School Safety Issues: Zero Tolerance." *School Policy Issues: School Environment*. Document #2299. Richmond: Virginia Commonwealth Educational Policy Institute. [electronic bulletin board]. Available from www.ecs.org (cited July 21, 2006).

Mosher, Frederick C. 1982. *Democracy and the Public Service,* 2nd. ed. New York: Oxford University Press.

Mulagan, Richard. 1997. "The Process of Public Accountability." *Australian Journal of Public Administration 56* (1): 25–36.

Nakamura, Robert T. and Frank Smallwood. 1980. *The Politics of Policy Implementation*. New York: St. Martin's Press.

Nalbandian, John. 1991. *Professionalism in Local Government: Transformations in the Roles, Responsibilities, and Values of City Managers*. San Francisco: Jossey-Bass.

National Conference of State Legislatures. 2004. "Legislative Budget Procedures: A Guide to Appropriations and Budget Processes in the States, Commonwealths, and Territories" (January 23). [database online]. Available from www.ncsl.org (cited May 28, 2006).

National Governors' Association. 2005. "NGA Statement Regarding Cuts in Vital Human Service Programs" (October 28). [database online]. Available from www .nga.org (cited May 26, 2006).

2006a. "Enhancing Competitiveness: A Review of Recent State Economic Development Initiatives—2005" (May 8). [database online]. Available from www .nga.org (cited May 26, 2006).

2006b. "Policy Position: Post Office Relocations and Closings" (March 1). [database online]. Available from www.nga.org (cited May 26, 2006).

National Security Agency. 2006. "Membership of the National Security Agency." [database online]. Available from www.whitehouse.gov (cited May 31, 2006).

Neustadt, Richard E. 1990. *Presidential Power: The Politics of Leadership.* New York: Free Press.

New York Civil Liberties Union. 2000. "*NYCLU v. Giuliani:* First Amendment Cases" (April 6). [database online]. Available from www.nyclu.org. (cited June 22, 2006).

Nodine, Thad R. 2006. "The Governors Speak–2006." *Honolulu Star Bulletin* (May 4). [database online]. Available from www.starbulletin.com (cited May 28, 2006).

Norquist, Grover G. 1993. "The Unmaking of the President: Why George Bush Lost." *Policy Review 63* (Winter): 10–25

Offgang, Kenneth. 2002. "Supreme Court Upholds Davis Veto of Rosenkrantz Parole." *Metropolitan News-Enterprise* (December 17). [database online]. Available from www.metnews.com (cited May 29, 2006).

Osborne, David and Ted Gaebler. 1992. *Reinventing Government: How the Entrepreneurial Spirit Is Transforming the Public Sector.* Reading, MA: Addison Wesley.

O'Toole, Laurence J. Jr. 2000. "Different Pubic Managements? Implications of Structural Context in Hierarchies and Networks." In *Advancing Public Management: New Developments in Theory, Methods, and Practice,* edited by Jeffrey Brudney, Laurence O'Toole, Jr., and Hal Rainey. Washington, DC: Georgetown University Press.

2005. "American Intergovernmental Relations: An Overview." In *Public Administration Concepts and Cases,* 8th ed, edited by Richard J. Stillman, II. Boston: Houghton Mifflin.

Papademetriou, Demetrios. 2003. "The Mexico Factor in U.S. Immigration Reform." Migration Policy Institute. [electronic bulletin board]. Available from www.migrationinformation.org (cited November 24, 2005).

Patterson, Thomas E. 2004. *We the People: A Concise Introduction to American Politics.* New York: McGraw Hill.

Peters, Guy B. 2001. *The Future of Governing*. Lawrence: University Press of Kansas. 1993. "Tragic Choices: Administrative Rulemaking and Policy Choice." In *Ethics in Public Service*, edited by Richard Chapman. Edinburgh, UK: Edinburgh University Press: 43–57.

2001. *The Future of Governing*. Lawrence: University Press of Kansas.

Peters, Paul. 2006. "Changing of the Guard." *Missoula Independent* (May 25, 2006). [database online]. Available from www.missoulanews.com (cited May 26, 2006).

Peterson, Janice and Barbara Smith. 2002. "Economic Security in Old Age? Retirement Income and Today's Workers." Paper presented at the Annual Conference of the Western Social Science Association, Albuquerque (April 10–13).

Peterson, Kurt W. 2002. "Religious Right." *St. James Encyclopedia of Pop Culture*. San Francisco: Thomson-Gale Group.

Pincus, Walter. 2006. "Panel Requires Annual Disclosure of Intelligence Budget." *Washington Post* (May 28). [database online]. Available from www.washingtonpost.com (cited June 1, 2006).

Pinkele, Carl F. 1985. "Discretion Fits Democracy: An Advocate's Argument." In *Discretion, Justice, and Democracy*, edited by Carl F. Pinkele and William C. Louthan. Ames: Iowa State University Press.

Platt, Rutherford H. 1999. *Disasters and Democracy: The Politics of Extreme Natural Events*. Washington, DC: Island Press.

Posner, Paul L. 1998. *The Politics of Unfunded Mandates: Whither Federalism?* Washington, DC: Georgetown University Press.

Powell, Mark R. 1999. *Science at EPA: Information in the Regulatory Process*. Washington, DC: Resources for the Future Press.

Reeves, T. Zane. 1986. "Administrative Discretion and the Action Agency's War on Poverty." In *Administrative Discretion and Public Policy Implementation*, edited by Douglas H. Shumavon and H. Kenneth Hibbeln. New York: Praeger, 115–127.

Reske, Henry J. 1997. "Senate Judiciary Chair Says He Won't Approve Activist Judges." *ABA Journal 83* (2): 28.

Revkin, C. Andrew. 2006. "A Young Bush Appointee Resigns His Post at NASA." *New York Times* (February 8). [database online]. Available from www.nytimes.com (cited July 7, 2006).

Richmond, Todd. 2006. "Wisconsin Governor Vetoes Legislative Oversight of Casinos." *New York Times* (May 26). [database online]. Available from www.nytimes.com (cited May 28, 2006).

Roberts, Deborah D. 2003. "The Governor as Leader: Strengthening Public Service Through Executive Leadership." In *Classics of Public Personnel Policy*, 3rd ed. Edited by Frank J. Thompson. Belmont, CA: Thomson Wadsworth.

Roig-Franzia, Manuel and Spencer Hsu. 2005. "Many Evacuated, but Thousands Still Waiting." *Washington Post* (September 4). [database online]. Available from www.washingtonpost.com (cited May 27, 2006).

Rosenblum, Victor G. 1972. "On Davis on Confining, Structuring, and Checking Administrative Discretion." *Law and Contemporary Problems* (Winter): 49–62.

Rourke, Francis E. 1984. *Bureaucracy, Politics, and Public Policy,* 3rd ed. Boston, MA: Little, Brown.

Saillant, Catherine. 2006. "Budget Ordinance Is Illegal, Court Says." *Los Angeles Times* (May 19). [database online]. Available from www.latimes.com (cited May 22, 2006).

Savas, Emanuel S. 2005. *Privatization in the City: Successes, Failures, Lessons.* Washington, DC: Congressional Quarterly Press.

Scherer, Ron. 2004. "Property Taxes Rising Nationwide." *The Christian Science Monitor* (December 3). [database online]. Available from www.csmonitor.com (cited May 22, 2006).

Schoenberger, Robert. 1996. "Some Say Clinton's Appointees Are Too Liberal; Professors Report Middle-of-the Road Decisions." (July 29) *Daily Cougar* 61 (133). [database online]. Available from www.stp.uh.edu (cited June 20, 2006).

Schroeder, Christopher H. 1996. "Letter: Opinion for the Counsel to the President." U.S. Department of Justice (September 11). [database online]. Available from www.usdoj.gov/olc (cited May 31, 2006).

Schwarzenegger, Arnold. 2005. "Statement of Decision, Request for Clemency by Stanley Williams" (December 12). [database online]. Available from www .governor.ca.gov/govsite (cited May 10, 2006).

Scutari, Chip. 2006. "GOP Anxious as Governor's Vetoes Pile Up." *Arizona Republic* (May 8). [database online]. Available from www.azcentral.com (cited May 8, 2006).

Shane, Scott. 2005. "Key U.S. Intelligence Official Tells All; Lets Annual Budget Figure Slip Out." *San Francisco Chronicle* (November 8). [database online]. Available from www.sfgate.com (cited June 1, 2006).

Shapiro, Martin. 1986. "APA: Past, Present and Future." *Virginia Law Review* 72: 452–454.

1994. "Controlling Administrative Discretion." In *Foundations of Administrative Law,* edited by Peter H. Schuck. New York: Oxford University Press.

1994. "Discretion." In *Handbook of Administrative Law,* edited by David H. Rosenbloom and Richard D. Schwartz. New York: Marcel Dekker, 501–517.

Sherman, Jerone L. 2006. "Shackle Policy Under Review by Pennsylvania Sheriff." *Pittsburgh Post-Gazette* (May 5). [database online]. Available from www.officer .com (cited May 24, 2006).

Shumavon, Douglas H. and H. Kenneth Hibbeln. 1986. "Administrative Discretion and Public Policy Implementation." In *Administrative Discretion and Public Pol-*

icy Implementation, edited by Douglas H. Shumavon and H. Kenneth Hibbeln. New York: Praeger.

Simonich, Milan. 2004. "Expulsion Part of Solution; Officials Say It Isn't a Quick Fix, But It's a Powerful Tool for Discipline." *Pittsburgh Post* (October 22). [database online]. Available from www.post-gazette.com (cited January 23, 2006).

Singer, Peter. 2004. *The President of Good and Evil: The Ethics of George W. Bush.* New York: Plume.

Singh, Ravi Inder. 2003. "Authority and Disclosure in Managerial Agency Problems." (PhD. Diss., Stanford University).

Skiba, Russell J. and Reece L. Peterson. 2000. "School Discipline at a Crossroads: From Zero Tolerance to Early Response." *Exceptional Children 66* (3): 335–347.

Southern Center for Human Rights. 2006. "No More 'Room and Board' Fees for Pre-Trial Detainees at the Clinch County Jail." Press release, Southern Center for Human Rights (April 17). [database online]. Available from www.schr.org (cited May 24, 2006).

Spitzer, Robert J. 1988. *The Presidential Veto: Touchstone of the American Presidency.* Albany: State University of New York Press.

Stepan, Alfred. 1999. "Federalism and Democracy: Beyond the US Model." *Journal of Democracy 10*: 19–34.

Stidham, Ronald, Robert A. Carp, and Donald R. Songer. 1996. "The Voting Behavior of President Clinton's Judicial Appointees." *Judicature 80* (July–August): 16–20.

Stillman, Richard J. 1974. *The Rise of the City Manager: A Public Professional in Local Government.* Albuquerque: University of New Mexico Press.

Stone, Deborah. 2002. *Policy Paradox: The Art of Political Decision Making.* New York: W. W. Norton.

Stumpf, Daniel. 2006. "Answers to Common Questions About the Mt. Soledad Cross and the Controversy Surrounding It." *San Diego Citybeat* (May 16). [database online]. Available from www.sdcitybeat.com (cited May 17, 2006).

Sullivan, John. 2002. "Briefing: Investigations; Paterson Ex-Mayor Convicted." *New York Times* (July 7). [database online]. Available from www.nytimes.com (cited June 26, 2006).

"Superintendent of Public Instruction" 2006. [database online]. Available from www.library.ca.gov/CCRC (cited May 28, 2006).

Sutton, Robert P. 2002. *Federalism.* Westport, CT: Greenwood Press.

Svara, James H. 1985. Dichotomy and Duality: Reconceptualizing the Relationship Between Policy and Administration in Council Manager Cities." *Public Administration Review 45*: 221–232.

1994. *Facilitative Leadership in Local Government: Lessons from Successful Mayors and Chairpersons.* San Francisco: Jossey-Bass.

2002. "Mayors in the Unity of Powers Context: Effective Leadership in Council-Manager Governments." In *The Future of Local Government Administration The Hansell Symposium,* edited by H. George Frederickson and John Nalbandian. Washington, D.C.: International City/County Management Association.

Taylor, Frederick W. 1923. *Scientific Management.* New York: Harper and Row.

Taylor, Troy. 2003. "Bath House John, Hinky Dink, and Others: Chicago's History of Graft and Corruption." *History and Hauntings.* [electronic bulletin board]. Available from www.prairieghosts.com/graft (cited June 22, 2006).

Terry, Don. 1995. "Chicago Housing Agency to Be Taken Over by U.S." *New York Times* (May 28). [database online]. Available from www.nytimes.com (cited May 20, 2005).

Titmuss, Richard M. 1987. *Welfare Rights Law and Discretion in the Philosophy of Welfare: Selected Writings of Richard M. Titmuss.* London: Allen and Union.

Toews, Otto B. 1981. *Discretion and Justice in Educational Administration: Towards a Normative Conceptual Framework.* Winnipeg: University of Manitoba Press.

Toppo, Greg. 2003. "School Violence Hits Lower Grades." *USA Today* (January 12). [database online]. Available from www.usatoday.com (cited May 22, 2006).

Turley, Jonathan. 2006. "Reckless Justice: Did the Saturday Night Raid of Congress Trample the Constitution?" Testimony before the Committee on the Judiciary. U.S. House of Representatives. Second sess. (May 30). [database online]. Available from www.judiciary.house.gov (cited May 31, 2006).

U.S. Department of Homeland Security. 2004. Fact Sheet: Arizona Border Control Initiative. Press Release. [database online]. Available from www.dhs.gov (cited November, 24, 2005).

U.S. Department of Justice. 2002. *Thomas v. Chicago Park District No. 00-1249.* 2006. "Former Mayor of Lynwood Sentenced to Nearly 16 Years in Prison for Conviction on Federal Corruption Charges: Associates Receive 10- and 6-Year Sentences" (March 20). [database online]. Available from www. losangeles .fbi.gov (cited June 23, 2006).
28CFR36.104. "Nondiscrimination on the Basis of Disability by Public Accommodations and in Commercial Facilities." Revised 1 July 2002.

U.S. Department of Labor. Bureau of Labor Statistics. 2006. "State and Local Government." [database online]. Available from www.bls.gov (cited May 17, 2006).

U.S. Government Accountability Office. 2005. "Unfunded Mandates: Analysis of Reform Act's Coverage and Views on Possible Next Steps." [database online]. Available from www.gao.gov (cited April 14, 2005).
1981. *Requests for Federal Disaster Assistance Need Better Evaluation.* CED-82-4. Washington, DC: GAO.

U.S. Citizenship and Immigration Services. Office of Policy and Planning. 2003. "Estimates of the Unauthorized Immigrant Population Residing in the United

States: 1990 to 2000" Washington, DC. [database online]. Available from www.uscis.gov/graphics/shared/statistics (cited November 24, 2005).

"Under the Law: The U.S. Constitution Does Not Grant Members of Congress Immunity from Lawful Prosecution." *Houston Chronicle* (May 30). [database online]. Available from www.chron.com (cited May 31, 2006).

Van Alstyne, William W. 2004. "The Demise of the Right–Privilege Distinction in Constitutional Law." *Harvard Law* Review *81*: 1439. [database online]. Available from www.constitution.org (cited August 31, 2004).

Van Riper, Paul. O. 1958. *History of the United States Civil Service.* New York: Harper and Row.

Vaughn, Jacqueline and Hanna J. Cortner. 2005. *George W. Bush's Healthy Forests: Reframing the Environmental Debate.* Boulder, CO: University Press of Colorado.

Villaraigosa, Antonio. "Villaraigosa Delivers His First State of City Address." (April 17) [database online]. Available from www.nbc4.tv/politics (cited April 18, 2006).

"Voting is Crucial." 2005. *Pittsburgh Post-Gazette* (November 6). [database online]. Available from www.post-gazette.com (cited May 24, 2006).

Walker, Robert S. 2006. "Talking Points of Robert S. Walker." Testimony before the Committee on the Judiciary. U.S. House of Representatives. Second sess. (May 30). [database online]. Available from www.judiciary.house.gov (cited May 31, 2006).

Wallin, Bruce. 1996. *Revenue Sharing as a Public Investment.* Washington, DC: Economic Policy Institute.

———. 1998. *From Revenue Sharing to Deficit Sharing: General Revenue Sharing and Cities.* Washington, DC: Georgetown University Press.

Warshaw, Shirley A. 1997. *The Domestic Presidency: Policy Making in the White House.* Boston: Allyn & Bacon.

Watson, Leonard E. 1981. *Managerial Discretion: A Key Concept for the Principal Commonwealth Council for Education Administration.* Armidale, N.S.W. Australia.

Watson, Jack. 1993. "The Clinton White House." *Presidential Studies Quarterly 23* (3): 429–436.

Weixel, Gordon. 2006. "Voters to Decide Sales Tax Hike." *Bismarck Tribune* (May 14). [database online]. Available from www.bismarcktribune.com cited May 22, 2006).

Weko, Thomas J. 1995. *The Politicizing Presidency.* Lawrence: University Press of Kansas.

Weissert, Carole S. 1994. "Beyond the Organization: The Influence of Community and Personal Values on Street-Level Bureaucrats' Responsiveness." *Journal of Public Administration Research and Theory 4* (2): 225–255.

West, William F. 1985. *Administrative Rulemaking: Politics and Processes.* Westport, CT: Greenwood Press.

White House. 2006. "Fact Sheet: President Submits Line Item Veto Legislation to Congress" (March 6). [database online]. Available from www.whitehouse.gov (cited July 21, 2006).

———. 2006. "President Bush's Cabinet." [database online]. Available from www. whitehouse.gov (cited May 31, 2006).

White, Leonard D. 1926. *Introduction to the Study of Public Administration.* New York: Macmillan.

Wilgoren, Jodi. 2006. "Corruption Scandal Loosening Mayor Daley's Grip on Chicago." *New York Times* (January 6). [database online]. Available from www.nytimes.com (cited January 6, 2006).

Wilkinson, Todd. 2005. "Past is Prelude: Whose Interests Should National Parks Serve?" *New West* (December 2). [database online]. Available from www.newwest .net (cited July 9, 2006).

Willoughby, W. F. 1927. *Principles of Public Administration.* Baltimore, MD: Johns Hopkins University Press.

———. "Transition." (January 17). [database online]. Available from www.presidency .ucsb.edu (cited July 8, 2006).

Woodward, Bob. 1987. *Veil: The Secret Wars of the CIA 1981–1987.* New York: Pocket Books.

Zola, Irving Kenneth. 1993. "The Sleeping Giant in Our Midst: Redefining 'Persons with Disabilities'." In *Implementing the Americans with Disabilities Act: Rights and Responsibilities of All Americans,* edited by Lawrence O. Gostin and Henry A. Beyer. Baltimore: Brookes Publishing Company: xvii–xx.

Index